John Papajohn

John Spiegel

TRANSACTIONS
IN FAMILIES

Jossey-Bass Publishers
San Francisco · Washington · London · 1975

TRANSACTIONS IN FAMILIES
A Modern Approach for Resolving Cultural and Generational Conflicts
by John Papajohn and John Spiegel

Copyright © 1975 by: Jossey-Bass, Inc., Publishers
615 Montgomery Street
San Francisco, California 94111
&
Jossey-Bass Limited
3 Henrietta Street
London WC2E 8LU

Library of Congress Catalogue Card Number LC 74-6740

International Standard Book Number ISBN 0-87589-237-X

Manufactured in the United States of America

JACKET DESIGN BY WILLI BAUM

FIRST EDITION

Code 7437

The Jossey-Bass

Behavioral Science Series

Preface

The field of family therapy has expanded rapidly over the past twenty-five years. (See Sager and Kaplan, 1972; Boszormenyi-Nagy and Framo, 1965; Group for the Advancement of Psychiatry, 1970; Howells, 1971; Christensen, 1964; Spiegel and Bell, 1959; Lidz, 1965.) Its growth as a distinct discipline has been based on a considerable amount of work in both the development of theory and the creation of innovative therapeutic intervention strategies. In the theoretical realm, work has proceeded from three discrete approaches to the family as a target for therapeutic change. In the first of these, the family is viewed as an aggregate of related yet separate individuals whose interaction needs to be understood from the perspective of the personality organization of the members who constitute it. Traditional psychological theories such as psychoanalysis (Lidz, 1965; Ackerman, 1966) and learning theory (Stuart, 1972; Patterson, 1971) have been employed to conceptualize individual disordered behavior in the context of the family matrix. Therapeutic change is predicated on the degree to which family members can be helped by the therapist to alter their disordered interactions by changing those aspects of their individual thinking, feeling, and acting that are contributing to the family disequilibrium and causing the dysfunctioning of one "sick" member. In the case of psychoanalytically oriented family therapy (Lidz, 1965; Ackerman, 1966), this change is brought about through the achievement of insight by family members into their disordered perceptions of and feelings about the others in the family. In the case of behavior therapy the focus is on the manifest behavior, or acting, of individual family members, which needs to be altered directly through "contingency contracting'" and other methods so that patterns of mutual frustration and punishment can yield to alternative patterns of mutual reinforcement.

The second approach to the family as a target for therapeutic change is based on social psychological rather than individual psychological theory. The family is viewed as a social group with structural and functional characteristics that are independent of the individuals who constitute it. The work of Wynne (1963a, 1963b) and Bateson (1960, 1956) typifies this second approach. Bateson employs communications theory to explain disordered behavior among family members, and his original theoretical work generated a wealth of creative research by those who employed his concept of the double bind in understanding disordered interactions in the family. (See Haley, 1959a, 1959b; Jackson, 1965; Watzlawick, 1963.) Wynne's formulations, while they postulate psychoanalytic concepts such as the ego, are based primarily on social psychological concepts such as social role. He sees the disordered thinking of schizophrenic patients as caused by their inability to develop separate identities within families where considerable role confusion and a lack of true complementarity are concealed under a facade of pseudomutuality.

The third approach to the family as a target for therapeutic change is based on broad multicausal models in which the family is viewed as a subsystem of the social and cultural milieu in which it is embedded. The work of Howells (1971), for example, is based on "ecological systems," considerations in which a reciprocal pattern is postulated between the psychologically disordered behavior of an individual, the interactions occurring in the nuclear and extended families of which he is a member, and the social and cultural systems of which his family is a part. Howells has operationalized his concepts in the form of a mental health delivery system. The work of Howells and others is based on a broad range of research studies that link social and cultural system characteristics with the structure and functioning of families, on the one hand, and the psychological functioning of the individuals constituting families, on the other. (See Pavenstedt, 1967; Minuchin, 1967; Rainwater, 1970.)

Spiegel attempts to integrate the three approaches described above into a unified theoretical framework. His formulation of transactional systems theory is described in detail in Spiegel (1971). This theory, in the ecological systems tradition, is based on the assumption that cultural, social, psychological, and biological events constitute a field of transacting processes in which change in one part is related to change in the others. Intrapsychic conflict in an individual family member, for example, would be expected, from a transactional point of view, to be systematically related to social role conflict among family members, as well as to the incongruent cultural value orientations, or culture conflict, that characterizes the relation of the family to the sociocultural environment in which its members live and work.

In *Transactions in Families* we illustrate the application of this theoretical model in the study of immigrant families in the United States. The ethnic family provides a good medium for examining the complex interrelation among cultural values, social role structure and functioning, and intrapsychic process as they relate to mental health and illness. While the salience of these variables is evident in all families in conflict, they are especially visible in ethnic families in the process of adapting to the American social system.

Transactions in Families is organized around case histories of three ethnic families (Puerto Rican, Greek-American, and Italian-American) undergoing the acculturation process in the United States. In the Puerto Rican family, a first-generation immigrant to New York City has reacted to the stress with a schizophrenic break. In the Italian-American family, a third-generation son of American-born, Italian-American parents is being treated for a neurotic disorder. In the Greek-American family, a second-generation daughter born of Greek parents in the Boston area is hospitalized with a psychotic reaction. The psychological disorganization exhibited by the "sick" member is examined in each case through an in-depth analysis of the family structure and functioning.

When members of the same family abandon old world values and adopt, at different rates, those of the American core society, conflict in role relations is inevitable. This process is especially evident in the intergenerational conflict between foreign-born parents and their native-born children. Also, a husband-wife relation in an ethnic family is often characterized by different rates of acculturation. While one spouse experiences accelerated upward social mobility in American middle-class terms, the other adheres to the ethnic values and life style of his foreign-born parents or grandparents. The interpersonal confusion and marital conflict this situation creates is rarely understood as a conflict in cultural values and instead is labeled by the family therapist as an interpersonal power struggle precipitated by the insecurity or neurotic personality of one or the other marital partners.

The current changing value structure of American society itself complicates the situation for the ethnic family even more since it has become increasingly difficult for them to discern what American values are. For example, their children often demand to be free to drop out of a system that their parents have struggled so long to become a part of. The children's energies are absorbed in social protest against a social system whose inequities and "totalitarianism" they become committed to fighting. Thus, social protest and psychological disabilities are two sides of the same coin. They reflect strain in interaction patterns both within the family and between the family and the community.

The major contribution of *Transactions in Families* is in providing a theoretical framework within which an effective therapeutic technology may be developed. With the theoretical constructs provided here therapists can order the relevant cultural and social characteristics of a family and can include them in planning intervention strategies and in developing therapeutic techniques. Therapists can identify and conceptualize those sources of stress that are based in cultural and social conflict. And, regardless of particular psychological orientations, therapists will be able to focus their techniques on the relevant areas of stress.

In Chapter One, the theoretical framework within which the three family case histories are analyzed is described. This chapter is based on a report prepared for the Group for the Advancement of Psychiatry, Committee on the Family, by Spiegel and F. Kluckhohn (1954). It continues to be the most lucid presentation of the main theoretical underpinnings on which the subsequent research work was carried out and the three subject families were studied.

These subject families represent three phases in a program of continuing research marked by progressively more sophisticated methods of inquiry. The first of these, the Puerto Rican family of Mario Corosa, was analyzed by Spiegel and members of the Group for the Advancement of Psychiatry, Committee on the Family, in the initial research effort. (See Group for the Advancement of Psychiatry, 1970.) This research was designed to test the efficacy of transactional systems theory in ordering behavior—in this case, among members of a Puerto Rican family in which severe psychopathology was manifest. The focus in this case history therefore is on employing the theoretical constructs presented in Chapter One in the conceptualization of the family processes involved in Mario's illness. The data for the analysis of the family were collected through the use of the Family Case History outline, which was also developed by the Group for the Advancement of Psychiatry, Committee on the Family.

In the second phase of the research the emphasis shifted to the clinical application of the theoretical constructs—to the diagnosis and treatment of an ethnic family in which a member manifested a neurotic disorder. The Italian family, the Tondis, was one of a sample of Irish-American, Italian-American, and Old American families studied in a participant-observation research project conducted through the Social Relations Department at Harvard University in conjunction with the Children's Medical Center in Boston and directed by Spiegel and Kluckhohn. The data were derived primarily through clinical interviews with family members and through direct participation in the daily activities of the subject families. (For a detailed description of the method employed in this research project, see Spiegel, 1971, ch. 6.) The case history of the Tondi family focuses more on social role than does the case analysis of the Puerto Rican family. This change in focus reflects later conceptual development within the transactional systems framework.

In the third phase of the research, begun at Harvard, the methodological focus shifted to an empirical, controlled study of a sample of thirty-four Greek-American families undergoing the acculturation process. The research compared families with mentally ill members and a matched sample of families without a history of psychopathology. The data in this study were obtained in a more systematic manner than in the previous efforts through the use of the Family Case History interview guide. The presentation of the Constantine family, therefore, contains more historical detail, less of the clinical detail which was provided in the analysis of the Italian-American family, and more emphasis on the complex interrelationships between the family members. Papajohn, as project director of the study, was responsible for its design. (For a detailed description of the methodology employed in this research, see Papajohn, 1974.)

Our major intent is to describe the application of transactional systems theory through its use in the in-depth analysis of these three ethnic families undergoing the acculturation process. We attempt to present the case histories in a graphic manner so as to capture some of the feelings of the family members as they struggled with the conflicting demands of two divergent cultures. Previous writings in this area of ethnicity and mental health have been either scientific research papers directed to the academic community exclusively or fictional works directed to the general reader and therefore, although based on the case histories, not intended to contribute to a scientific understanding of the issues. We try here to bridge these forms in a way that will engage the interest of both professional readers and those individuals interested in ethnic issues who are not involved with treatment or theoretical considerations.

Chapters Four, Six, Seven, Eight, and Nine were written by Papajohn. Chapters One, Two, Three, and Five were written by Spiegel, Chapter One in conjunction with F. Kluckhohn and Chapters Two and Three in conjunction with the Group for the Advancement of Psychiatry, Committee on the Family.

The nature of the research on which this volume is based required the collaboration and support of many coworkers and other individuals. We are indebted to all of them, without whose help the book could never have been completed. We want to mention especially some of those who were directly involved in one of the various phases of our research over the years: Florence Kluckhohn, Ezra Vogel, Norman Bell, Albert Treischman, Israel Zwerling, Marilyn Mendelsohn, Doris Seder Jacobson, and Helen Friedman.

We also thank the Publication Committee of the Group for the Advancement of Psychiatry and its chairman, Alexander Saryan, for permission to reprint sections from its report *The Case History Method in the Study of Family Process* (1970), which appear revised in this volume as Chapters Two and Three. Our thanks also to Jason Aronson, Inc., New York City, for permission to publish in this volume as Chapter Five a revised version of "The Tondis: A 'Sick' Family" from Spiegel (1971).

We are indebted also to the Massachusetts Department of Mental Health and the Veterans' Administration for their assistance in facilitating our research effort in the various institutions under their jurisdiction. The National Institute of Mental Health made substantial contributions in support of the early stages of the research. The Marcus Foundation of Chicago provided continuing support for later phases and made it possible for us to bring our work to its conclusion.

Waltham, Massachusetts　　　　　　　　JOHN PAPAJOHN
November 1974　　　　　　　　　　　　JOHN SPIEGEL

Contents

Tables and Figures

TABLES

xvii

FIGURES

Transactions
in Families

A Modern Approach for Resolving
Cultural and Generational Conflicts

1

Integration and Conflict in Family Behavior

In 1950 the Group for the Advancement of Psychiatry formed a committee to look into the subject of family behavior. Although an extensive literature already existed in a number of fields (see Waller and Hill, 1951), the job of the committee was to bring the subject specifically into psychiatric focus.

The difficulty at the outset was how to derive data and materials based not on the study of sick or well individuals but on the study of family processes. It is easy enough to study individuals against a family background when the dynamic principles are never clearly specified. The influence of the father or the mother or the sibling on the individual being examined can be studied without consideration of the totality of relations. To change the object of inquiry from the individual to the family, however, necessitates different methods of observation and different conceptual tools (see Lindemann, 1950). From this altered perspective, the family is seen as a fairly well-defined, organized entity with a life history and dynamic principles of its own. Because of this altered perspective, the Committee faced a new problem. It had set itself the job of finding out something about the normal and pathological physiology of the family, so to speak, without knowing anything about its anatomy—its structure and function. It seemed fruitless to acquire extensive observational data without undertaking this fundamental step.

But this apparently simple task presented a whole new series of complications. Families exhibit the most astonishing variance in their structure and function. If one examines variance dependent only upon ethnic, class, and regional differences in the United States, and excludes the variance found in other societies, the range is still quite remarkable. In addition, differences in lateral extension (the range of collateral relatives such as aunts, uncles, and cousins) and in vertical extension (the range of generations, such as grandparents, great-grandparents, and grandchildren) make it difficult to know where to locate the boundary of The Family.

In seeking factors to correlate with this variation in lateral and vertical extension, the Committee found that the structure of the family is inextricably associated with the structure of the society of which it is a part. Small family groups are associated with the urban middle-class and its continuous demand for maximum mobility, both geographical and social. Continuity of generations is found in upper-class families with their family portraits, traditions, and hierarchical systems. Collateral relatives prove important in rural areas and in certain ethnic groups.

This aspect of the complexities involved in a study of family dynamics becomes even more prominent when we consider the functions of the family. Not only are various and differing functions assigned to the family in different social milieus, but even those functions that are apparently universal, such as the socialization of children, the satisfaction of sexual needs, and the biological and material maintenance of the members of the family, are carried out in such various ways with such differing implications that it is impossible to obtain meaningful patterns without reference to the surrounding social system. The responsibilities and attitudes of a father toward his child, his wife, and his mother-in-law cannot be divorced from his other roles in the society. For example, he can perform differently, and somewhat different functions are expected of him, depending on what his occupational role is—farm owner, factory worker, airplane pilot. A mother's attitude toward and relations with her children vary, among other factors, with her ethnic origin, as well as with her decision to stay at home or to increase the family income by going to work.

Since no generalizations regarding the structure and function of the family can be obtained apart from an understanding of the particular social structure with which it is integrated, a new dimension was added to the work of the Committee: an understanding of social systems. The structure of a social system, however, especially a system as broad and complex in development and in function as that of the United States, proved to contain as much variance as that found in families and individual personalities. And similarities and variations in socal patterns are related to another level of human behavor, the variations in values of a culture and subcultures. For instance, the significance and structure of the United States occupational system become clear only when considered in the light of the tremendous value placed on planning for the future, on personal achievement based on hard work, and on individual initiative. Relations between parents and children frequently reflect a belief in the potential for goodness, dignity, and worth of the individual. There is no escaping the ubiquitous and penetrating effect of cultural value orientations on every aspect of human behavior.

The process of adding new dimensions to the work of the Committee focused attention on a way of viewing human behavior that is not easily perceived in the context of purely clinical work with emotionally disturbed individuals. In clinical work one tends to study the distortions of a reality known to the observer and the maladapted behavior based on such distortions in psychologically disturbed individuals. The field of observation is intrapersonal and interpersonal in the sense of a series of small two- or three-person clusters composing the social relations of the patient, including the relation with the therapist. In this setting, fairly satisfactory explanations of human behavior can be derived from conceptions based upon purely intrapsychic mechanisms, such as those of integration, defense, and disintegration. However, as soon as the area of observation is widened to include larger human groups such as the family, the environment as a given constant disappears. In its place there emerges a field of transaction that is not intuitively known or easily discoverable by the observer, especially insofar as the observer is a part of the field. The structure of the field at any given moment depends on components contributed by the physical universe, the biological situation of the individuals transacting within the field, the intrapsychic status of these individuals, the small groups formed by these transacting individuals, the extended social system, and the system of values existing at that time and in that place. The extensiveness of this field of transaction and the variety and intricacy of the network of interlocking systems of which it is composed constitute a cognitive problem for the observer. The attention falters in trying to span so large an area, and common sense and intuition fail to supply adequate and easily summoned cues for a definition of the situation. (For a detailed development of Spiegel's transactional theory, see Spiegel, 1971.)

Psychiatrists lack patterns for perceiving phenomena of such magnitude and complexity. They have to construct conceptual patterns that can encompass the field of transaction as the necessary background for a complete and realistic description of human behavior. They must add to their already existing stock of concepts related to physical, chemical, biological, and psychological events a new cluster of concepts, of equal scientific rigor and seriousness, related to the group-dynamic, sociological, and cultural-anthropological descriptions of events. Such additions go further than what is usually meant by the terms *interdisciplinary* and *multiprofessional*. The concepts basic to other disciplines must be integrated so that they become a part of the psychiatrist's cognitive orientation toward reality—or at least as much so as physical, chemical, and biological concepts are at present.

Transaction, furthermore, is distinct from the concepts denoted by the terms *self-action* and *interaction*. Self-action signifies behavior springing from the internal, preset, wound-up condition of a detached, organized entity, like a clock. The concepts of instinct and of the hereditary development of the organism are self-action concepts. Interaction refers to the effect the behavior of organized, detached entities such as billiard balls or gas molecules has on each other. The notions of classical physics, like the Newtonian laws of gravity, are based on interaction concepts. The term *interpersonal relations* is also based on interaction concepts insofar as it describes the effects of discrete personalities on each other's behavior. Transaction, however, describes the interpenetration and mutual, reverberating, and reciprocal effects of processes that can no longer be considered organized, detachable entities. It is here rather a question of system in process with system. Biochemical systems have this characteristic, as do most of the processes that are denoted by the term *homeostasis*. The equilibrium-maintaining, self-correcting systems involved in cybernetics and communications engineering are also transactional in orientation.

The various sciences concerned with the study of human behavior do not distinguish among self-action, interaction, and transaction. Human behavior becomes transactional, however, either when viewed macroscopically, that is, as a system of human relations constituting a human society, or microscopically, that is, as a system of psychosomatic processes in which no one individual behaves as a completely self-directing (autonomous, self-acting) or even completely self-conscious (aware of the influence of others, interacting) entity. Looked at in this way, a complex network of processes determines behavior, not an individual personality or a group.

In a way, transactional concepts imply a study of function at the cost of structure. Structure appears as but a static cross-sectional version of function. And although it becomes increasingly difficult to characterize, structure does not disappear altogether. Events must still occur somewhere in space in some sort of orderly relation to each other. Such considerations moved Spiegel to characterize the persistent, structurelike aspects of transactional relations as a field of transaction.

Analysis of Family Processes

Our purpose is to analyze family life with reference to the processes responsible for the mental health or illness of its individual members. For this it is necessary to develop concepts concerning the family. First, the term *family* must be closely defined; the variations of rule-of-thumb definitions must be eliminated. And insofar as the family is associated with the mental health of the individual, concepts must be developed for detecting and describing the states or conditions of the family that favor good or bad health. Lastly, since not all families are the same, we must find methods to distinguish the normal—dominant or variant—from the pathological or deviant states that are conducive to illness.

To work with concepts relatively unfamiliar to psychiatrists, we need a frame of reference within which to locate them. This can be constructed from the set of reference points briefly sketched here.

(1) The family is a collection of individuals. One point of reference, therefore, is the individual, including everything we know about his somatic and psychological functions.

(2) The family is an organization, a group. Another point of reference, therefore, is the small primary group, with its characteristic action processes and group dynamics.

(3) The family is a major unit of the social system. It has structural and functional characteristics that extend throughout the social system in a network of articulation with other subsystems such as the occupational and educational systems. Thus, a third point of reference is the social system.

(4) The family is an agency for the transmission of cultural values. Its form and function are intimately connected with the specific value orientations of a given culture. Accordingly, a fourth point of reference is the system of values characteristic of a social system.

(5) The family exists in a particular locale, or territory. The contrasts between a rural and urban environment may be of considerable significance in indicating variance in family structure and function. The geographical setting is thus a fifth point of reference.

These five reference points provide a convenient descriptive conceptual frame that allows easy identification of the point of view from which the family is being considered. It is a part of our thesis, however, that they can also be considered as a system of interrelated and more or less integrated component parts. When looked at this way, the individual, the group, the social system, the cultural values, and the geographical location are all foci of organization in one integrated system or field of transaction.

Thus, a married woman may or may not be a mother, and

a mother may or may not be married, depending on her biological and psychological state and her ideological outlook. If she is a mother, her parental attitudes vary according to her geographical location and status in the social system; she has techniques for taking care of her child that differ if she lives alone or on a farm with her husband nearby from those she uses if she lives in a city with a husband who travels for long periods. Other factors also produce variations in parental attitudes and child-care arrangements. The farm wife who has ten older children delegates much more responsibility than does the wife of a traveling salesman and the unmarried, working mother, in different ways, who has two children under five.

In spite of the differences between these mothers, they may resemble each other in their attitudes toward disciplining and spoiling their children. These attitudes will be strongly influenced by the cultural value orientations of the women. For example, if the mothers derive their values from one of our more severe ethics, it is quite likely that they will consider their offspring basically evil and in need of severe training and repeated punishment in order to be turned into reasonable human beings.

The primary point is that the foci of organization in the total field do not vary independently of each other. No matter where the focus of observation is directed—at the individual, the family as a group, the family as a part of the social system, the value orientation of the individual, family, subgroup, or social system, or the geographical setting—the other foci of organization are always implied. Because they are in a state of transaction and reciprocal influence, they cannot be divorced from one another, and any description of human behavior must take account of the contributions of all these foci of organization.

We intend here to confine ourselves to two foci—the social system and the cultural value orientations—that seem to be of the greatest strategic importance. To a lesser extent we shall discuss some of the effects of the geographical setting on the family.

Relation of Family to Social System. Extensive cross-cultural surveys have shown that some form of family is found in every society. (See Murdock, 1949.) Every known society has institutionalized sexual and parental roles into a formal pattern of small nuclear groups integrated with other nuclear groups in an extended kinship system. The patterns vary with respect to size and kinship lines, but the basic structure is universal. Furthermore, in all societies the family system is structurally related to all other units of the social system. It is universally integrated with systems such as residence, community organization, the stratification system (that is, the class structure), the occupational system, the educational system, and the religious system of the society. Often, it is integrated with the power structure or political system of the society.

For example, the family in American society is integrated with the occupational, social class, and educational systems. The class position of the family in the United States—especially the middle-class family—depends very much on the position held by the father in the occupational world. But it is also true that his job depends on certain qualifications attained through education and training. Furthermore, the education one receives depends largely on the social and economic status of the family. Family status, class position, occupational position, and educational attainments are all interdependent.

However, the smooth functioning of these interdependencies in the time axis depends on the individual and his personal qualities. The child of the well-established, upper middle-class family who loses occupational status because he lacks the intelligence to train for a job commensurate with the status of his family, is likely to put a strain on his family. Some member undoubtedly will object to or be unhappy about this person's menial job. However, if ways are found that allow him to maintain his occupational status despite his lack of ability for the job, then strains of another kind are produced. The structure of the social system is seriously threatened when occupational positions are given to persons not qualified for the jobs.

There is also a universal connection between the family, the rules of residence of the community, and the composition of ethnic groups. In almost all societies the members of a nuclear family group, that is, husband, wife, and their children, live together in the same residence. Whatever the physical or architectural nature of the dwelling place, it is nevertheless a place—a territorial location. From the point of view of the individual, it is primarily the family that determines where he lives and calls home. These determinations are important because local, regional, and national sentiments contribute to his sense of personal identity. From the point of view of the social system, the family is the basic unit of regional organization of the community, state, or nation.

Particularly important for our objective is the structural relation between nuclear and extended family groups, rules of residence, and ethnic groups. The nuclear or primary group, as stated before, consists usually of husband, wife, and their children. A kinship system integrates such nuclear groups both through vertical extension—that is, by continuity of generations in time—and through lateral extension—the collateral relatives of the present generation. The residential patterns of the group or subgroup prescribe what permutations and combinations of vertically or laterally extended relatives live together. In our American society, for example, especially for urban groups of an industrial community, the prevailing pattern prescribes the residential isolation of nuclear families from all relatives, collateral or generational. The husband who has to house and feed his mother-in-law or the wife called upon to find room for a sister-in-law—to say nothing of distant cousins, aunts, or grandparents—feels sorely abused as a general rule. In other societies, however, sharing household facilities with a wide assortment of relatives, near and far, is regarded as a natural design for living.

The relation between the family and the system of residence is also structurally integrated with the ethnicity of the community. An ethnic group is, in one sense, a system of extended and related family groups. A concept of race based on clear-cut distinctions is invalid in any strict sense; specific traits are found to be diffused through many different ethnic and racial groups. Nevertheless, it is also true that the members of an ethnic group tend to be more closely related to each other biologically than they are to members of other ethnic groups. Thus, the composition of the family is of structural significance to the related ethnic group, and, conversely, the ethnic group frequently determines the structure of the family. This reciprocal relation is also integrated with the residential structure of the community. Families that are ethnically related frequently tend to live, for some generations at least, in the same location. In crowded urban communities, this closeness often leads to considerable strain if not outright social conflict.

Clearly, then, the universality of these structural interrelations seems to indicate that the family has functions of fundamental importance to the total society. They meet certain requirements that cannot be satisfied in any other way.

Of the many interrelated functions that the family performs for the individual and for the social system, two are apparently allocated specifically to the family. The rest are shared, in varying degrees, by other organizations. The two functions are reproduction and socialization of the children. Survival of the species requires a mechanism for the constant introduction of new members. The biological processes of humans, which would in themselves apparently satisfy this prerequisite, are not intrinsically sufficient. The social organization that supports the species requires for its perpetuation that the new members be recruited in an orderly and systematic fashion. There is no doubt that every society universally ascribes a rank order—a destiny—to its children at the moment of birth through the mechanism of the family. Children cannot be potentially "anybody" with a random, anything-is-possible kind of future ahead of them. In order for the structure and function of the social system to be maintained, children must be introduced into it with an ascribed social status. They must have a place to begin and a range of future goals selected from the total system of roles of the particular society.

This extensive selectivity and ordering of possibilities is accomplished through the legitimization of the parents. (See Malinowski, 1930.) It is not actually the children who have to be legitimate, but the parents; the raising of children within families must be assured to the social system. Thus, the invariant insistence on the legitimacy principle is not primarily for the sake of controlling sexual behavior. In many societies extramarital and premarital sexual intercourse are positively sanctioned. The legitimacy is invoked primarily to preserve and transmit the entire system of status relations and the integrative mechanisms that maintain its structure, by allocating the newcomers to the appropriate status.

The second function of the family is the socialization of the children once they have arrived and have been legitimately assigned their initial status. This functional prerequisite is closely associated with an important aspect of the biological focus of organization, namely, the prolonged dependency of the child. The dependence is actually both biological and psychological and stands in a reciprocal relation with another established biological fact, that is, the apparent lack of innate behavior, and the extraordinary plasticity of the human child. Because our children bring so little predetermined behavior into the world with them, and have so much to acquire, they need a great deal of time to learn how to play their roles in life. By the same token, they can be taught a wide variety of behavior. And since much of it is mutually exclusive, once it has been learned it cannot easily be unlearned or relearned or transferred to a different kind of social system. Plasticity diminishes with maturation.

This functional requirement, determined by the prolonged immaturity of the child, is apparently better satisfied by the family system than by any other institutional arrangement, at least to this point in the history of mankind. Efforts have been made to socialize children exclusively in institutions where the parental roles are shared by a number of different individuals. By and large, these efforts have not been as successful as some form of family. The very diffuseness and discontinuity of the roles does not permit the child to develop a clear idea of his status and identity. The child's need for a stable, enduring relationship with significant parent figures based on affection—a need that is assumed to be basic—is not well met.

It is within the framework of mutual love and interpersonal security—that is, relations relatively free from anxiety, exploitation, and intimidation—that the child can best learn the social role behavior and the techniques of adjustment for situations he will meet as an adult. These roles are learned by imitation and identification. Assuming that the family is not in itself a deviant one, the roles thus acquired will turn out to be appropriate for the social system in question.

At this point it is necessary to be more specific about the use of the concept of role as a conceptualization of human behavior. (For a detailed development of Spiegel's concept of social role, see Spiegel, 1971, chs. 3 and 4.) If one is describing the behavior of an individual in a known situation, anyone with common sense and intuition immediately apprehends and judges the behavior as either appropriate and realistic or as inappropriate, maladaptive, or unrealistic. This immediate cognitive ability to relate behavior to situations is possible only for situations within one's own culture. Under such circumstances, the observer or the participant intuitively assigns the culturally appropriate roles to all who are participating in the situation. No need is felt for analytical dissection of the behavior patterns. In a strange situation, however, as in a foreign land, lack of prior experience makes such automatic allocations of behavior patterns impossible to achieve, and therefore the observer does not know how to define the situation. He does not know how to understand what is going on until it can be explained to him in terms of the roles being played, the motives activating them, and the goals implied in them.

The primary structural components of the social situation, as far as its human participants are concerned, can be conceived as a system of roles. (See Neiman and Hughes, 1951; Parsons, 1951, pp. 36–45.) A single individual obviously plays many roles—for example, in the occupational system, a school teacher; in the family, a wife, mother, daughter; in the economic system, a consumer; in the political system, a citizen, party member, voter. Each particular role is culturally patterned, that is, it is tailored to fit the needs of the social system or subsystem in question. There are norms for each role that all persons in the role are expected to follow. There is, of course, always individual variation; no two people ever perform exactly alike in any given role. Role expectations orient the responses of the participants somewhat as a magnet orients randomly distributed iron filings along the lines of magnetic force. The limited range of response, analogous to the field of force, results from the reciprocal roles the other participant or participants are forced to assume in relation to the one who initiates the new situation. The initiator, who plays the lead and structures the role situation, may be doing something as innocuous and informal as changing the subject of conversation, asking a question, or greeting another on the street. Nevertheless, by so doing, he specifically orients and limits the possible behavior of the others in the transaction. Although the process of learning new and more appropriate role responses is never finished, it is in childhood especially, that roles appropriate to the various statuses are learned through reciprocal transactions with the parents.

Another significant aspect of role playing is that it is a form of communication. As such, it depends on a system of cues, signs, symbols, meanings, and values shared by the participants in the situation. Without sharing, communication in the sense of meaningful interpretation of, and response to, the roles of the others would be impossible. Because of the cognitive and evaluative aspects of a shared system of meanings and values, each role is accompanied by a set of complementary or counterroles based on reciprocity within the cognitive and evaluative systems. In other words, the enacting of a role is associated in the individual with a set of expectations of reciprocal role responses on the part of others. The particular responses in the others then determine further aspects of the role playing on the part of the originator. To a certain extent, these counterrole responses either gratify or frustrate the expectations of the initiator and are interpreted as approval or disapproval of the role behavior of the initiator. What is an expectation on the part of the initiator, that is, how he expects the other to respond to his role behavior, is a sanction on the part of the participant, that is, he approves or disapproves the role of the initiator, and vice versa.

Role behavior, then, on the part of two or more individuals involved in reciprocal transaction both defines the situation and regulates it. The regulation is established both by the effect of the sanctioning function implicit in the counterrole response and through the functioning of the shared system of meanings and values that orient the actions of the participants.

There is probably no difficulty in perceiving the central importance of role playing in the socialization of children. Role theory looks at the problem of child training from the point of view of the social system, especially as it is embodied in the family. Its specific contribution is that it makes it possible to describe the development of the child from the point of view of a multiplicity of object relations. Because it is based on a transactional system, inclusive of the self and others, it can prove to be a useful link between the intrapersonal systems of id, ego, and superego, and the interpersonal systems of primary groups such as the family, on the basis of which the former derives its characteristic stamp. Such a link also provides a mechanism whereby cultural value orientations can be described simultaneously from the points of view of the individual and of society. Because of this application, it opens up immense vistas for cross-disciplinary collaboration and research.

There is one other way in which role theory is significant to the aims of this analysis. It provides a method for defining the structure of a situation in terms of the roles of the participants. In this way it establishes the possibility of analyzing the state of a transaction system. The system may be stable and persistent, changing in an adaptive fashion, enduring with difficulty because of inner conflicts, or disintegrating. Where families are the system under scrutiny, it is our stated intention to discover methods for detecting states of deviance and pathology and to distinguish them from various states of stability or adaptive change that have healthier implications for the emotional adjustments of the members. The description of the family in terms of the roles of its members supplies an analytical method for approaching these variations in structure and function. The roles can be inspected for incompatibility and conflict both as an internal system and in relation to the integration of the family with the other parts of the social systems.

Spiegel categorized social roles with special reference to the family as a social system. This categorization makes it possible to specify the locus of conflict within a family and the shifts occurring in the family interaction process from one role system to the other. (For a detailed description of this framework, see Spiegel, 1971, chs. 3 and 4.)

Social roles can be divided into three major categories: Formal, Informal, and Fictive. Formal roles can be characterized in several different ways. They include the major activities that every society needs to regulate in order to survive. Some, like age and sex roles, concern straight biological functions and are universally ascribed to every member of the society. These roles are initially learned through family transactions. Not for one moment can most people safely step out of the behavior expected for their age or sex. Some, like domestic or family roles, are almost as universally and inevitably ascribed; for everyone is born into a family, and most people create new ones. Still others, like occupational, religious, and recreational roles, are more episodic; that is, one does not need to occupy all of them all the time. They are acquired through effort, achievement, or failure throughout a lifetime. (See Linton, 1936, ch. 8.) They too are strictly patterned and required for most people.

Informal roles, on the other hand, are more occasional and more the choice of the individual than Formal roles. Some concern transitional occasions, that is, with getting out of one situation and into another. The sick role, for example, is a transitional role; it occurs at a certain occasion and the sick person may or may not agree to accept the role. On the other hand, some people, usually called malingerers, may take the sick role when they are not actually sick. At any rate, the sick role is informally patterned in every society in order to get the sick person back into a state of health. Visitors, guests, and travelers are also examples of transitional roles.

Another group of Informal roles are the character roles. These include heroes and villains, liars and cheats, exhibitionists and voyeurs, sadists and masochists. Such designations are usually thought to result from traits of character, but the given behavior cannot take place without the reciprocal behavior of a role partner. Every hero must have his admirers; every exhibitionist must locate his voyeur; just as every masochist needs to find his sadist in order to enjoy his role in life. But such roles are not required of anyone by the social system. They may be adopted by a person or assigned to him—we may assign the role of a fool to someone we do not like, for example. Such adoptions and assignments, then, are part of the informal workings of social groups.

The third category, Fictive roles, includes roles that are not pragmatically related to the ongoing work of any social system or group but instead serve the interests of imagination or play. For the most part, they are occupied deliberately on the basis of pretense— a girl plays the role of mother to her doll or a boy plays the role of cowboy. Fictive roles allow fantasy behavior in everyday life and thus serve to relieve the stress and strain of reality for adults as well as children. Every society sanctions such roles provided they are accompanied by a communication that says in effect: this is not serious; this is in jest or play. When Fictive or fantasy roles are taken without this accompanying signal, then we say that the person who shows such behavior and the group that accepts such behavior are pathological. For example, the person who pretends to be the prophet Elijah for the sake of amusement or satire is looked at quite differently from the person who says he *is* the prophet Elijah and the group of followers who accept this claim.

Apparently no organized group can supply the variety and interplay of ascribed and acquired roles to so few individuals as the family. In residential institutions for children, the roles are strung among a wide variety of parent substitutes who have attained their position by achievement. The lack of ascriptive foci for the roles undermines the emotional poignancy of interpersonal relations. No one really belongs to anyone.

It is this factor of belonging by right of membership that underlies a group of functions the family shares with other parts of the social system. These functions include the satisfaction and integration of biological and psychological needs, the performance of subsistence and maintenance functions, the observance of cultural and religious rituals, the more formal education of the children, and recreational activities.

There is enormous cultural diversity in the degree to which these functions are allocated to the family or shared and assigned to other institutions. In the United States, for example, education and recreation are shared with the schools, subsistence activities are shared with the occupational structure. The middle-class, urban family as a whole participates very little in these functions. Individual members of the family, taking advantage of the elaborate division of labor in the industrial community, enact these roles through group membership in other organizations or through purchase of services. In all societies, however, all these functions are performed to some extent by the family. Even in our highly specialized communities, functions such as cleaning, helping with homework, and watching television are performed in the home.

From the point of view of the social system then social roles conceptualize behavioral processes of transaction among individuals. It is only by looking at the whole social system that one can segregate parental roles from occupational and recreational roles. From the point of view of the individual, however, these same social roles appear related to inner needs and drives. A role is a socially regulated way of satisfying instinctual needs in an organized system of action. If this is true, then any discussion of the functions of the family must include not only the description of the particular configuration of roles that characterizes this primary group and depends on the social system in which the family functions, but it also must deal with the way these roles satisfy certain crucial needs of the individuals composing the family. Because there is no uniform conceptual system for characterizing the instincts, drives, or needs of the individual, we shall discuss individual needs in a very general, nonspecific fashion.

The socialization of children is a process that covers—from the psychological focus—a cluster of intimately related individual needs. The biological need of the child for continual nourishment and physical maintenance during the prolonged period of dependency has already been mentioned. More important, perhaps, is the child's need for love, approval, and security. This latter need can tentatively be further specified as the need for a consistent pattern of rewards and punishments in the context of a basic emotional acceptance and understanding of the child by its parents or parent substitutes.

These needs of the child cannot be adequately discussed without simultaneous consideration of the individual needs of other members of the nuclear family—siblings, mother, and father. The mother-child pattern of transaction is the process that has been most extensively studied in this area. The early symbiotic nature of the mother-child relation and the gradual loosening and differentiation of the relation with the changing needs of both mother and child have been stressed. (See Benedek, 1949.) The significance of the child as an emotional object for the mother and the unconscious identification of the child with various significant objects from the mother's past life have also been emphasized. The mother-child relation, however, is not isolated from other family processes. Here especially, the needs of the father vis-à-vis both mother and child, and of the mother toward child and father, introduce complexities into family processes. Mother and father need love (according to the specific cultural patterning), security, understanding, and sexual satisfaction in their relations with each other. But this system of needs is continuously modified by the competing systems of mother-child and father-child. Where there is more than one child, further imbalance is introduced by multiple assemblies of such triangulated need systems. Some of the most pressing problems in the etiology of mental health and ill health arise from degrees of good or bad fit among the triangular relations that constitute the internal structure and function of the nuclear family.

It is evident that the conceptual items in the theory of social roles are not made from whole cloth but are already embedded in our everyday language as a sort of preconceptual wisdom. It is impossible, for example, to make generalizations about the distribution of needs or drives among the various members of the family without referring to the social role of the individual member under observation. We must talk about the generalized father, mother, daughter, or son in order to have a way of locating the observed drive in time and space. Needs are already specified to social roles in the ordinary currency of our discourse. Our problem, then, is to distinguish the various social roles from the point of view of their adequacy—their capacity for integrating particular needs. This problem may turn out to be something of an artificial one created by a concealed value assumption since we do not as yet know the degree to which the needs or drives that we can perceive (as well as the very act of observation) are shaped by the cultural patterning processes of a particular society. It is well to remind ourselves repeatedly that the observer is himself a part of the total field and is influenced or thrown off balance by it at the moment of observation as well as later in moments of reflection and conceptualization. Nevertheless, so far as one can discern in the present state of our knowledge, roles can be matched for the degree of satisfaction they provide and for their manner of organizing particular needs.

From this point of view it would appear that the family role relations of husband-wife, father-mother, parent-child, and so forth are the most appropriate ways of organizing and satisfying the particular needs of the individual discussed above—at least for our society. At the same time it is quite clear that these role relations do not exhaust the ways of organizing the satisfaction of the same needs. So far as its total function in the social system is concerned, the family shares this function with other social structures characterized by variant social roles. In the matter of sexual satisfaction, for example, the husband-wife role parallels other variant role relations such as those with prostitutes, the brief affair, or homosexual partnerships. Regarding the socialization of children, we have already mentioned social structures, such as orphanages and the foster family, that share some of the aspects of this function with the family. For example, the school system is strategically important for the more formal cognitive and group-oriented aspects of child training. Obviously much more could be said about the relations between individual needs and role structuring, but for our present purposes it is only necessary to emphasize that although the degree of sharing of these functions varies from society to society, in every known society the family remains the central and apparently indispensable agency for satisfying such individual needs.

To account for the various forms these universal aspects of family structure take in different societies and subgroups, it is necessary to discuss cultural value orientations. Not until this focus of organization with the total field of human behavior has been presented will a groundwork be laid to frame a typology of families—that is, to make descriptive comparisons between various types of families within a society with a view to isolating unhealthy and deviant from healthy dominant or variant types.

Family Value System. Cultural anthropologists must receive most of the credit for pointing out the tremendous variability in human behavior as determined by cultural patterns. This variation not only includes moral standards and mores but also extends to the subtler issues of motivation and patterns of interpersonal relations. The variations in existential judgments and systems of belief, such as those found in various religious orientations, philosophies, and science, are not new to us; but the cultural anthropologists integrated them in a new way with other cultural patterns, such as child-rearing practices. As a result of the novel synthesis, we now have a clearer understanding of the relation between the psychology of the individual and the culture in which he develops and to which he is adapted. (For an excellent discussion of the relation, see C. Kluckhohn and Murray, 1953. Another approach is found in Linton and Kardiner, 1939; Linton, 1945; Kardiner, 1945. Also see Frank, 1948.) And it is no longer possible to assume that generalizations based on observations of one culture have a universal applicability.

A number of anthropologists have developed slightly varying concepts for dealing with the generalized meanings in a cultural tradition; and they have all shown that a knowledge of the differences in these meanings is important to our understanding of individual behavior in varying cultural traditions. Almost all the concepts also stress the critically important fact that, despite the individual's lack of conscious awareness of most of his cultural values, they greatly influence his motivational system and action patterns.

But in spite of the new insights provided by the concepts, most of them have had a limited usefulness in the analysis of the relations between psychological and cultural processes. For the most part, the difficulties in using them arise from the absence of a systematic theory of cultural variation and the consequent tendency to rely too heavily on empirical generalizations. The concepts have been both too particularized to single cultures to permit systematic comparisons between cultures and too grossly generalized to allow for an analysis of variations within cultures. All too frequently the persons who have ably demonstrated a uniqueness in the value systems of different societies have ignored the fundamental universality of human problems and its correlate that human societies have found approximately the same answers for some problems.

Also, in most of the discussions of the common value element in the many patterns of a culture, the dominant values of peoples have been overstressed and variant values of peoples largely ignored. These two concomitant tendencies have produced interpretative studies that are, in spite of their brilliance of insight, oversimplified, static representations of social structures and processes. Variation for the same individual when he plays different roles and variation within whole groups of persons in a single society have not been adequately accounted for. Yet it is precisely this kind of variation that is crucial for the conceptual integration of psychological and social or cultural processes.

For our treatment of family patterns, we shall use the classification scheme and theory of variation that is based primarily on those previous concepts of variability but that differs in that it rests on several assumptions that postulate a systematic variation in value orientations both between and within cultures. (The theory of cultural value orientations used here was formulated by F. Kluckhohn, using C. Kluckhohn's definition of value-orientation. The later comprehensive development of the theory appears in F. Kluckhohn and Strodtbeck, 1961.)

Before presenting these assumptions, it is necessary to define the term *value-orientation*. The definition being followed is mainly that of C. Kluckhohn (1951, pp. 409, 411). "It is convenient to use the term value-orientation for those value elements which are (a) general, (b) organized, and (c) include definite existential judgments. A value-orientation is a set of linked propositions embracing value and existential elements . . . Since value elements and existential premises are almost inextricably blended in the overall picture of experience that characterizes an individual or a group, it seems well to call this overall view a "value-orientation," symbolizing the fact that the affective-cognitive (orientation) elements are blended. More formally, *a value-orientation may be defined as a generalized and organized conception, influencing behavior, of nature, of man's place in it, of man's relation to man, and of the desirable and nondesirable as they relate to man-environment and interhuman relations* . . . Like values, they vary on a continuum from the explicit to the implicit."

The first of the major assumptions for our classification and theory of value-orientation variation, which relates to the number of value-orientation areas, is that there is a limited number of common human problems for which all peoples in all places must at times find some solution.

The second assumption is that although there is variability in solutions of the problems, this variability is neither limitless nor random but occurs within a range of possible solutions.

The third assumption, which provides the key for the analysis of variation, is that all variants (all alternatives) of all solutions are in varying degrees present in the total cultural structure of every society. There will be, in other words, in every society, not only a dominant profile of value orientations, which is made up of those orientations most highly evaluated, but also variant or substitute orientations that are universal.

Four problems have been tentatively singled out as the crucial ones common to all human groups. These problems are stated here in the form of questions, and each is answered with the name that will be used henceforth for the range of orientations relating to the question. What is the modality of human activity? *Activity orientation.* What is the modality of man's relationship to other men? *Relational orientation.* What is the temporal focus of human life? *Time orientation.* What is the relation of man to nature? *Man-nature orientation.* The ranges of variability suggested as a testable conceptualization of the variation in the value orientations are given in Table 1.

Table 1.

VALUE ORIENTATIONS

Modalities	*Preferences*		
Activity	Being	Being-in-becoming	Doing
Relational	Lineal	Collateral	Individualistic
Time	Past	Present	Future
Man-nature	Subjugation-to-nature	Harmony-with-nature	Mastery-over-nature
Human nature	Evil	Neutral Mixture of good and evil	Good

The modality of human activity is the first of the common human problems in the value orientation system, and the range of variation in solutions suggested for it is the threefold one of Being, Being-in-becoming and Doing.

In very large part this range of variation has been derived from the distinctions made long ago by philosophers. However, there are important differences. In the conceptual scheme of value orientations, the terms Being and Becoming are expanded to a three-point range of Being. Being-in-becoming and Doing are here much more narrowly defined than they usually are by philosophers. Furthermore, we hold to the view that this range of orientations varies independently from those that deal with the relations of man to nature, man to time, and man to basic human nature. The tendency of philosophers, writing with different aims, has been to treat these several types of orientations as relatively undifferentiated.

The three preferences center on the problem of the nature of man's mode of self-expression in activity. Each mode is definitely considered to be a type of activity. The differences between them are not, therefore, those distinguished by the dichotomy of active-passive, for example.

The Being orientation is a preference for the kind of activity that is a spontaneous expression of what is conceived to be given in the human personality. As compared with either the Being-in-becoming or Doing orientations, it stresses a nondevelopmental conception of activity. It might even be phrased as a spontaneous expression in activity of impulses and desires; yet care must be taken not to make this interpretation too literal. In no society, as C. Kluckhohn comments, does one ever find a one-to-one relation between the desired and the desirable. The concrete behavior of individuals in complex situations and the moral codes governing that behavior usually reflect all the orientations simultaneously. A stress upon the "isness" of the personality and a spontaneous expression of that "isness" is not pure license, as we see if we turn our attention to a society or segments of a society in which the Being orientation is dominant. Mexican society, for example, is clearly one in which the Being orientation is dominant. The wide-range patterning of fiesta activities alone shows this. Yet never in the fiesta, with its emphasis on spontaneity, is there pure impulse gratification. The value demands of other orientations, such as the relational orientation, for example, create codes that restrain the activities of individuals in very definite ways.

The Being-in-becoming orientation shares with the Being a great concern with what the human being is rather than what he can accomplish, but here the similarity ends. In the Being-in-becoming orientation, the idea of development, so little stressed in the Being orientation, is paramount.

Erich Fromm's conception of "the spontaneous activity of the total integrated personality" is close to the Being-in-becoming type. "By activity," he states, "we do not mean 'doing something' but rather the quality of the creative activity which can operate in one's emotional, intellectual, and sensuous experiences and in one's will as well. One premise of this spontaneity is the acceptance of the total personality and the elimination of the split between 'reason' and 'nature' " (Fromm, 1941, pp. 258–59). A less favorably prejudiced and, for our purposes, a more accurately limited statement would be: the Being-in-becoming orientation emphasizes the kind of activity that has as its goal the development of all aspects of the self as an integrated whole.

The Doing preference is the dominant one in American society and there is little need for an extensive discussion of it. Its most distinguishing feature is a demand for the kind of activity that results in accomplishments that are measurable by standards conceived to be external to the acting individual. That aspect of self-judgment or judgment of others that relates to the nature of activity is based mainly on a measurable accomplishment achieved by acting on persons, things, or situations. What does the individual do and what can he or will he accomplish are almost always the primary questions in our scale of appraisal of persons. "Getting things done" and finding ways "to do something" about any and all situations are stock American phrases.

Fromm also considers this orientation to be different from the one he defines in his concept of spontaneity, but he does not accord it an equally favored position. Instead he condemns it as a fertile source of neurotically compulsive behavior. While few would disagree that the Doing orientation of Americans leads to a comparison and competition with others that is often extreme and intense, we do not as yet know just how often the competition either leads to or reflects compulsion in the technical sense of the term.

The second common human problem treated in the conceptual scheme is the definition of man's relation to other men. This orientation has three subdivisions: the Lineal, the Collateral, and the Individualistic.

All societies and all groups must give some attention to all three principles. All societies must acknowledge that individuals are biologically and culturally related to each other through time. There is always a Lineal principle in relations that are derived from age, generational differences, and cultural tradition. Collaterality is also found in all societies. The individual is not a human being outside a group. One kind of group emphasis is that put upon laterally extended relations. These are the immediate relations in time and place. Individual autonomy also cannot be and is not ignored by even the most extreme type of collectivistic society. The fundamental question is always that of emphasis.

For some types of problems it may be sufficient to differentiate only between the individual and the collectivity. In most cases, however, it would appear highly important to know what kind of collectivist preference is being stressed. A society that places its major emphasis on the Lineal preference—as do, for example, the Japanese and some upper-class Americans—will have quite different evaluations of right and proper relations from the society that puts a first-order emphasis on the Individualistic preference—as do, for example, most Americans.

There will always be variability in the primacy and nature of goals according to which of the three preferences is stressed. If the Individualistic preference is dominant and the other two interpreted in terms of it, individual goals will have primacy over the goals of either the Collateral or Lineal group. When the Collateral preference is dominant, the goals—or welfare—of the laterally extended group have primacy for all individuals. The group in this case is viewed as being moderately independent of other similar groups, and the question of continuity through time is not critical. When the Lineal preference is most heavily stressed, it is again group goals that are of primary concern to individuals, but the goal of continuity through time is uppermost. Both continuity and ordered positional succession are of great importance when Lineality dominates the relational system.

How the continuity and ordered positional succession are achieved in the Lineal system is separate from the preference as such. It does in fact seem to be the case that the most successful way of maintaining the stress on Lineality is through mechanisms that are either actual hereditary ones based on biological relatedness or ones that are assimilated into a kinship system. The English, for example, maintained into the present time a strong Lineality by consistently moving successful members of their more Individualistic middle class into the established peerage system. Other societies have found other but similar mechanisms.

Three obvious preferences define man's place in time—the third common human problem. There is always a Past time to be reckoned with, a Present time in which we live, and a Future time that lies ahead. No society does or can completely ignore any of the three time periods. Yet societies differ greatly as to which of the three dimensions they make dominant.

Mexican-Americans are a people who emphasize Present time. They pay little attention to what has happened in the past, and regard the future as a vague and most unpredictable period—planning for the future or hoping that it will be better than either present or past is not the Mexican-American way of life.

Traditional China was a society that put its main emphasis on Past time. Ancestor worship and strong family tradition were both expressions of this orientation. So also was the Chinese attitude that nothing new ever happened in the present or would happen in the future.

Many modern European countries also tend to stress the past. Even England—insofar as it has been dominated by an aristocracy and traditionalism—shows this emphasis. One of the chief differences between ourselves and the English is our somewhat varying attitudes toward time. We have difficulty in understanding the respect the English have for tradition, and they do not appreciate our disregard for it.

Americans, more than most people in the world, place an emphasis on Future time, a future that we anticipate to be "bigger and better." This attitude does not mean we have no regard for the past or fail to give thought to the present. But few Americans ever want to be called old-fashioned. We do not consider the ways of the past to be good just because they are past, and we are seldom content with the present. This makes us a people who place a high value on change.

The fourth common human problem is man's relation to nature. This dimension is also characterized by a three-point range in variation—Subjugation-to-nature, Harmony-with-nature, and Mastery-over-nature. These variations are well known from the works of philosophers and cultural historians and need little explanation.

In years past, Mexican-American culture in the American Southwest gave us an example of a definite Subjugation-to-nature orientation. Traditionally, the typical Mexican-American sheepherder believed firmly that there was little or nothing a man could do to protect either land or flocks when damaging storms descended on him. He simply accepted the inevitable. One finds the same fatalism in Mexican-American attitudes toward illness and death. "If it is the Lord's will that I die, I shall die" is the way they express it, and Mexican-Americans have been known to refuse the services of a doctor because of this attitude.

If the conceptualization of the man-nature relation is that of man's Harmony-with-nature, there is no real separation between man and nature. One is but the extension of the other; both are needed to make a whole. This orientation seems to have been the dominant one in certain periods of Chinese history.

A third way of conceptualizing this relation is that of man's Mastery-over-nature. With this view, clearly characteristic of many Americans, natural forces are to be overcome and put to the use of human beings. We span our rivers with bridges, blast through mountains to make tunnels, make lakes where none existed, and do a thousand and one other things to exploit nature and make it serve human needs. In general, this attitude indicates an orientation based on overcoming obstacles. It is difficult for us to understand the kind of people who accept the obstacle and give in to it or even the people who stress the harmonious oneness of man and nature.

In this delineation of the ranges of value orientations, attention has been focused mainly on dominant orientation emphases. But important as it is to know what is dominant in a society at a given time, it is also important to our understanding of the dynamics of that society that we know the variant orientations. Individuals and groups who live in accordance with variant rather than dominant orientation patterns are essential to the maintenance of the society.

Variant values are, as has been indicated in our third basic assumption, not only permitted but actually required. It has been a common misconception that all behavior and certain aspects of motivation that do not accord with the dominant values should be treated as deviant behavior. Lack of adequate criteria has often led us to confuse the deviant, who, by his behavior, calls down the sanctions of his group, with the variant, who is accepted and required. In a society like ours, a wide range of variation lies beneath the surface of what has often been called our compulsive conformity. The dynamic interplay of the dominant and the variant is one of the outstanding features of American society although it has been little analyzed or understood. We laud or condemn the melting pot ideology and accept or reject what we frequently term the contradictions of our society, but we have not examined carefully the processes that create what we so readily judge.

We cannot here treat the kinds of variations or the reasons for them. However, it is a central theoretical proposition in all that is to follow on the analysis of family systems, that there is an ordered cultural variation (or web of variation) in all social systems.

Innate human nature (the fifth common problem) is logically characterized as evil, good and evil (simply neutral or a mixture of good and evil) and good. The subprinciples of mutability and immutability increase this basic threefold classification to six possibilities. Human nature can, for example, be conceived to be evil and unalterable or evil and perfectible; as good and unalterable or as good and corruptible; as an invariant mixture of the good and evil or as a mixture subject to influence. Thus, one may rightly question the validity and usefulness of the three-way classification suggested for the range of this orientation. However, the three categories do seem adequate as a first approximation in making major differentiations. Furthermore, some of the finer distinctions noted in specific values and behavior patterns may be derivatives of an interrelationship between human nature and other of the orientations. Other desirable distinctions perhaps also can be achieved by using the derivatives of a cross-classification of the basic three-way categorization and the twofold subcategorization.

Leaving aside possible derivations, let us illustrate from American culture itself some of the major variations. The orientation inherited from Puritan ancestors and still strong among many Americans is that of a basically evil but perfectible human nature.

According to this view, constant control and discipline of the self are required if any goodness is to be achieved, and the danger of regression is always present. But some in the United States today, perhaps a growing number, incline to the view that human nature is a mixture of good and evil. They would say that although control and effort are certainly needed, lapses can be understood and need not always be severely condemned. This latter definition of basic human nature appears to be more common among peoples of the world, both literate and nonliterate, than is the one held to in the historical past of the United States. Whether any total societies are committed to the definition of human nature as immutably good is to be doubted. Yet the position is a possible one, and it certainly should be found as an alternative definition within societies.

Integrations in Mexican-American Family Patterns

We have now completed sketching in the main elements in the theoretical framework we propose to use for the analysis of the family as a system of behavior. We consider this behavioral system to exist in a transactional field of interdependent systems. However, for the sake of simplicity and convenience we intend to confine this analysis to an examination of the interdependence of only four of the five systems transacting in the total field: the geographical place or territorial reference of the transacting systems; the system of cultural value orientations; the extended social system, existing in that place with reference to the particular system of cultural value orientations; and the family, as a system of social role patterns, interdependent with the place, the values, and the social system.

Since the transactional field is a unity of interpenetrating processes, each of these four systems is molded by the others; each one is reflected in all the others. No linear causal chain of events connects them, only reverberating processes that take place between and among all of them. In order to bring out as clearly as possible how this happens, we propose to compare two very different assemblies of these systems. The first is the pattern of family life among the Mexican-Americans of the American Southwest. The second is the role patterning of family life in a dominant middle-class large urban center in the United States. We believe that the contrast is sufficiently vivid to reflect clearly both the invariant and variant relations that we would like to make explicit.

The Mexican-Americans of the Southwest are, of course, a part of total American society. Although currently undergoing a dramatic change, they have had until quite recently displayed an order of value orientations in startling contrast to dominant middle-class American values. (Adapted from F. Kluckhohn, 1952.) Ignoring for the moment the variant and deviant values within each of the groups, we can outline the contrasts in dominant value orientations as shown in Table 2.

Table 2.

MEXICAN-AMERICAN AND ANGLO-AMERICAN VALUE
ORIENTATION PROFILES

Modalities	*Mexican-American*	*Anglo-American*
Activity	Being	Doing
Relational	Lineal	Individualistic
Time	Present	Future
Man-nature	Subjugation-to-nature	Mastery-over-nature

The Mexican-American system of value orientations is reflected in and maintained by a certain kind of social system and family role structuring. First, the social system and the family system coincide to a large degree. The social system is formed to a much larger extent than in other communities by a network of interrelated families. Although the pattern is now changing rapidly, the Mexican-Americans lived characteristically in small village units. Although economic and other pressures have pushed many of them into urban centers and have disrupted some of the old patterns, still, even in towns and cities today, they tend to live, wherever possible, in some kind of interrelated group.

In the villages, most of the persons are related to each other by blood and marriage ties, and the village is often no more than a large group of interrelated families. In one village in New Mexico every family has the same surname. Within this network of biologically related people, the occasional unrelated person is not apt to have an easy time. Until he can establish some kind of relation, he remains an outsider about whom there is always some concern and even suspicion. In part, such hostility results from the fact that social control in these villages is exercised mainly through the family. It is not shared, as in other communities, with agencies like the police and law courts.

The extensive interrelatedness of the Mexican-American village community is achieved by wide-range recognition of kinship ties both vertically (through the generations) and laterally (to include, for example, even fifth and sixth degree cousins) and also, by a general extension, to include everyone even remotely related. Neither the pattern of relatedness nor the actual number of relations differs greatly from the situation in other communities. What is different is the strength of the ties that bind them all together. The basic nuclear family of husband, wife, and children exists as it does in all societies. Yet, a true Mexican-American would feel extremely impoverished if the only relatives he had about him were his wife and children. His nieces and nephews arc almost the same to him as his sons and daughters, and his cousins differ little from his brothers and sisters. Everyone disciplines nieces and nephews as readily and as efficiently as his own children—to say nothing of feeding and caring for them. There is a general and almost casual sharing of children. Since it is felt that a family without children—four to ten are preferred—is not a family, the unfortunate couple without children will usually take one, two, or three of those belonging to sisters or brothers or, in fact, anyone with too many. Some 10 to 12 percent of the children in one village, for example, were found to be living with persons other than their parents. Mexican-Americans do not have the anxieties about adoption that many Anglo-Americans have. And their relative unconcern about who gets which child reflects the low value they place on individualism.

The authority lines—the Lineal accenting of relational values—in the Mexican-American family system are definite and firm. The old people are the rulers; the male sex is clearly dominant. Respect for and obedience to age are bred into the Mexican-American child at an early age and are never forgotten. Sons do not expect to become independent upon reaching maturity. Only the eldest son is permitted by custom to have any kind of authority and responsibility, but even he must remain subservient to the father's control until death or infirmity of the father necessitates his taking control of the family affairs. This special training of the oldest son is so pointed that the younger brothers and sisters treat him more as a father than as a sibling. The social mechanism that shapes the role of the oldest son is concerned with preserving the continuity of authority by age. With such large families, it often happens that the father dies before all the children have reached maturity. The oldest son then moves into the father's position, and all is supposed to go on as before.

The authority relations centered about age and other ascribed roles are not confined to the family system in the Mexican-American community. They are generalized and extended to include a kind of feudal relation called the *patron-peon* system. One powerful and dominant family, the head of which is the *patron,* rules the whole village in much the same way fathers rule the families. Those under control of the *patron* are sometimes called *peones* —or more frequently simply *la gente* (the people). Between *patron* and *peones* there is a relation very similar to that which existed between the lord of the feudal manor and his serfs. Beyond the *patron* there is still another authority—the village saint. The interest of the Mexican-American Catholic in his own particular *patron* saint is far greater than his interest in the more abstract aspects of the religion. The saint is considered most responsible for everyone's welfare and a big annual fiesta is given for him. In this way, the Lineal accenting of relational values is synchronized with the man-nature range of value orientations, with regard to which the Mexican-American views himself as subservient to and dependent upon forces in nature.

We have already mentioned the dominance of men in the Mexican-American family system as an example of the importance of ascribed characteristics. It is true that in the larger towns and cities the Mexican-American women today do take jobs and assume many of the achievement aspects of the Anglo-American women. In the villages, however, the Mexican-American woman has only one career to look forward to—that of wife and mother. There is none of the equality between the sexes however problematical that is so signficant in the Anglo social system. Instead there is a clear-cut division of labor and of rights and obligations. The lives of most women in the villages were, traditionally, so circumscribed that they were not permitted even to market in the village store. The store was a meeting place for the men—hence neither safe nor proper for the women. Men and children bought all supplies.

Yet, despite the restrictions, the female role offers Mexican-American women great security. They expect their marriages to be permanent, and they usually are. They know exactly what is expected in every aspect of their roles. By the age of twelve almost every village girl is quite well trained for her future job of house-wife and mother. She moves easily into her adult role without having to face such vexations and anxiety inducing problems as what sort of a boy to marry or whether to choose a career instead of marriage.

According to dominant American standards, the Mexican-American patterns of living undoubtedly seem exceedingly repressive. Considering the Mexican-American orientations, however, the picture is quite different. While familial ties—both Lineal and Collateral—bind them on every side and keep them dependent, there is a definite security and safety in that dependence. Even the *patron,* who has the authority to demand obedience to himself and his commands, has many obligations to his people. He often manages the economic affairs of families, guides and counsels in times of crisis, and has the major village responsibility.

Within individual families great stress is placed on group cohesion. Each member of the family is responsible to all the others in accordance with his particular position. Without this extensive interdependence Mexican-Americans could not long maintain their Present time orientation to life. It is one thing to accept each day for what it is and enjoy it when one has many relatives to depend on if things should go badly. This attitude may be quite destructive, however, if independence and responsibility for self are prevailing rules. An example of this attitude was recorded by F. Kluckhohn. The families of a father and two married sons constituted a single economic unit. Once they had been a land and livestock-owning family in which all members had worked at a common task. When all the property was eventually gone, the old patterns still persisted —even though from our point of view each of the individual family heads was now an independent wage earner. The three families maintained a common larder, and all continued to contribute to the support of all. At no time did the three wage-earning men work simultaneously. When two of them had moderately good jobs, the third was certain to be on a trip or vacation or simply resting at home. Since two could make all that any of them required or needed, why should all three be driving ahead? Indeed, there was nothing in particular to drive toward. That which is is good enough; the future is of small concern.

Correlated to this point of view, and of equal importance, is the acceptance of the inevitable. The whole system of relations, including those of the family, but especially those of *peones* to their *patron,* tends to preserve what exists and leaves little room for achievement or ambition. Change is not expected, and improvement is scarcely even a dream. The family's standard of living remains the same generation after generation with only microscopic alterations. *Peones* remain *peones,* younger brothers stay in their places, and for a woman to challenge masculine dominance is unthinkable.

Thus we see that Mexican-American value orientations are —or were—fully expressed in the structure of family patterns. It is also evident that, reciprocally, family patterns foster and maintain the system of cultural values in a transactional field. It is central to our thesis, however, and to our search for factors responsible for mental health in families, that the transactions between the two systems are not always well integrated. There is undoubtedly security in the Mexican-American patterns, but there are also definite strains and inadequate fits among the tightly knit relations. The child is accepted for himself as few American children are. He is not driven or urged to be independent and ambitious. On the contrary, training is consistently—except in the case of the oldest son— toward a lack of initiative and responsibility. There is much evidence that this emphasis is too rigid. Although we are not considering the impact of biological variation on family patterns, there is no doubt that the Mexican-American values are a hardship on those children constitutionally endowed with greater reactivity, vigor, and energy. The most frequent conflicts occur in the relation between the older and younger brothers. Recent research in the area has shown that family relations have undergone considerable change. This change is especially apparent in the breakdown of the oldest brother-younger brother relation and the consequent intense conflict within or disruption of the family.

There has been an increasing shift from Lineally organized relations to Individualistic ones, but as yet little or no change has occurred in other Mexican-American value orientations. Disorganization within the structure of the family and in the personalities of family members is the striking result of the process. Delinquency among adolescents has increased rapidly, divorce has become more common, in-group taboos have broken down, and, perhaps most important of all, one notes attitudes of bewilderment and hopelessness in many of those who are middle-aged or older. Only a few at any age level have become thoroughly acculturated in the ways of Anglo-American life. A majority are seeking new patterns of adaptation, which, it seems certain, will also not be free from strain —an Individualistic relational orientation simply does not fit well with either a Being activity or a Present time orientaton. It is one thing to live in the present and act in accordance with certain feelings when one has a Lineal family system that assures both economic support and firm regulatory norms for the impulse life; it is quite another when the individual or the small nuclear family lives alone.

Integrations in American Middle-Class Family Patterns

Mexican-American family patterns, as they were, are good representatives of what is often termed a familistic society. In contrasting them with Anglo-American family patterns, it is important to keep in mind that the Mexican-American situation is not atypical. A majority of the peoples of the world tend to be familistic to some degree. They tend to emphasize either the Lineal or Collateral relational principle rather than the Individualistic one. It is the American pattern that is more atypical—due in large part to its extreme stress on Individualistic relations. However, there are other ways in which the dominant American profile of value orientations is unique. We have already mentioned the extraordinary emphasis on Doing in the range of the activity orientation and the accenting of Future time. Indeed, this latter orientation goes so far that we often appear to have forgotten how to enjoy the present for its own sake. Perhaps this accounts for the existence of what David Riesman has called our "fun morality"—a compulsive search for enjoyment through ritualized and institutionalized entertainment in which having fun, having a good time, has to be planned for and "achieved" (Riesman, 1950). But if one has to plan to enjoy the future, spontaneity tends to be vitiated by the time the future becomes the present.

Other possible difficulties flowing from the severe stress on these value orientations will be taken up shortly in our examination of American family patterns. Here it is sufficient to point out that there is a good deal of harmonious interlocking of the value orientations in the ramification of roles that constitute the social system. The emphasis on achievement requires considerable planning for the future, step-by-step planning of the means-ends patterns by which future success may be secured. (This preference for distant aims also tends to place a great premium on the young—those with the most future ahead of them.) And it is the individual around whom all the planning centers who reaps the rewards. Without a sanctioning of Individualistic over Lineal and Collateral relations, the individual would never be free to realize his plans, to leave his family, his home town, or his job for a better situation. Along with the planning and achievement values goes the optimism derived from the emphasis on man's Mastery-over-nature. The conviction that we can always improve matters by thoughtful care and planning and the belief in progress through scientific achievement give our industrial, job-centered society its characteristic stamp and support the system of mobile occupational roles through which the plans for achievement are realized.

In observing how the dominant American value-orientations are reflected in the patterns of American family life, we face problems of selectivity and special emphasis. It is possible to speak of The American Family only if we realize that we mean the ideal or typical family of the dominant middle class although no single family type can be said to be representative of all America. Variation in American families results from having within one nation large groups of people with quite different cultural backgrounds. There are also families midway between those of clear-cut ethnic background and those dominantly American. We can distinguish differences of another kind among families of varying economic levels.

It is this diversity that leads to the stress on a dominant or typical family pattern. We could not hold our differences together for long if there were not at the same time a strong sense of conformity and oneness. Thus, there exists a kind of consensus regarding the relations and roles that should exist in the Good Family. There is, in other words, a kind of model family—other families are judged by it and many strive to become like it. This model is the typical family of the middle class.

The typical middle-class family of today is a small nuclear family. A father, a mother, and two or three children at most has been the numerical pattern in recent years. In addition to being small, this typical family is in many ways an isolated one. It is an independent unit, both economically and socially. Even though its members always recognize relatives—grandparents, uncles, aunts, and cousins—the relational bonds are not, in most cases, strong ones. Although personal preference may, and often does, make them strong, there are no binding rules—such as there are in Mexican-American society—that make it necessary always to accept and get along with relatives.

In relations between siblings in the typical American family, for example, it is easy to assume that the bonds of affection and antagonism experienced by siblings as they grow up will gradually lead to and become permanent attachments in adulthood. Yet, in actuality, by the time they are thirty-five or forty years old, many of them are closer to their associates and friends than to their brothers and sisters. The separation and emotional distancing may be screened by sentimentality—that is, an increasing emphasis on symbolic aspects of relations that are losing substantive content—and last-minute gestures on birthdays and anniversaries, but they are there all the same. This gap is frequently reinforced by the actual physical separation incident to the vigorous geographical mobility of middle-class Americans. Also, it is often widened by a social distance. One sister's husband is successful, another's is not. As a result they live in different social orbits and seldom meet. Even if the two sisters maintain their relation, it is unlikely that their children will have much in common or have many contacts with each other. In other cases, it may be simply that the interests of the family of one sister are different from those of the other. With relations as distant as those between cousins the instances of weakened bonds are still more numerous and more frequent.

The weakening of the Lineal bonds among the generations is still more poignant. The son or daughter who moves away from parents both geographically and occupationally comes to sense an ever-deepening emotional chasm in the relation. In part this is due to the child's straining against his dependent needs in order to fulfill the demands for independence and self-reliance occasioned by our value orientations. In part it is associated with the general sentimentalizing of family relations that serves as a substitute for the lost closeness of parent and child. Mother's Day is an example of one sentimental bridge that helps us ignore the chasm below. An analyst of American life has called our Mother's Day customs a rite of atonement.

While we are not placing a value, positive or negative, on our own value orientations and the customs in which they are reflected, it must be pointed out that, in some ways, American family patterns put severe strains on individuals. Since our aim is to present a method for dissecting the malintegrations in family patterns that underlie the mental ill-health of the individual, it is necessary to attempt to pinpoint some of these strains.

One area of strain is the situation of older people in our society. Excluded from living in the homes of their children, retired from jobs often because of age, and cut off from the occupational interests that have absorbed their creative energies for many years, older people tend to become increasingly isolated from meaningful relations. As the life span grows longer, the interest span for these persons shortens. To some extent we have, through social security measures and insurance, overcome their need to rely financially on their children. But the gap that severs dependent relations between generations makes it likewise impossible for the aged to rely emotionally on their children. Whereas the Mexican-American or Chinese parent would expect not only to live with his children but to receive their continued respect and devotion, older people in our society can expect to be told that they are old-fashioned, that their opinions are out of date, and that their capacity to give helpful advice based on long experience is strictly limited. With our impatience for the future and our restless pursuit of change, the wisdom of an older generation is not likely to count for much. Thus, the rewards of intense planning for the future—if a person lives long enough—follow the law of diminishing returns.

The sequence of relations observed by Parsons and others with respect to the so-called American youth culture points to another kind of strain in the society (Parsons, 1949, chs. 10 and 11). It is not generally understood that the behavior of the more or less typical American adolescent is not universal. In many other societies adolescence is a period of fairly smooth transition to adulthood. The defiant independence, the gyrations from idealism to cynicism, from lush romancing to hard-bitten, stripped-down sexual aims, and from cringing conformity to last ditch nonconformity are attitudes largely unique to our own social system. And throughout adolescent attitudes is woven a belief in the power of the gang, the adolescent peer group with its own unique and frequently spectacular behavior patterns.

Parsons points out, in discussing the origin of the power of the peer group, that the adolescent in our society is caught on the horns of a dilemma. On the one hand, he grows up in a small, nuclear family in which all his dependent needs are satisfied in relation to a few persons. Consequently, the libidinal attachment, especially to the mother, grows very strong. On the other hand, the child is expected to become a self-reliant, independent adult. How is he to resolve this problem of discontinuity between childhood training and adult expectations? The shadow of this dilemma is seen in almost every form of adult neuroses. Adolescence is the time when the first tentative solutions of preadolescence must be made workable. If the individual waits until he attains adult status, it may be too late; the solutions may not be forthcoming, and shame at not being able to make the grade may wither further experimentation. He may then become increasingly trapped within his family, wooed perhaps by a mother who cannot let him go and scorned by father and friends who cannot tolerate his staying.

The adolescent peer group, then, is the mechanism through which the most workable solutions are provided. Instead of violently rupturing his ties to his parents as adulthood approaches, he gradually begins to transfer them to his peers. When his own lack of experience and uncertainty make it difficult for him to get along without support, the peer group will back him up whether or not his parents approve or disapprove of his behavior. Further, the adolescent in our society is considerably inhibited in his attempts to try his wings and discover his own abilities and natural bents—in the words of Erikson, to determine his personal sense of identity (Erikson, 1950)—by the prolonged period in school.

School is considered by most people to be chiefly a preparation for life rather than an experience in its own right. Because of the technical requirements of our culture, it must be continued long after the adolescent has reached the point where he must determine his identity. As a result, however, the adolescent is sealed off from many aspects of the adult world that he is expected to be able to identify with and to master. Perhaps this isolation from the adult world is the reason many young people develop neuroses—or don't discover their existence until after graduating from school.

At any rate, youth culture provides a framework of behavior between the world of the child and the world of the adult. Roles in the peer group are distributed among those aimed at pleasure, play, and fun, and those whose goal is a serious project. Even when the latter verges on a delinquent or deviant goal—depending on the nature of the group—it nevertheless shows an orientation toward the planning, organization, and achievement that are so important in our system of values.

Another source of strain in family patterns is the role of the father. One aspect of his role is the tremendous responsibility he must bear for the welfare of his wife and children. In many societies—the Mexican-American, and Chinese, for example—no man is made to feel that he alone is solely responsible for the well-being of his family. There are parents, brothers, even uncles and cousins, to be called on in times of crisis. Many American men, however, would rather borrow from a friend or even a stranger than from a relative, so strong is the push toward independence. While welfare agencies and other community mechanisms for emotional and financial support are becoming more acceptable, they still encounter the resistance toward accepting help or charity that is associated with our value system.

The great resourcefulness and responsibility required in the father role is well integrated with the Doing aspect of his orientation toward life. As a result he is apt to concentrate highly on his business or occupational role. This concentration, however, is not so well integrated with other family roles. He must usually, for example, spend an enormous amount of time away from his home and family. Thus, the amount of role sharing—of real companionship—between husband and wife is reduced below the optimum, and the pair find themselves driven increasingly apart. Also, with the father out of the house so much, the son is thrown together often with the mother, and mutual bonds are intensified. Also, because the mother must do most of the training and controlling of the children, she tends to assume a disproportionate amount of moral authority for the whole family. For the son this means that the distribution of internalized traits that compose psychological identifications with his parents is heavily weighted toward the mother. The resulting feminine identification—especially the feminine superego—as well as the strong affective tie toward her, constitute mechanisms difficult to integrate later with the initiative and aggressiveness demanded by the ego ideals of our value system. This situation is not helped by the fact that the father's occupation is often a mystery to the son. The father's occupation is obviously a focus of great interest and, therefore, an important way of identifying the father and of identifying with him. Yet middle-class occupations take place, for the most part, far from home and are difficult to describe operationally. How many middle-class sons know what their active fathers really do on the job?

None of these strains, however, is as severe as that found in the wife-mother role. Indeed, if we were asked to point to the most strategic spot in the American family system for an effecting of constructive change in it, we would certainly single out the female role. (Some of the basic concepts undergirding the women's movement were anticipated by F. Kluckhohn. For a more detailed analysis of the strain of the woman's role in American society, see F. Kluck-hohn, 1952.) There are many reasons for the choice, and the whole of the female role problem, including the difficulties in both the husband-wife and the mother-child relation, is exceedingly complex.

Compared to the male role, that aspect of the total female role that we label the wife-mother role is not well established in the dominant value system. The mother of a family is not expected to take an individualistic, autonomous role as the father is in the occu-pational system. She is expected to have a Collateral orientation in which she puts the interests of the group as a whole above whatever individualistic interests she may have. She is, much more than the father, expected to play a representative role in her relations out-side the family. She may, for example, be representative in the sense of being a husband's status symbol. Thorstein Veblen pointed out long ago that the American woman, in certain strata of society at least, is the symbol of a husband's or father's ability to pay and is in herself an item of conspicuous consumption. More often today, the mother is expected to take the representative role at parent-teacher meetings, in the church, and in community affairs. There is even a rapidly growing trend, especially in suburbs, for women to take a far more active part than men in community governmental affairs.

Some women find a great deal of satisfaction in this role. However, many do not, and there are two main reasons for this. The various activities are often so diffuse that women cannot easily concentrate on occupational goals, a characteristic part of the dom-inant American achievement pattern. Also, almost all of the spe-cified activities are defined mainly as women's activities—men do not participate. Such a definition not only leads to further segrega-tion of the sexes but also tends to put the activities themselves in a position of second-order importance—as though men should tend to the truly important (i.e., economic) affairs in American life, while necessary matters of lesser importance could be safely left to women.

In the all-important occupational system, there has been an increasing acceptance of women. Nevertheless, expressions of grave concern—often condemnation—about the working mother are still heard. Delinquency and psychological disturbances in children, as well as the high divorce rate, are frequently attributed in large part to the mother working outside the home. The American mother is not, in other words, expected to have an active part in those aspects of American life that best express the Doing activity and Future time orientations. Hers is a vicarious participation that depends on what a husband, a father, or a son, and not she herself, accomplishes.

The frustrations that result from these variant definitions of the woman's role are further reinforced by the facts that women have been poorly trained for the domestic area of the wife-mother role and that this area has been increasingly demeaned over the years as a prestige role.

In most respects, American girls are trained through adolescence to play individualistic and competitive roles very similar in nature to the masculine role. The girl child goes to school with boys and competes for many of the same goals. Of course, she may find a doll and carriage under the Christmas tree while brother finds a train, but in spite of this, she is expected to learn to look after herself. At the same time, the hope is expressed that she will not remain independent and therefore will not need to use much of what she has learned. Instead, she is expected, either at the time of marriage or certainly after children are born, to give her attention to motherhood and household duties, for which she has had little or no training.

This lack of training, together with a lack of traditional methods for child rearing, creates great anxiety in many women about the mother role. Many American women desire children and have definite aspirations to be good mothers. Moreover, in society at large, the idealization of woman is primarily an idealization of her motherhood. There is, in other words, considerable pressure for women to be good mothers, and there are high prestige rewards for achieving the goal. But just what being a good mother means or how to become one are questions many women find difficult to answer. Too often the mother compares herself and her children with friends or neighbors and their children; and she anxiously follows the latest theories of child care and training. Motherhood, like almost everything else in the society, becomes both competitive and instrumental, or, as some suggest, professionalized.

The difficulties encountered in playing the mother role are enormously increased by the low evaluation placed by most women themselves and by society on the domestic component of the wife-mother role. In earlier periods of American history, the housewife and mother roles were one. Today in the minds of men and women alike, the two components are fairly clearly separated, and the attitude toward the housewife aspect is markedly negative. The home, as a house to be managed, is constantly pictured as a mild variety of penal institution. Almost everyone defines housework as drudgery —something that one does because one has to. The prestige rewards accorded domestic interests and accomplishments are not at all comparable to those that can be won in the occupational system or in other kinds of activities. Of all the evidence supporting this conclusion, the most telling is the common phrase, "I am 'just' a housewife."

Since being a housewife is usually part of the mother role, it is not unusual for mothers to convey to children the idea—consciously expressed or unconsciously made known by behavior—that mother deserves so much because she has given up so much and done so many things she really did not enjoy.

Even in cases where women willingly accept the housewife role, as a necessary aspect of motherhood, one sees instances of maladjustment when the children leave home and go on their way. The mother's job in our kind of society, especially when families are small, does not long endure. Mead has commented, "Every social pressure to which she, the mother, is subjected tells her that she should not spoil her children's lives, that she should let them lead their own lives, that she should make them independent and self-sufficient. Yet the more faithfully she obeys these injunctions, the more she is working herself out of a job. Some day, while she is still a young woman . . . she will be alone, quite alone, in a home of her own" (Mead, 1949, p. 337).

In an action-oriented, future-minded society, having no job engenders a feeling of uselessness that in turn creates emotional disturbance. Women whose children have grown up and gone often exhibit disoriented behavior and emotional stress. Some respond by clinging to children; others try to fit into jobs with the outmoded skills they learned and used years ago; others become unnecessarily fussy housewives; some are merely restless. Whatever the response or the degree of disorientation, it should be plain that the demands of a role that is patterned rather inconsistently in terms of both dominant and variant value orientations are not easily met. There is considerable confusion in the minds of many women as to just what is expected of them, and the confusion affects all family relations.

In this section, we have stressed the existence of problems not to demonstrate that the dominant family system is falling apart but rather to set up an analytical model for isolating some of the processes related to psychological strain and ill health. If it were our purpose, we could also demonstrate successful integrations within family patterns, and among the family, the social system, and the system of value orientations. Given our basic values, the typical roles within the middle-class family structure appear, on the whole, to be well fitted to the functions of the family within the larger social system. The system of individualistic roles and autonomous functions within the family is remarkably well suited to, and good preparation for, the degrees of freedom and independence our industrial society calls for.

2

Contrasts in Puerto Rican
and American Values

The family case history of Mario Corosa, a Puerto Rican who suffered a psychotic reaction after immigrating to New York City, is the first to be analyzed from the vantage point of the theoretical perspectives outlined in Chapter One. In order to understand the adaptation problems of Puerto Ricans immigrating to the United States, it is necessary to examine Puerto Rican culture, particularly its value system, in relation to American culture. In this case, we examine the Puerto Rican working-class culture from which Mario derived and that of the American middle-class culture to which he attempted to adapt in New York City.

The contrast between these two patterns is presented in Table 3. Even a casual glance at the items reveals the amount of cultural distance migrating Puerto Rican families may have to traverse in order to accommodate to the culture of American cities.

While these patterns are not thought to describe all Puerto Rican working class or American middle-class families (since families and individuals in both settings have variant values), the patterns do describe the dominant trend within each setting. The American middle-class rather than working-class pattern has been

Table 3.

PUERTO RICAN WORKING-CLASS AND AMERICAN MIDDLE-CLASS
VALUE ORIENTATION PROFILES

Modalities	Puerto Rican Working-Class			American Middle-Class		
Activity	Be	$>^a$ Do	$>$ BiB	Do	$>$ Be	$>$ Bib
Relational	Coll $>$	Lin	$>$ Ind	Ind	$>$ Coll	$>$ Lin
Time	Pres $>$	Fut	$>$ Past	Fut	$>$ Pres	$>$ Past
Man-nature	Sub $=^b$	With	$=$ Over	Over	$>$ Sub	$>$ With
Nature-of-man	Evil $>$	Mixed	$>$ Good	Neutral Mixed $>$ Evil		$>$ Good

Abbreviations: Be, BiB, Do stand for Being, Being-in-becoming, Doing;
Lin, Coll, Ind stand for Lineal, Collateral, Individual; Past, Pres, Fut
stand for Past, Present, Future; Sub, With, Over stand for Subjugated-
to-nature, Harmony-with-nature, Mastery-over-nature.
[a] $>$ indicates that the solution to the left is preferred to that on the
right.
[b] $=$ Indicates that there is no clear preference between the solutions
to the left and right.

selected because it is the pattern toward which immigrant families
usually aspire.

The activity dimension involves those aspects of the personality in action that are most valued. Puerto Rican society emphasizes Being. The individual is expressive and feelings are aired,
usually with considerable dramatic flair. Tempers fly, laughter rings
out, tears flow. One knows where one stands in the feelings of
others. Children are freely scolded and punished; they are also
freely and effusively loved. No one is expected to control his feelings except before strangers. As for actions, they are controlled by
the group in accordance with the Collateral principle. Since the
individual is not expected to be able to control himself, violence
may break out, requiring calming or control by the collateral group.
In the second-order position, probably because of recent economic
progress and initiative within the Commonwealth, is Doing. Energy

employed toward achievement and success is appreciated, but this is still secondary to the expressive needs of the individual. Work may be called off if tensions grow, if there is a ceremonial occasion, or if there is illness in the family. The Being-in-becoming solution in Puerto Rico is important mainly for the wealthier classes with the leisure to develop their interests in a variety of directions.

The preference for Doing in American life is obvious. Initiative and striving for success are expected of everyone. Parents watch themselves and their children for evidence of progress; progress competition is the spice of life. Education is viewed as the main path to success, and the higher rungs of education depend on achievement at lower levels. Consequently, work and study come before play. Being, however, is encouraged in recreation, when the compulsive attention to success is temporarily relaxed. If one is freed from watching one's step in order to get ahead, as at a game or party, then expressiveness can be trotted out; one can, in modest doses, even make a fool of oneself. Being-in-becoming in the United States is of importance only to variant groups—to artists, musicians, and some intellectuals. To most others, it has the flavor of dilettantism or self-indulgence. (For a close correspondence to the Being-in-becoming orientation, see Reich, 1970.)

The relational dimension, concerning the ordering of relations within social groups, is of the greatest importance to family life. Collaterality is the principle that holds the Puerto Rican family in a web of horizontally extended relationships. The preference is for a high birth rate, large family systems, and close, intensely consuming relations. The child is trained for dependence on the family network and for obedience. Loyalty is demanded, in exchange for which the individual family member is offered reliable caretaking throughout his life. Whoever sticks with the system will be protected by it against a potentially evil outside world. Whoever leaves the system takes grave risks. Separation is cause for grief, preferably dramatically expressed; greeting after absence is reason for elaborate displays of tearful happiness. Within such a warm and controlling family, the individual scarcely exists; in the outside world, he is a representative and bears responsibility for the entire family's honor and reputation. With Collaterality firmly established, the second-order Lineal principle is brought into play for important decisions. The male is the dominant authority, both as husband and as father. This area gives rise to one of the principal strains in Puerto Rican family life, namely, the disparity between the presumed dominance of the male and the actual facts of the situation, a disparity that brings about exaggerated masculine pride and sensitivity.

The American middle-class pattern of preference emphasizes Individualism to a degree almost unknown anywhere else in the world. Children are expected to stand on their own two feet, make their own decisions, and learn self-control from an early age. They are trained to experience separation (for example, being sent to summer camp) as a normal event, one that tests their ability to manage by themselves. In contrast to the large Puerto Rican family, where it is quite proper for any of several relatives to discipline a misbehaving child, the American child is responsible only to himself and his immediate family. Nuclear families of parents and children are themselves expected to be relatively independent of extended kin. Collaterality, the second-position preference, is regarded as necessary for restricted occasions. In recreation, for example, one should forget about himself for the good of the team or learn to be a good loser. In emergencies and crises, there is a closing of the ranks within families, communities, or even within the nation as a whole. The Lineal principle is avoided whenever possible. Generally, Americans do not like bosses and do not like being boss; they fulfill such roles, somewhat apologetically, only when a job situation requires it. Within the nuclear family too, husbands and wives usually avoid the Lineal principle, sharing responsibilities and reaching decisions by mutual agreement.

Every society must order its relations within time. In Puerto Rican families, the traditional preference has been for the Present time orientation, a preference characteristic of most peasant societies. In such societies, the past is not well differentiated from the present or the future, and life is perceived as a vast, self-repeating cycle of events. Time boundaries are demarcated by seasons (rainy versus dry), celebrations (fiestas), holidays, anniversaries, and other recurring occasions. There is little point in hurry because no future is conceived as pressing down with inexorable demands. There is little expectation of change in the course of life and no positive appreciation of novelty for its own sake. In the Present time preference, change is regarded as something accidental.

American middle-class culture places a heavy emphasis on the Future. Americans plan ceaselessly for a future pictured in terms of a vastly extended perspective. Parents plan the children's education before they are born and plan for their own old age over a period of years. American middle-class persons watch their clocks and calendars to make sure they will not be late when the future arrives. They look forward to what novelties the future will bring, confident for the most part, that they have planned change to their own betterment. They value their children as representing the future just as they neglect their elderly who have little future remaining. The second-order position of Present time means that it is the preference for a crisis. In stressful situations, everyone stops worrying about the future and attends to the immediate problem. In some other circumstances too, particularly in recreation, Present time considerations prevail; in a party or game, it is thought important to have fun and to forget the future with its compulsive concerns. Past time is given little importance, as shown in the American hostility to tradition. What few traditions Americans preserve are being constantly reinterpreted in the light of new circumstances.

At the present time, Puerto Rican society demonstrates a lack of ordering within the man-nature dimension that refers to the relation of man and nature or supernature. The reasons why there is no clear preference are not really clear. Eighty-five percent of the population of the Commonwealth is nominally Roman Catholic, and the Church's position is clearly that the individual human is subjugated to the Deity, needing constant help to overcome the sinfulness toward which his human nature leads him. But ecclesiastical organization on the island is not strong; the number of Spanish-speaking priests is rather small; anticlerical feeling tends to run high; and religious observances are deemed interesting mainly to women. The situation is complicated by remnants of belief and custom inherited from the native Indian population or transferred from Africa at the time of the slave trade. These beliefs and customs have crystalized into a strong belief in spiritualism, a movement with its own institutional forms and practices, largely of a

Harmony-with-nature cast. Finally, recent economic and industrial development, backed by science and technology, has dramatically increased confidence in the Mastery-over-nature position. No one of the three solutions can claim precedence. Individuals and family groups move around among the three positions with remarkable ease; they may call on the Church and clergy for weddings and baptisms, look for cures for illnesses or assurances of good luck from spiritualist practitioners, then seek out physicians or other technical specialists for the same problem.

Americans clearly prefer the Mastery-over-nature solution, most conspicuously symbolized by the satellite program and the flights to the moon. It is believed that man, with the help of computers, can engineer most large problems toward a successful outcome. For small problems, there are professionals and experts listed in the Yellow Pages. For problems such as chronic illness and death, where science and technology do not work, there is a disjunctive turning, through religious ceremony, to the second-order Subjugated-to-nature solution. Even there, however, the Mastery-over-nature solution is so strongly preferred, that death tends to be regarded as a mistake, a failure of science and medical research to reach their goals. It ought not to have happened, and emotionally one often responds as though it had not happened. There is no room for lamentation over unhappy events brought about by forces beyond our control. This is in marked contrast to Puerto Rican custom where the Subjugated-to-nature position is still strong enough to produce an outpouring of expressions of grief at the death of a family member. Like the Being-in-becoming preference, Harmony-with-nature is important only to certain variant groups.

In respect to the basic nature of man dimension,[1] the first-order preference among Puerto Ricans is that man is born in a state of sin and has a large, almost ineradicable component of Evil in his nature. Since this is so, one must watch carefully for the intentions of others. One can try to be good through the help of the Church, the saints, and the Deity, or one can be influenced for good (or bad) by local spirits. Nevertheless, one needs to be always on

---

[1] This fifth value orientation modality represents a later stage in the development of Kluckhohn's theory; see Kluckhohn and Strodtbeck, 1961.

guard. It is particularly important to remain on good terms with the collateral group, for this group is the main guarantee of protection against outside (outgroup) hostile forces.

Middle-class Americans tend to see man as either a mixture of Good and Evil or as Neutral. The latter concept is becoming more and more prevalent, probably because of the gradual education of the public by psychiatrists and the teaching of the behavioral science point of view of child development in colleges. Children are looked at as neither good nor evil, but as products of their early experiences and of the environment in their homes. This concept, of course, shifts the burden to the parents, who feel responsible for providing an environment in which the child can blossom into an achieving, independent, future-oriented, self-controlled, middle-class citizen. In spite of the growth of preference for a Neutral view of man's nature, there is still a strong second-order preference for man as Evil but perfectible. This preference often causes parents to vacillate, feeling one moment that they ought to punish a misbehaving child to show him there are rules he must obey, and feeling guilty the next moment for not having offered a sufficiently appropriate model so that he would learn without punishment. The possibility that man is innately Good but corruptible exists only in the third-order least-preferred position, supported by a few nostalgic idealists who believe that man could be Good if it were not for the corrupting influences of urban life and modern times. (See Wells, 1969.)

No culture is perfectly integrated, and strain can arise from any of several sources. The various dominant or first-order value choices may not fit well together. Or, the first-order preferences may cease to fit the actual circumstances of social life because of rapid cultural change resulting from internal or external forces. Or, when large numbers migrate, the values of the immigrants may clash with those prevailing in the country of adoption. When there is malintegration both within the original value profile of the migrating group and within the value pattern of the adopted country, the strain is doubled or tripled. Two interrelated sources of strain in Puerto Rican life have been selected for discussion, and are presented as they affect generalized masculine-feminine sex-role patterning and, more specifically, the structuring of husband-wife and parent-child roles. (See Lopez, 1973, and Hatt, 1952, for comprehensive analyses of the historical and cultural antecedents of contemporary Puerto Rican life.)

The first strain arises from the fragility of collaterally structured groups. The Puerto Rican family, with its laterally extended chains of relatives, is easily fractured by internal tension. The break most often occurs between the husband's relatives and the wife's relatives, placing a terrible strain on the husband-wife bond. The break may also come between siblings or between a parent and a child. Wherever it occurs, the rupture produces great anxiety in the family members most closely affected because of their training for dependency on the family and the multiply-reinforced need to preserve collateral relations at all costs. The fragility of the laterally extended family results from its great size and from the absence of a stable pattern of authority in the male line.

Problems of male authority, a second source of strain in Puerto Rican life, are associated with a long-standing history of weak support for legal marriage in Puerto Rico. The origin of acceptance for alternate male-female household units is obscure. At any rate, the norms of the culture support both consensual (common-law) marriage, unblessed by either religious or legal sanction, and the maintenance by the male of a mistress with whom he does not live but by whom he may have children. In some cases, a man may be supporting a legal wife, a consensual wife, and a mistress, all of whom have borne him children.

This pattern of polygamy is costly to the structure of the collateral groupings. It is also costly in purely economic terms since the man is expected (and usually tries) to support his wives and their children. And although he usually accepts the responsibility of fatherhood toward his children, both legitimate and illegitimate, he is able to be a father, in the sense of providing an adequate role model, toward only some of them. He is unable to spend the necessary amount of time in the various households where his children live to function adequately as a parent in all of them. Thus, a son may not often be exposed to his father, but live in close proximity to his mother.

Under these circumstances, the son's identification with his mother is apt to be strong, and his character structure uncon-

sciously apt to be patterned in large part along feminine lines. Consciously, however, he usually has a strong identification with the
absent father, an identification encouraged by whatever collateral
male relations the son can maintain and by the *machismo* image so
important within the culture. *Machismo* refers to a pattern of belligerent masculinity and sexual dominance that the Puerto Rican
male is expected to display under any possible situation of challenge. Though its overcompensatory quality is apparent to those
outside the native culture, to those within, a failure to display
machismo in appropriate circumstances may result in social disgrace and ostracism.

The degree of male dominance thought to be suitable for a
husband to maintain would fit better with first-order Lineal and
Past time value choices. Lineal values support authority lines more
firmly than do Collateral values. Lineality endorses ordered positional succession over time, an oldest son replacing an infirm or
dying father, from the Crown Prince down to the lowliest subject.
Past time values provide the sanction of tradition for such inheritance of authority and responsibility in the male line. In a Present
time Collateral system, there is no sanction of the transmission of
authority to any particular son; all the sons, therefore, are likely to
compete for dominance. Given a son's genetic problem with masculine identification, the problem of settling the question of dominance in the Collateral system, and the difficulty of managing two
or more households of wives and children, it is not surprising that
the male asserts himself through a hypertrophied, self-reassuring
masculinity when faced with a challenge to his authority or to his
sexual competence.

What is the source of such challenge? Quite often it is the
wives, who are the first to sense the intrinsic weakness of the male's
position. Since wives are required to be submissive, the challenging
must be subtle. Frequently it is expressed through a wife's managing to take care of household affairs without consulting her husband. The husband-wife roles feature much segregation of tasks
and responsibilities, with the husband the nominal authority for
major decisions. The husband's frequent absence from home make
sharing tasks a practical arrangement. But they also provide the
opportunity for the wife to make decisions and to carry out plans

without consulting her husband. This arrangement is facilitated by her own collateral relatives, especially the women, who are usually around to help. Gradually, then, authority and responsibility shift to the wife and her female relatives, and a masked matriarchy is established. The husband either settles into this matriarchal system, comfortable as long as his authority is not overtly challenged, or he rebels and seeks solace with a consensual wife or a mistress.

Just as every social system has its strains, it also has compensatory mechanisms. The balance may be uneasy, but it is at least a working equilibrium. In Puerto Rico, the system of checks and balances within the family works. The collateral family network may cause hardship to one or another of its members, but, just as often, it provides him with its own special kind of support and protection.

The system works haltingly, however, for Puerto Ricans arriving in cities on the mainland, and the pressure to change over to the American family style is constant. A collateral network of relatives cannot easily be maintained in the cut-up, overcrowded tenements of metropolitan slums that are designed for small, nuclear, independent families, which are preferred as the dominant American value. Isolation is the price of this independence, and the loneliness of isolation is one of the strains of American life. This strain can be compensated for by rewards accruing to those who master the uprooted, wandering, but achieving path toward upward mobility and financial success; for new immigrants, though, there may be a long interval before there is even the faintest foretaste of this compensatory success. There may be special strains if only one side of the family network immigrates. If it is the wife's family, the matriarchal pattern may attain unusual force; if it is the husband's, his dominance over his wife may become unbearable to her.

The situation is often exacerbated by problems of employment. The job market for unskilled and semiskilled labor, the primary attraction for Puerto Ricans arriving on the mainland, is variable, sometimes glutted; the Puerto Rican male may find himself recurrently unemployed. If the collateral family system has arrived intact in the new environment, a small business like a grocery store, the family *bodega,* may be set up and managed with all the relatives pitching in. Sometimes the husband finds employment in a service or manufacturing job, earning higher wages than were possible back home. Even these more successful ventures, however, often fail to result in a comfortable living standard, since higher costs of living quickly consume earnings. (For an excellent summary of Puerto Rican life in New York City, including social, political and economic aspects of their adaptation to that city, see Glazer and Moynihan, 1963, pp. 86–136.)

The high birth rate required by the collateral family system in Puerto Rico is usually maintained after migration. A family of many children is, of course, difficult to support and particularly difficult to house in a crowded city. The decrepit brownstone tenements of New York's West Side absorb and expel these burgeoning families before they can establish any stable relations with neighbors, any sense of belonging, or any network of those community controls that regulate internal impulses within the native culture. Wandering in and out of the job market, moving his family frequently in a frustrating search for housing, the Puerto Rican husband may easily find his fragile sense of masculine identity further weakened.

In Puerto Rico, the male was known to everyone in the community and in turn knew everyone. In the streets of an American city, he is largely unknown and knows hardly anyone. He may end up barely recognizing himself. Self-recognition is also impaired by the change in his wife. In Puerto Rico, unmarried girls are vigilantly watched by their parents, who protect their virginity against the wicked natural tendency of males, married or unmarried, to seduce them. Girls are kept at home and carefully supervised. They marry at an early age to escape this surveillance and immediately begin having their own families. From then on, with the assistance of numerous female relatives, they keep busy with child rearing and domestic tasks, while the husbands are working or displaying masculinity in the company of others.

In the United States, however, the wife may not have collateral relatives near her to help with the child rearing. She keenly feels the burden of many children and may deeply resent her husband's absence and his propensity for manly displays outside the home. She soon discovers, however, that, if her husband is not able to maintain the family's income, to manage its affairs effectively, or to give her the help she needs, the city's welfare agencies will come to her aid. She is not as dependent on her husband as in Puerto Rico and, therefore, under less obligation to fulfill his demands for passive, compliant behavior. The American pattern of feminine equality and relative independence is soon borne in on her. As she finds the means to assert herself and her rights, she further reduces her husband's concept of himself as a self-respecting male. The strain on the marital bond sometimes becomes disruptive.

New conditions on the mainland also affect relations between parents and children. Shrinkage of the collateral network makes it impossible to supervise children constantly outside the home. Since self-control is not expected and since children are not assumed to be individuals capable of getting along by themselves, the world of the city streets seems especially evil and threatening as, indeed, it often is.

The situation is most critical with respect to adolescent girls. It is impossible to supervise them strictly at all times. And the centrifugal impact upon families of American schools and the established, highly valued dating patterns are usually able to pry a girl away from the watchful eyes of her parents. Parental anxiety over the possibility of seduction and premarital pregnancy is enormously magnified, resulting either in attempts to increase supervision and control or in the abandonment of vigilance in the face of the American system, however immoral it seems. In either event, the anxiety is often transmitted to the daughter, who becomes strongly tempted to act out her parents' expectations of what will happen during her contacts with boys.

The control of sons is also difficult. The absent or careless father and the idea of compulsive masculinity have a damaging effect on the growing boy's sense of male identity. The situation is magnified in the United States where there may be no other male relatives available as role models. Masculinity, then, comes to be represented by the peer group and the street gang. The gang satisfies the need for impulse expression and an exhibitionistic display of male power, perhaps involving violence, to overcome internal uncertainties and weaknesses. The gang also channels the need for mastery away from the school situation. With or without a gang's influence, school performance is seriously jeopardized by the value patterns of Puerto Rican youths. Present time, Being, and Collateral values are not conducive to planning and hoarding energies needed for application in intellectual areas. In addition, language difficulties and the middle-class expectations of American school teachers work against the success of Puerto Rican students. Their dropout rate, like that for all minority groups, is high. The gang, with its imaginative names, its projects, legal or illegal, and its team spirit, supplies an alternate climate for achievement. In a pale and corrupt way, the aims of the gang imitate the success motif of American society, while simultaneously satisfying the need for feelings of territoriality and community and for knowing who is who in one's neighborhood. Peer groups and gangs are sources of anxiety for Puerto Rican parents. Sometimes they try to tighten controls, but that strategy usually fails. Resenting the domineering father and the overprotective mother, a boy may stay away from home as much as possible, eventually ending up in the domineering and overprotective hands of the police and court authorities.

In this examination, potential areas of stress confronting the newly-arrived, working-class Puerto Rican family appear overwhelming. There is no doubt, however, that many families arrive in this country with a background of education and a set of values more concordant with American middle-class patterns. Such families suffer fewer strains. There is no doubt, furthermore, that second-generation parents and their children make the cultural transition to middle-class roles with less difficulty than the first generation. On the other hand, some areas of strain have not been covered by this description. No reference, for example, has been made to skin color and the problems of race relations that Puerto Ricans experience.

The inspection of cultural sources of strain in family processes is appropriate to many currents of contemporary life. Family factors intermingle in the formation of character structure. To understand a person, one must understand his family. To appreciate the form and function of the family, one must understand its cultural determinants, which are of the utmost importance in assessing integration and conflict within a family and the psychic health and illness of its individual members.

3

Case Study of a Puerto Rican Family

The study of the Mario Corosa family conducted by members of the Committee on the Family of the Group for the Advancement of Psychiatry required a total of eighteen months for its completion. Contacts between the investigators and the subjects were maintained for an additional fifteen months. Besides the focal family, relatives were seen in both New York and Puerto Rico. (See Group for the Advancement of Psychiatry, 1970, pp. 323–329, for a description of the Family Case History outline employed in ordering the data collected.)

The investigators tried to conduct a naturalistic observation of the family and did not undertake family therapy or individual psychotherapy with any family member. The members of the Corosa family were told that the investigation was aimed toward gathering information about patterns of family life among Puerto Ricans, and they agreed to cooperate. It became apparent, however, that they believed the interviews were treatments for the husband's "craziness." As a result of psychotic episodes, he was treated under other auspices both before and during the period of investigation.

General Background

The investigators first met Mario and his wife Rosa in the office of the hospital to which she had brought him in a raving condition two months earlier. "I'm going to die!" Mario had shouted the day he entered the hospital. "She is going to kill me!" Rosa indicated that he was habitually given to outbursts of verbal and physical violence. This time, however, he had been incoherent and out of control for six days—since hearing of his mother's unexpected death in Puerto Rico. He had returned to the island for the funeral and behaved wildly there, trying to throw himself in his mother's grave, saying that he was "with" his mother, that she was "on top" of him. He remained incoherent and excited on returning to New York, talked of dying, and began to confuse his wife with his mother.

To define the presenting problem, the investigators consulted hospital admission notes about Mario. On admission, he had been restless and distracted and was apparently hallucinating. The admission diagnosis was acute schizophrenic reaction. At the time we first met Mario and Rosa, however, the gross psychotic symptoms had disappeared, and he had been discharged.

Besides Mario and Rosa, the household included a school-age son, Mario, Jr., and daughter, Cara, two years younger. All four were born in Puerto Rico. The family moved to New York when Cara was nine months old. Mario was Protestant; Rosa and the children were practicing Catholics.

Before we proceed in outlining the family background a contrast is in order between the traditional psychodynamic approach as it would be applied in the conceptualization of the origins of Mario's psychotic illness and the transactional considerations which are described in the remainder of this chapter. The process manifesting itself in Mario's psychotic behavior would, in the usual clinical diagnostic approach, be first labeled in terms of the most salient phenomena of the illness. The next step would be to formulate the intrapsychic dynamics, that is, the forces and counterforces, conscious and unconscious, determining his cognitive and emotional behavior.

Among a large number of psychiatrists, despite a wide consensus about the intrapsychic determinants of Mario's character structure and of the manifest psychopathology, there would probably be some disagreement about the clinical diagnosis, about the ordering in importance of the psychodynamic sequences identified, perhaps even about the presence or relevance of a particular sequence. Thus, "acute undifferentiated schizophrenic reaction," "chronic schizophrenia, paranoid type," and "homosexual panic in a passive-aggressive character disorder" were three diagnoses conferred upon Mario at different times in the course of his illness. The presenting symptoms, it will be seen, can be described essentially as regressive, marked by lack of control, excitement, confusion, with few restitutive or reparative symptoms. The prepsychotic personality picture was of a pseudo-masculine, hyperaggressive, impulsive behavior style. Character structure was of a mixed neurotic type, with emphasis placed by different supervisors of Mario's therapy on his intense dependent needs, his marked castration anxiety, and his deep yearnings for a passive-feminine adaptive mode.

Genetic determinants can be cited to support each of these formulations, including the incapability of Mario's mother, particularly with the many siblings born in rapid succession after him, to provide an adequate nurturing experience in infancy; the harsh, poorly controlled physical punishment meted out to offenders by both parents; the combination of seductive behavior of the mother and the father's near-paranoid jealousy. The mother's death, which precipitated Mario's psychotic episode, may be seen as representing, at one level, the loss of Mario's unconscious dependency object ("I'm a part of Mother and therefore I too will die"). At the same time, and in the presence of an excess of rage at the abandonment, it also represented the loss of a powerful source of external control. Finally, it represented the loss of Mario's oedipal object in a setting already marked by heightened passive-feminine longings and exaggerated defensive pseudo-masculine needs. The treatment program, including choice of drugs, the type and frequency of psychotherapeutic contact, and the nature and extent of family or community resources to be utilized depended on which formulation seemed most valid to the therapist.

Whatever the seeming differences in dynamic formulations, clinical diagnoses, and treatment programs, they are indeed more alike than different. Most fundamentally, they share at least one feature—they all limit themselves to a basic view of Mario's illness as residing within himself. Though the histories obtained on the occasions of his hospitalization did refer to his family of orientation and even to his family of procreation, the references were limited to two-person units within these families and, furthermore, merely alluded to the influence of the important "other" upon the patient.

The alternative family diagnostic approach involves a system of cross-references among the cultural, interpersonal, psychological, and biological determinants of family function—all in the context of the structure of the family field.

At the time the investigation began, Mario, who had eight grades of schooling, was the owner and operator of a neighborhood grocery store, purchased from his wife's brother-in-law two years previously. Before that, he had worked for about seven years as a TV repairman. He kept his store open seven days a week, until 10 P.M. on all days but Sunday. The net income of the store was estimated by investigators to be between $5000 and $7500 per year. Rosa, who had ten grades of schooling, helped in the store on weekdays from about noon until late afternoon when she returned home to prepare dinner for the children and to spend the evening with them. Before Mario purchased the store, she had been a sewing-machine operator and had suffered severe arthritis attacks that she attributed to her working conditions. The family was bitter about having been denied compensation for this condition.

The family lived in a seven-room apartment on the second floor of a two-family house, their sixth residence since coming to New York. Each change of address had represented some move upward although all their apartments had been in predominantly Puerto Rican neighborhoods. Their apartment was neat, moderately clean, somewhat run-down, in a section of the Bronx that had declined from its previous standards.

Mario was good-looking, rather more youthful in appearance than his thirty-five years. Even when most relaxed, he appeared tense and restless; he was a chain smoker and a voluble talker. He was quite articulate and obviously of at least normal intelligence. Rosa was short and mildly obese, with a pretty face and sweet smile. Although she dressed without regard to style, she was very neat. She appeared placid and slow moving, seemingly agreeable and dependent. She spoke fluent English and was very alert, more energetic than her first impression suggested.

Mario, Jr., twelve, was small for his age, handsome, fidgety, and thought by the family to be "nervous like his father." He performed well in school. He was broody, touchy, and had trouble controlling his anger. He had nightmares and was preoccupied with fears about injury to his body. After some initial shyness, he became friendly and verbal with the investigators. Cara, ten, was plump and pretty and handled herself with poise. She had been kept back a year at school and was in the fourth grade. She appeared quite bright and was open, friendly, and talkative with the investigators.

Mario, Sr. appeared to be the isolate in the family group. He was rarely with his children except on Sunday evenings. His contacts with his wife were limited to those times when they were together in the store, the late evenings on weekdays, and Sunday evenings when the whole family was together. He made it clear that he was master of his household, but it seemed that Rosa actually made most major decisions and regulated the family's life. Mario appeared to resent the fact that his children, especially his son, had to work less hard than he had as a boy. Rosa seemed to be allied with the children and more lenient with them. The interviewers sensed that Mario would check with his wife before making pronouncements about family matters; once he had spoken though, the others gave the appearance of obeying. The children seemed to be close to each other. Their father was frequently harsh with them, especially with Mario, Jr., and father and son exhibited more strain between them than did any other pair in the family.

The wife and children were markedly relaxed in referring to the period when Mario, Sr. was "crazy." At the time of his father's hospitalization, Mario, Jr. had been the most frightened of the three, thinking his father was being taken away to be shot.

In the early stages of the investigation, the interviewers administered tests to Mario and Rosa. Mario was overbearing, guarded, and grudgingly cooperative during testing. He seemed a suspicious, negativistic individual during testing, whose nonchalance, defiance, and superior pose masked deep feelings of inadequacy and vulnerability. He achieved a Verbal I.Q. at the upper end of the Dull-Normal range, but various responses indicated a greater potential. He revealed grandiose notions and themes suggestive of antisocial trends. He revealed himself as a passive, impulsively acting-out individual with underlying depression and strong latent homosexual tendencies.

Rosa was task oriented and cooperative during testing. She had only occasional difficulties and then made facetious comments or laughed nervously. Generally she strove to do her best and answered questions promptly, neatly to the point, and, seemingly with unwavering confidence. She achieved a Verbal I.Q. at the Average level, but analysis of her subtest scores revealed superior ability for abstract thinking with a nearly mental defective level of function in Comprehensive performance. Some of her responses reflected naivete, niggardly tendencies, concern with aggressive urges, exhibitionistic impulses, touchiness, and self-contempt. She possibly viewed her husband's psychotic behavior as abandonment, which resulted in the frustration of her dependence needs and a regressive shift to an adolescent type of homosexual liaison for gratification.

Interaction testing could not be completed, so no conclusive measure of their joint intellectual function and potential could be obtained. Those data that were gathered suggest that marital interaction brought pressure to bear on Mario, evident in his regression and bizarre behavior. Much of his disturbance seemed to be related to his need to be dominant. Rosa's problem seemed to be to avoid conflicts with him, with the result that she sometimes gave in to his responses to close the issue, though occasionally writing her own answer on a piece of paper. Rosa unquestionably emerged as the dominant partner in the dominance pattern. It seems that Mario, although impulsive and aggressive in stance, was basically passive, whereas Rosa, though quiet and restrained, was characteristically aggressive.

Although the focal family consisted of only four members, both Mario and Rosa had originated in large and convoluted families. Collecting data about their history was, therefore, a complicated and time-consuming task. We suggest that the reader, in order to identify clearly the various relatives discussed in this section, refer frequently to Figure 1. The schematic representation of the family networks is a useful adjunct to the written material. (See Group for the Advancement of Psychiatry, 1970, pp. 251–261, for a description of the use of the family field chart in family diagnosis.)

Mario's paternal grandfather, Pablo (H III A), was a farmer who owned land and also a retail bakery. He and his wife produced five children; the only one still alive at the time of the investigation was Mario's father, Sandor. Mario had heard stories of his father's brothers' wildness, including the tale that two of them had killed each other in a fight. Sandor (HF) vehemently denied these stories. There had, however, undoubtedly been trouble in the family. Pablo had a brother who forced him off his land and paid only one hundred dollars for the property, which was worth much more. This eviction occurred at the time Sandor moved to Ponce, where he was to meet his future wife (HM).

Roberto Hass, Mario's maternal grandfather (H III B), the son of a German immigrant to Puerto Rico, owned a liquor store in Ponce. He and his wife, the daughter of an emigrant from Holland, produced six children before her death in 1916. Mario's mother, Catalina (HM), was the fifth child, and the sixth was Mario's Aunt Cara, for whom his daughter was named. After his wife's death, Roberto lived with another woman and the two had a daughter, Amelia, living in Philadelphia at the time of the investigation and on good terms with the family. Roberto himself died in 1947.

At the time of the investigation, Mario's father was living in Ponce, Puerto Rico, where he was visited by one of the investigators. He had been a railroad worker and, for a long time, owned a grocery store in Ponce where he and his wife had raised their family. After selling the store in 1947, he bought and sold cattle for a time. In his retirement, he remained active, doing odd jobs on his own property. He was a Catholic. He was a short, wiry man, rather like Mario in his rapid speech and his aggressive manner and gestures.

Mario's mother, Catalina, was born and raised in Ponce and lived across the street from the store where Sandor worked as a young man. She was in good health during their courtship. After their marriage, however, she had nervous attacks whenever they argued; she would cry, scream, and fall breathless. The couple's arguments were mostly about their eight children, Maria, Lotta, Roberto, Mario (H), Alfonso, Johnny, Hector, and Juan. Sandor and Catalina never got along well. Mario blamed his father's temper but added, "You can't blame one in an argument." He indicated that his mother was the family disciplinarian. When Mario was first asked to describe his mother, he paused briefly and said, "She was all right as far as I was concerned. (Pause.) I have a lot of

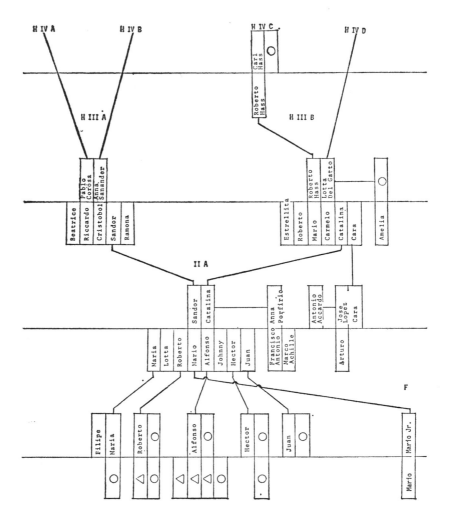

HIVA   HIVB   HIVC   HIVD

Carl Hass

Roberto Hass

HIIIA   HIIIB

Beatrice | Riccardo | Pablo Corosa | Cristobol | Anna Sanander
Sandor
Ramona

Estrellita | Roberto | Mario | Carmelo | Catalina | Cara
Roberto Hass | Lotta Del Gatto
Amelia

IIA

Sandor | Catalina

Maria | Lotta | Roberto | Mario | Alfonso | Johnny | Hector | Juan

Francisco Anna Antonio Porfirio
Marco Achille

Antonio Accardo

Jose Lopez
Cara

Arturo

F

Filipe | Maria
Roberto
Alfonso
Hector
Juan

Mario Jr.

Mario

—— Direct lines of ascent
—— Indirect lines of descent

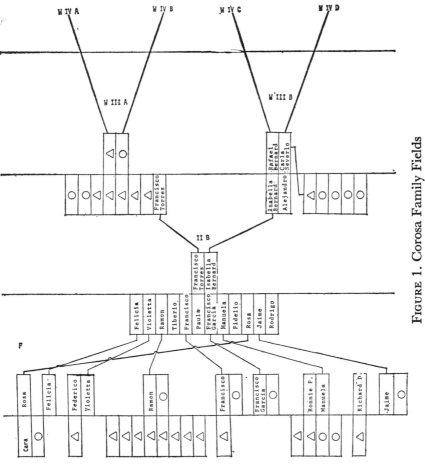

FIGURE 1. Corosa Family Fields

problems with my wife—you know we separated once." Mario's sister Lotta told the interviewer that she could not remember a single occasion when her parents slept in the same room.

Several members of the family mentioned Sandor's jealousy of Catalina, sometimes accompanied by threats of violence. Every time Catalina left the house, Sandor would check on her movements. He was even jealous of visiting male relatives. For the last fifteen years of their marriage, Sandor and Catalina were separated, Catalina moving to the vicinity of San Juan with all the children except Maria, who had already married. Occasionally, Sandor would visit the family and stay in their house. On one such occasion when Mario (H) was seventeen, he remembers Sandor waving a gun and threatening to shoot Catalina in the course of an argument; the others in the family were terrified, but Mario walked up to Sandor, said firmly, "Give me your gun," and took it away.

After Catalina's departure from Ponce, Sandor established a common-law marriage with Anna Porfirio that produced two sons. The two separated because of Sandor's temper according to Mario's sister Lotta and his Aunt Cara, and they had no contact except that Sandor provided money for the support of the children.

There is some mystery about changes in the family that occurred in 1947; the sale of the store, the separation of Sandor and Catalina, her move to Rio Piedras near San Juan. It seemed to investigators that Sandor had sold his store, at a time when business was booming all over Puerto Rico, to raise money for Catalina's house near San Juan, even though her move was equivalent to her leaving him. The modern, prosperous-looking house in a quiet, well-to-do neighborhood was ultimately left by Catalina to her daughter Lotta, who was living there when the investigation here was begun.

Sandor seemed to the investigators to be a tragic figure; he had apparently hoped to live with his family in the new house, but Catalina would not allow him. Although Mario had invited him to come and live in New York, Sandor said he couldn't get away because of unfinished business. In conversations, he ventured the opinion that men were paying a heavy price for progress in immorality, war, and the dissolution of the family life. He spoke dramatically of arrangements in an ideal family where the man made all important decisions. When asked where he would turn for help in a crisis, he mentioned his children, particularly Lotta and Mario, and friends in the neighborhood.

Of Mario's seven siblings, three (Maria, Roberto, and Juan) were living in the United States, the other four in Puerto Rico. It is striking that when the news of Catalina's last illness reached them, all those in this country were able to gather on short notice for the trip to Puerto Rico.

Mario and his brothers and sisters were very varied in respect to educational attainment, ranging from Juan, who completed only seven grades of school, to Hector, who received a B.S. degree from the University of Puerto Rico. Of the five who did not complete high school, four were living in the United States; all three who had at least completed high school remained in Puerto Rico. All were married except for Lotta, aged forty at the time of the investigation, and Johnny, who was living with Lotta in the house left by Catalina.

Among the siblings, the investigators received most information from Lotta. She seemed nervous and frightened that Johnny would leave the house to get married; Hector had lived with her formerly but left when he took his degree at the university. She described her childhood as unhappy. She referred to a love affair that had embittered her life, and she seemed distrustful of men. Her mother had, apparently, tried to discourage all dating for her. Her attitude toward Sandor was ambivalent. She was sharp, cynical, and critical of everything he said, but seemed to evince much tenderness and affection for him behind a facade of near hatred. She wore her mother's wedding ring on her own fourth finger. Once, when Sandor was not present, the investigator commented that, despite her efforts to be hostile, she was obviously fond of her father. She replied that she didn't want to know the details of her parents' quarrel and separation and that, if she knew, she would end up by hating her father.

The family's religious activities deserve special comment. Catalina was Presbyterian and Sandor, Catholic; they were married in the Catholic Church because Catalina had agreed that the children would be raised as Catholics. Maria, the first born, however, was baptized Presbyterian, though the later children were all baptized in the Catholic Church. Of all the children, only Maria considered herself Catholic at the time of the investigation. Some members of the family were obviously involved with spiritualism, including Mario, who ordered herbs from his sister Lotta to make prescriptions for friends in New York. Lotta thought that Rosa's influence had caused her brother to become interested. Lotta confessed to attending spiritualist services regularly although, paradoxically, she also attended mass from time to time. Sandor felt that he was protected by "good guides" and threatened by evil spirits. Some conversation with Aunt Cara (HMS) indicated that she may have been a spiritualist medium at one time and had suffered seizures during seances.

Rosa's paternal grandparents were said, by her mother, to have been a wealthy couple who squandered their money on lavish living, leaving nothing to their children. Her maternal grandfather (W III B), Rafael Bernard, had come from France as a young man and lived on his inheritance from his parents. He married a widow with five children; they had two children together, one of whom was Isabella, Rosa's mother.

The investigators were able to interview Isabella (WM)', then living in New York. She was small, wiry, very dark-skinned with marked Indian features. Her upper teeth were missing and she smoked cigars. She claimed to be seventy-two but looked older. She was a vigorous woman with a lively sense of humor. She reported that she had had a happy childhood; she had been her mother's favorite and well loved by her older half-sisters. The family lived on a farm with cattle and horses and had enough money and help to make life relatively easy for them. She went briefly to private school but refused to continue. Her mother died when she was thirteen.

Rosa's father, Francisco Torres, was the youngest of eight children in an economically comfortable family. He and Isabella grew up in Arroyo together but did not marry until their midtwenties. Francisco died in 1941. He was reported to have been very short (4'4"), white-skinned, black-haired, and handsome. He had little schooling but, among all the siblings, was the only one who could read and write. He was a railroad worker. Isabella described him as a model husband. Rosa reported that he gambled and drank, although he was well liked and respected by all. The couple produced twelve children: Felicia, Violetta, Ramon, Tiberio, Francisco, Paula, Francisco Garcia, Manuela, Fedelio, Rosa (W), Jaime, and Rodrigo. Eleven lived to become adults, and nine were alive at the time of the investigation.

Both Rosa and Isabella agreed that Isabella had been the stricter parent. Francisco was affectionate and indulgent. Isabella appeared to be a strong figure in the family, still playing a prominent role in her children's lives. In 1950, after most of her children had migrated to New York, she followed them there; her apartment in a run-down Puerto Rican section of the Bronx became a center for family gatherings. At various times, one or another of her children had lived with her; at the time of the investigation, a grandchild, Rosita, was living there, apparently quite content with the arrangement.

Felicia, the oldest of the children born to Isabella and Francisco, married a laborer in Puerto Rico and died in childbirth in 1949. It was her daughter, Rosita, who was living with Isabella, though the father was eager for both Isabella and Rosita to come and live with him in Puerto Rico. Violetta, the second child, and her husband, Frederico, had owned the grocery store that Mario and Rosa owned at the time of the investigation. They sold it in order to move to Florida because of their son's rheumatic heart disease. The sixth child, Paula, died in 1944 following a severe illness, and Rodrigo died in infancy. Of the remaining children, those from whom information was forthcoming were living in New York; the youngest, Jaime, was with Isabella, following a separation from his wife.

Much of the focal family's social life centered around Isabella and the rest of Rosa's family in New York. Isabella appeared to be venerated by her children and grandchildren. She referred to Mario as the "crazy one," but spoke of him affectionately, somewhat more so than of Rosa. She blamed Mario's family, whom she considered difficult and vindictive, for the focal family's troubles.

Mario's side of the family had never been particularly fond of Rosa, but their attitude toward the whole focal family was not clear. Mario's contacts with his siblings had apparently diminished since their mother's death. Lotta in Puerto Rico seemed aggrieved that he had not written to her to acknowledge a gift. At the time of Catalina's funeral, Mario and his brother Roberto concluded a two-year period of not speaking to each other, and Mario mentioned his distress over Roberto's insulting comments about Sandor when they were in Puerto Rico.

Little information could be collected about Mario's earliest years. He described himself as not too close with any of his siblings. He was most frequently with Roberto, with whom he had fought. He also fought with Johnny because, Mario asserted, Johnny didn't show sufficient respect for their parents. Mario remarked that his own son, Mario, Jr., was like Johnny. Mario claimed to have been his father's favorite, beaten less frequently than the others and trusted with more responsibilities. Sandor confirmed this and cited Mario as the most responsible and hard-working of the children. Sandor described Mario as a good child, active and "nervous," who got on well with his siblings. Mario's Aunt Cara spoke of Mario's closeness to his mother, Catalina, and there were indications that Mario and Lotta had been very close when they were growing up. Mario's own early memories were a sequence of rather traumatic episodes, including several illnesses.

Mario quit school in the eighth grade to help in the family store. He described himself as not very bright, though Lotta and Sandor thought he had been quite bright but that a bad encounter with an eighth-grade teacher had precipitated his leaving school. Mario's adolescence was most dramatically marked by the separation of his parents when he was about sixteen. Since Maria had married and Roberto and Lotta were in the service, he was left the senior sibling. He did much of the household maintenance and helped his mother with the chores. "If she was sick, I used to do the cooking—you know, I liked taking care of Mother when she was sick, and when she was well I would do anything she asked me to do." He wanted to join the service, but his mother insisted that he stay home. He had applied to trade school to become an auto mechanic but was not accepted; instead, he was given a place in an electrical school where he discovered, on the first day, that he was "afraid of electricity." (He later became a TV repairman.) He quit electrical school and returned home to help his mother. Lotta remarked that he was the closest of all the children to Catalina. Mario confided everything to his mother. In his late teens, he held a series of jobs, finally working in a clothing store owned by Rosa's brother-in-law. Rosa, who lived in Guyama, occasionally stayed with her sister and would visit the store, where the two met.

Rosa was described as having been an easy, quiet, not very active baby, and as a good, conforming, quiet child, loved by all her family. The one exception was, perhaps, Manuela, five years older; the two girls often fought. Rosa, during interviews, was amused and giggly in describing Manuela's bad behavior, as she was in talking of anyone who was nonconforming, hostile, "crazy." Rosa's father preferred the girls, his favorites being Rosa and Violetta. Rosa said that her mother preferred the boys, particularly Francisco. Isabella confirmed this and also evidenced some preference for Violetta. Francisco Garcia was the one child who angered their father, because he was rough and active. Once he accidentally hit his mother on the head with a rock; his father then hit him with a broom handle. On another occasion, he accidentally caused Rosa to fall and break her clavicle.

Rosa's parents had not argued. Isabella was the stricter of the two and had preached to her children that the man of the house was always right. Rosa talked more affectionately of her father than of Isabella, but admired her mother for being friendly and calm and felt that she, Rosa, resembled the mother. Among her sisters, Rosa was especially close to Paula when they were children.

An event that Rosa remembered as especially traumatic, along with the broken clavicle, was having Fidelio accidentally crush the top of one of her fingers with a hammer when she was five years old. She felt pain for months. The nail grew in wrong and had to be pulled out. The nail continued to be deformed and Rosa expressed annoyance with its ugly appearance at the time of the investigation.

Rosa started school at six, having already learned to read and write. She was considered bright and she accelerated by combining the second and third grades in one year. Because there were so many children in the family, she had few household responsibilities. When she was eleven, her mother started Manuela and her in cleaning, washing dishes, and caring for their own clothes, tasks that Rosa enjoyed. The family went to church regularly on Sundays. Rosa attended doctrine classes at the church daily from age ten to twelve and later taught the class.

When Rosa was ten, her father died, and the family moved from Arroyo to Guyama, a move that changed Rosa's life considerably. In the former, more rural environment, Rosa had been able to play outdoors freely with many children, although she was permitted to play only with those boys who were members of the family. In Guyama, her social activities were confined to school and church and to visits to the houses of two girlfriends, with whom she remained friendly until she left Puerto Rico. Her activities were restricted more as she began to mature.

When Rosa was fourteen, her sister Paula died; Rosa cried during the interview when recounting this event. About a year later, she quit school. She had done well until her second year in high school when, although good in other subjects, she expected to fail at bookkeeping. She felt so averse to bringing home a failing grade that she left, despite her mother's efforts to dissuade her. Rosa blamed the teacher, saying that he had intimidated all the students. She had liked mathematics best of all her subjects and had hoped to become a bookkeeper. On leaving school, she went to Rio Piedras to live with her sister Felicia and her husband, who owned a clothing store and needed some help. Manuela had been there earlier but had been sent home for disobedience. Rosa took up a way of life that she was later to repeat with her husband. She would cook meals at home and take them to the store for Felicia to eat, then stay on to help. She enjoyed this period and the many outings on which she accompanied her sister and brother-in-law, a great change from her restricted life at home.

Mario was in love with Rosa before the two met, having seen her when she visited Felicia before coming to live in Rio Piedras. Once she moved to her sister's house, they saw each other frequently at the store. However, Rosa did not like Mario because he had "bad manners" and used obscene language. He began to improve his manners and his language and to pursue her for a date. She refused because she was not allowed to go out with boys. Often she teased him by agreeing to meet him and was amused when he waited in vain. Finally, Felicia permitted Mario to take Rosa to a show. He tried to make love to her, but Rosa held him off, out of respect for her sister and brother-in-law, although in Rosa's words, "He kept on until he got me."

The two dated secretly for about a year. When Felicia discovered this, she objected because of Mario's family. It was believed that his mother had treated a daughter-in-law badly. Rosa refused to give up Mario, and Felicia returned her to their mother. Isabella (WM) declined to interfere, and Mario was received as a regular visitor in their home. Mario and Rosa became engaged, and he visited her on Sundays for the next year. The couple planned to marry when Mario got a better job. When Mario's visits became less frequent, Rosa heard through his sister Lotta that he was seeing another girl. She wanted to break the engagement, but Mario persuaded her that Lotta was lying and threatened to kill Lotta. Relations between the two families seemed otherwise amicable.

At their wedding, Rosa, then nineteen, was, unknown to either family, four months pregnant. She and Mario had managed to have intercourse only once. She expressed great shame at having been married in a white veil and reported that she was too worried to enjoy her wedding. Isabella thought that Rosa looked very pretty and that Mario's family had fussed over her with great pleasure. Interviews in Puerto Rico, however, indicated that only Mario's Aunt Cara saw anything good in Rosa at the time of the wedding. Lotta repeatedly referred to Rosa as "two-faced" and grimaced whenever her name was mentioned.

During the early months of their marriage, Mario was a taxi driver. The couple had money difficulties and practically no social life. They ate their evening meals at the home of Mario's mother, and Mario paid for this. Friction developed between Catalina and Rosa, and the dining arrangement ceased. Isabella said that Catalina wanted to dominate the young couple and that "Rosa is nobody's fool." Rosa was nauseated and ill during her pregnancy, anxious lest her family discover her condition, and relieved when they found out and were only a "little mad." When Rosa was seven months pregnant, her sister Felicia died in childbirth, and Rosa became alarmed that she too would die. All the family were stunned by Felicia's death. Rosa eventually had an easy delivery, and there were few problems with the baby, Mario, Jr., until just before his second birthday when a gland burst in his groin. He was "leaking for two years," during which time he got penicillin shots every day, administered at a drugstore; he feared the store and screamed whenever he saw it.

During their three years in Rio Piedras, Rosa and Mario lived in three different residences, each move leading to improved housing. Mario continued driving a cab for one year; then his mother bought him a liquor and food store. Rosa and Catalina became increasingly hostile to each other. Rosa opposed the move to the liquor store but helped in the store. The couple began to argue frequently, mostly about Catalina's interference.

During her pregnancy with Cara, Rosa was ill with phlebitis. She was in labor three or four days. The day after the birth, Rosa had her tubes tied. Mario and Rosa were glad for a girl, and Mario, Jr. was "crazy about her." Family arguments continued, however. A crisis arose in 1952 when Rosa sent twenty-five dollars to her brother Fidelio in New York. Catalina said that Rosa was taking money from the store to support her relatives and to force Mario to sell the store to his brother. Rosa reported that Catalina asked Mario to leave her, and they separated for two weeks. By that time, Isabella and most of Rosa's siblings had gone to New York, so Rosa made plans to follow with the children. Mario begged for a reconciliation, and the whole focal family moved to New York.

The investigators discussed with relatives in Puerto Rico the circumstances of Mario's selling the store. One reason offered was that Mario had failed in business because he trusted his customers too much. (This was one of several reasons advanced to explain Sandor's selling his store some years earlier.) Another reason was that Rosa was "stealing" money to send to her "lazy brother in New York." It emerged that, just before the sale, a man with whom Mario had once fought, was killed in a fight outside the bar. Just after this episode, Alfonso "got" the business from Mario. Both Sandor and Lotta (HS) denied that Mario was suspected of being involved in the killing.

The focal family spent their first three months in New York with Isabella. Then Mario got a job in a TV repair shop, and they moved to a small apartment. For five years, they got on well. Troubles appear to have begun when Rosa took a job as a sewing-machine operator; Mario objected to her working and wanted all her money. In 1957, Rosa's brother Ramon migrated from Puerto

Rico and, with his wife and six of their eight children, moved in with Mario and Rosa. Mario said they could stay for six months. Rosa found this intolerable and threatened to leave with her children unless Mario evicted Ramon by Christmas. He did not, and Rosa moved out with Mario, Jr. and Cara. Mario succumbed to Rosa's demand, gave up the apartment he had originally shared with Rosa and her brother's family, and moved into the new one Rosa had taken.

In 1959, Mario wanted to use five hundred dollars banked in Rosa's name to buy a new car. Rosa insisted that the money was for an emergency and that they didn't need the car. Mario appeared at the factory where she worked and shouted at her until she left. At home, he hit her, kicked her, and threatened to "kill her like a dog." She left with the children and took him to court for assault. After two weeks, he begged her to return to him and she did. Mario admitted that he had really wanted to send the money to his father.

A more serious rupture occurred in 1960. According to Rosa, Mario had decided to return to Puerto Rico and was trying to sell their furniture. Rosa, in the presence of a friend, said to him, "You found me on the street and can leave me on the street." This enraged Mario. He punched her so hard that her face was "black and blue for five months." He went to Puerto Rico, stayed two weeks with his mother, then returned to New York. Meanwhile, Rosa had gone back to work and had found a new apartment in Yonkers. They were apart for six months, meeting at Isabella's where she brought the children to see Mario each week. He was to bring her support money. He threatened not to provide money unless she revealed her address. An emergency appendectomy for little Cara eventually brought them together again. Rosa reported that Mario did not hit her after that; she told him that, if he ever hit her, she would "cut his arm through." Four or five months after their reunion, they bought their grocery store and took up the pattern of life they were leading at the time of the intensive interviews.

Mario, Jr. had several visits away from his immediate family during his childhood. During Rosa's second pregnancy, he stayed in Guyama with his uncle Francisco Garcia. When Mario and Rosa separated just before their move to New York, Mario's family "took" little Mario for a few weeks, threatening not to give him back to Rosa. When he was five, he visited Catalina's stepsister, Amelia, for five months; Rosa liked Amelia and trusted the child with her. She also wanted him to have a visit with Catalina before he began school; Rosa reported that he complained that Catalina mistreated him. Mario, Jr. also made two-week visits to other relatives in Puerto Rico in 1958 and 1960.

The boy did well in school and sports and made friends easily. He visited his grandmother Isabella daily and was said to adore her, saving his allowance to buy her presents of cigars. Mario, Sr. usually talked to his son in screaming tones and often threatened him. Mario, Jr. had begun having nightmares three years before the interviews began.

Little Cara was treated gently by both parents. She did poorly in school because, according to Rosa, she missed many sessions with colds and had changed schools four times. She was left back in third grade while her parents were separated and Rosa moved to Yonkers. The school guidance counselor told the interviewer that Cara did not get on well with other children because she was a "tattler" and that she was able to do her school work but was quite lazy. She played with her friends and cousins but was not active in sports.

Contrasts in Values

In reconstructing the life experiences of the Mario C. family, in searching for the pattern that led to Mario's psychotic episode shortly before we met him, and in contemplating the attitude of his wife and children toward this episode, the investigators were struck by the severity of role conflict past and present. The retention by one partner of Puerto Rican working-class values versus movement by the other partner toward American middle-class values escalated the conflict to extremes.

The core of the problem in the Mario C. family may be located in the husband-wife roles, which exhibited many of the strains typical of working-class Puerto Rican family life. Mario was influenced by the usual machismo patterning of the male role. It was extremely important to him to be regarded as macho—an assertive, competent, sexually aggressive male—and to see himself in that light. During the early years of their marriage, while they were living in Puerto Rico, Rosa and her family tended to undermine his views of his own competence. The means for undermining were present in the typical collateral fragility of the extended family system. While they were in Puerto Rico, the point of rupture between the two extended families, with concomitant divisive effects on their marriage, was mainly provided by the mutual antagonism of Rosa and Catalina. Rosa complained that Catalina interfered in their lives; Catalina complained that Rosa stole money for her "lazy" brother in New York. As tension mounted, Catalina put pressure on Mario to leave his wife and their first separation occurred. Behind this overt fracture of the husband-wife bond lay the usual competition of the implicit matriarchal system. To whom was Mario to attach himself, his mother or his wife? To his own family or his wife's family? (See Figure 1.)

The issue was resolved on that occasion by Mario's return to Rosa and their subsequent migration to New York to live with Rosa's mother. It is probable that various factors operated to determine Mario's choice. Rosa's family represented a tightly knit, harmonious clan, in contrast to the fragmented units available to him in his own family. It was equally important that, whereas Rosa was unacceptable to Mario's family, Mario was relatively acceptable to Rosa's family. It may be that Rosa was unacceptable because Mario's role as male head-of-the-house was of such urgent importance to his mother and sister that they could not tolerate his wife; nor could they have permitted him the culturally acceptable solution of leaving Rosa and simultaneously escaping from his mother by forming a relation with a mistress, or a common-law wife. At the intrapsychic dynamic level, Mario's choice was between Rosa as an uncertain dependency object who was sexually acceptable, and his mother as a reliable dependency object who was sexually prohibited.

In New York, Mario settled down in the bosom of Rosa's family. With his mother far off in Puerto Rico, he was initially relieved of the strain of the competing collateral systems. In fact, Mario was happier with his wife's relatives than Rosa herself; for example, it was Rosa who objected to her brother and his family moving in with them and who insisted that Mario eject them.

Mario's inclination to accept collaterality in the household in the form of overcrowded hospitality was opposed by Rosa not only because of the discomfort and inconvenience but also because her values were slowly, hesitantly moving toward a more middle-class orientation. Because of this change, Rosa did not want to have as frequent or as close contact with her mother and siblings as Mario did. Her swing toward American middle-class orientation also made her decide to seek employment in an occupation outside the home. This decision precipitated intense quarreling between Mario and Rosa and signaled a further major step toward crisis in their family.

In the maternal environment of Rosa's family, Mario could maintain the machismo pattern outside the home without too much strain, but Rosa's steady drift toward independence from his domination constituted an increasing challenge to his masculine role at home. Mario's violent response to Rosa's working and her increasing control of family finances was, culturally speaking, merely an exaggeration of the customary reaction. As Mario's violence increased, Rosa's tendency to question his competence as a wage earner and husband also increased, producing a vicious circle of interaction.

When it became evident to Mario that his culturally legitimate masculine right to stormy and violent behavior would not bring about the expected submissiveness of his wife, he left her and returned to Puerto Rico to stay with his own family. Rosa, to emphasize her independence and her determination to assert her newfound rights, refused to let Mario have her address or to communicate with him. Expecting, however, that Mario would eventually ask to be taken back, she let it be known that he could return if he promised to refrain from further violence. The maneuver was, in effect, a manifesto demanding that Mario sanction her right not to live with him if he insisted on the Puerto Rican pattern of domestic abuse to obtain dominance. At the same time, undoubtedly anticipating the need for his cooperation in the purchase of her brother's store, she facilitated his return by appealing to him on the basis of the family's need for him. Because of Cara's illness, Mario gave in.

Following his return, Mario bought the grocery store, Rosa gave up her job to help him with the store, and their relations were again temporarily stabilized in a compromise pattern. Running a family business gave Mario some area for expressing his masculine assertiveness and gave Rosa some hope that the store would provide enough income for them to make adjustments to the American success pattern. Underneath the compromise, however, lay the strain of Rosa's chronic doubt that Mario could perform successfully and with restraint in the American pattern and her tendency to depreciate him because of that doubt.

This was the setting at the time of the death of Catalina and the sudden eruption of Mario's psychosis. In losing his mother, Mario lost the mainstay of his collateral support system. His siblings could not be depended upon to take him in and buoy him up when he had trouble with his wife and family. Furthermore, Catalina had endorsed and often prompted Mario's expression of masculinity through abusive demands for submissiveness from Rosa. Even though he was no longer able to enforce these violently because of Rosa's ultimatum, he still wished to do so, and Catalina's death removed the principal validation for his definition of his own masculinity.

With all this concern for his masculinity, it must be remembered that Mario himself had grown up within a typical masked matriarchy in which the mother represented control and constraint. Ordinarily, the release of such restraints is described in terms of the secondary gain of illness. In this instance, however, even more was involved. Mario's culture actively subscribes to the proposition that spirits may gain access to a person and influence his behavior in ways for which he is not responsible. This is an intrinsic feature of spiritualism and is akin to the voodoo culture of Haiti and other Caribbean societies. From the cultural point of view, the significance is that the person possessed by spirits is not ill, but merely possessed, and that a religious phenomenon must be dealt with differently from an illness and differently from deliberately bizarre behavior. In becoming psychotic, Mario was, in part, acting out a culturally prescribed role for which there were many precedents in his family. Both his mother and aunt were known for their susceptibility to seizures. He was unwittingly taking full advantage of his cultural prerogative; his psychosis represented a last desperate attempt to force his wife and her family to accept his male dominance.

This definition of the "sick" role was quite clearly perceived by Rosa and the children. His "craziness" was described to the observers with amusement and understanding. It was the use of his psychosis to get his own way, to control his family by threats and by physical attacks, that in the end could not be tolerated.

When we investigated the conflict between Mario and Rosa as a phenomenon of the nuclear family, influences from the extended family were mentioned only as background. But in our study, we concurrently appraised the extended families as systems in themselves. From this point of view, the problems of Rosa and Mario appear as reverberations of the strains in each of the two family systems, with value conflicts causing much of the trouble. Integration and conflict in any one nuclear family do not appear clearly and cannot be conceptualized with accuracy except as reflecting integration and strain in the larger system. To introduce a disease analogy, we would not be able to identify typhoid fever in an isolated patient except as a manifestation of a complex process involving definable systems of bacteria, food, typhoid carriers, feces, flies, and dwelling places.

Even a cursory inspection reveals clear differences in the life styles of Mario's and Rosa's clans. As a group, Mario's family members tend to show violence, dramatic overstatement, quarrelsome and suspicious behavior, and ambition. For the most part, they are hard-working, they value education, and they strive to improve their economic and occupational positions. But they are often outrageously manipulative in their relations with each other and with outsiders; at other times, they permit themselves to be manipulated unnecessarily. Rosa's family, in contrast, is characterized by a slow, somewhat genteel, downward social mobility. The family members stick together, giving each other much support. They seldom get angry or disappointed with each other; they accept life as it comes. Little or no emphasis is given to education or occupational achievement. The hysterical outbursts of spiritualistic possession and the appearance of animistic or folk medical practices of Mario's family are unknown in Rosa's family system.

These differences are associated with relevant variations in the manifestations of integration and conflict in both groups. The members of Mario's family are, for the most part, willing to help each other financially or in other ways whenever the help is associated with an improvement in life circumstances. This sort of aid is likely to be proffered even when it causes other serious strains. For example, Sandor used a large part of his life savings to buy a home for Catalina and the children, even though he knew that she was in the process of permanently separating from him. Catalina bought a liquor and food store for Mario despite her disapproval of his marriage and over the opposition of his wife. Mario tried to get five hundred dollars from Rosa, under false pretenses, to send to his father, even though father and son had had little to do with each other recently. The most spectacular of these family savings-and-loan operations occurred during the time of the investigation. The siblings permitted their sister Lotta to acquire Catalina's house by buying them off with a token compensation; because she was lonely and disturbed, they put up with her financial manipulation.

As a result of such help and prompting, several of Mario's generation of his family managed to improve their status. Three finished high school (Lotta, Alfonso, and Hector), and Hector graduated from the University of Puerto Rico. Three others had some high school education (Maria, Roberto, and Johnny), while two failed to complete the primary grades (Mario and Juan). Four managed to attain middle-class status in occupational and residential terms (Maria, Lotta, Alfonso, and Hector), in contrast to the other four, including Mario, who remained at the working-class level. It is interesting that among the four siblings who migrated to the mainland (Maria, Roberto, Mario, and Juan), only Maria achieved middle-class status, whereas, of the four remaining in Puerto Rico, all but Johnny rose to the middle class. Apparently the promised land failed to live up to its image for most of the migrating siblings, at least in the migrators' own generation.

Another sign of the integrative potential of Mario's family is the stability—Mario's excepted—of the children's marriages. There were no divorces or separations, and we have seen how steadfastly Mario struggled to maintain his marriage. His sister Lotta never married, but she seems to have been a special case. (In large family systems, it often happens that one child, usually a daughter, is selected to stay close to the parents and to be the caretaker for their old age. This child tends to be discouraged from marrying by parental disapproval of every known suitor; sometimes she is forbidden to marry. The record shows that Catalina not only

actively opposed a suitor, but frowned on any dating for Lotta.)`
The degree of marital stability shown by the other siblings is not
only atypical for Puerto Rican culture, but is also in marked contrast to the marital instability of their parents, Sandor and Catalina.

In contrast to these positive aspects of the family system are
negative features that weaken the fabric of their life style. Often the
support and closeness that one family member offers another is con-
ditional upon a slavish dependency and submissiveness enforced by
punitive measures. The violent parental conflict, to which Mario
was exposed during his childhood, was a prolonged struggle for
dominance. Sandor tried to master his rebellious wife by terrorizing,
brutal behavior. Both Sandor and Catalina beat their children
severely for challenges to their authority. The use of harassment to
establish authority and quash rebellion resulted in a kind of clinging, masochistic dependence among the children, alternating with a
defiant, domineering behavior. This oscillation seems clearest in
Lotta and Mario. Mario was known for his closeness to both parents and his desire to serve them; once he beat his brother Johnny
for not showing them enough respect. Yet it was Mario who defied
his drunken father and took away the gun with which Sandor was
threatening Catalina. In his youth, Mario was submissively close to
Lotta while Lotta was submissive to their mother; when Mario became engaged, Lotta did her best to break up the relation so as to
retain control over Mario. When she told Rosa that Mario was dating another girl, Mario learned of it and reacted characteristically
with a threat to kill Lotta. Much later, Lotta responded with bitterness to Hector's and Johnny's desire to leave her home to get
married.

The seams and cracks in the family structure, and the ce-
ment as well, are now clearly visible. It is a system that demands
and fosters achievement at the price of dependence—a paradoxical
combination. To maximize achievement requires a diminution of
dependence; but the attempt to resist dependence is interpreted in
this family as rebellion and countered with open punishment or
behind-the-scenes manipulation. Some of the family members were
able to juggle these contradictory directives, holding them in a kind
of equilibrium that permitted them to preserve their balance between the family and the outside world. We do not have enough

information to know how they did this. As usual, the successful adaptations among members of a large family attract little attention; and the observational resources available for this study were unequal to the task of gathering all the information needed for a full understanding of how the family system operated. Accordingly, we do not know what sort of personal and family relations are characteristic of Maria, Roberto, Alfonso, Hector, and Juan. We know only that, as reported by our chief informants, they experienced no difficulties.

What kinds of values can be associated with the paradoxical behavior features exhibited by Mario's family? If one assesses the probable value orientation profiles in the first three of the five categories discussed—activity, relational, and time orientations—then a most interesting pattern emerges. (See Table 4).

Table 4.

GENERALIZED COROSA FAMILY VALUE ORIENTATION PROFILES

Modalities	*Profiles*					
Activity	Be	$=^b$	Do	>	BiB	
Relational	Lin	>	Coll	>	Ind	
Time	Pres	$>^a$	Fut	>	Past	

Abbreviations: Be, BiB, Do stand for Being, Being-in-becoming, Doing; Lin, Coll, Ind stand for Lineal, Collateral, Individual; Past, Pres, Fut stand for Past, Present, Future.
[a] > indicates that the solution to the left is preferred to that on the right.
[b] = indicates that there is no clear preference between the solutions to the left and right.

There are several interesting aspects of this profile. First, the equal preference for Being and Doing and the preference for Lineal over Collateral relations diverge somewhat from the typical working-class pattern in Puerto Rico. Of more importance, however, is the awkward combination provided by the family's first-order choices. Time problems tend to be settled on the basis of the Present; thus there is a lack of ordered perception of change over time. There is no clear-cut preference for Being or Doing; in other words, both achievement and dramatic expressiveness are equally valued. Or, to put the issue differently, both are regarded as equally valid solutions for situations of tension or frustration. Group decision and control proceed on the basis of Lineal hierarchy; tension generated by this system of dictatorial command can be dissipated either through the creation of stormy emotional scenes followed by reconciliation, or through a maximum effort to achieve and thereby to win some freedom from the stringent demands of the control system. But the path to educational and occupational achievement is made difficult by the lack of a primary orientation toward the Future. This obstacle puts a premium on the attempt to achieve success through manipulating and victimizing rivals, a feature of many success-hungry, Present-time oriented, Lineally organized groups, such as gamblers and gangsters.

The pathological consequences of this configuration of values show up most conspicuously in Sandor, Catalina, Aunt Cara, Lotta, Roberto, and Mario. Sandor and Catalina spent most of their married life fighting until they separated; Sandor did not get along any better with his new common-law wife Anna Profirio, who also left him. Catalina and Aunt Cara were both subject to wild hysterical seizures that the family considered episodes of demonic possession. Lotta quarreled with, clung to, and manipulated her brothers and was defiant and disrespectful toward her father. Roberto and Mario fought continuously and refused to speak to each other for two years. Catalina constantly urged Mario to separate from Rosa and made her daughter-in-law's life as unpleasant as she could. When Mario tried to throw himself into his mother's grave, shouting, *"Esta encima de mi,"* he meant to convey the feeling that he was possessed by his dead mother's spirit. But his literal translation, "My mother is on top of me," conveys in the clearest fashion the dysfunctional properties of the Lineal, hierarchical, and domineering system of relations existing in the family.

As we noted earlier, the first choice of the Lineal solution is not characteristic of the dominant Puerto Rican value system. Our information is insufficient to explain how Mario's extended family developed such a strong Lineal orientation. Perhaps it is significant that Catalina's paternal grandfather emigrated from Germany and her paternal grandmother was born in Holland; both of these countries are characterized by a dominantly Lineal relational orientation. All we know about the inheritance of Sandor is that a struggle for dominance flourished among his siblings and that two of his brothers probably killed each other in a fight. In the preceding generation, there was a similar struggle among siblings; Sandor's father was forced off his land by an older brother and given one hundred dollars for property worth much more. Thus it seems that intensely stratified interpersonal relations and the use of force to maintain dominance descend from both sides of Mario's family.

In contrast to the variant preferences of Mario's family, Rosa's family is fairly well in line with the main directions of Puerto Rican life in the first quarter of this century. With the exception of the downward mobility on both sides of Rosa's family, the family's life style before migration was not distinguishable from that of many rural island families living on slowly decaying farms. Even the descent into poverty may not have been as dramatic as it is portrayed in retrospect. The story that the parents of Francisco, Rosa's father, were rich enough to "put gold coins out to dry" has the overblown, romantic sound of a family myth. That Francisco's father dissipated the family resources by living lavishly and not working probably approximates the truth. Either because of lack of interest or lack of knowledge, he failed to run the farm profitably.

Somewhat the same fate seems to have overtaken the parents of Isabella, Rosa's mother. Rafael Bernard came to Puerto Rico with an inheritance that he dissipated after purchasing a farm. He is described as well educated and well mannered, but "lazy." Isabella's mother is similarly described as a delicate refined lady of a good family. By the time of the marriage between Francisco and Isabella nothing was left of either family's fortune except the rundown farm on which they lived while Francisco supported his family as a railroad worker.

Marital relations between Isabella and Francisco were tranquil. He was amiable and hard-working but unambitious, and he liked to drink and gamble with his male friends on weekends; Isabella did not object. In the customary Puerto Rican fashion, she supported him as the ideal head-of-family while herself making all important decisions and carrying out most family responsibilities. The integration of the family rested on the implicit matriarchy, an efficient mechanism for the easy-going, extended family networks of the Puerto Rican farms and villages.

This easy, warm atmosphere prevailed in relations between siblings and parents. Rosa's father hated to discipline the children and left most of this to the mother. The children played with their cousins under the supervision of older relatives in a rural setting. A similar life style continued when, after the death of Francisco, the family left the farm and moved to a village. Later, Isabella and all her children and their nuclear families migrated one after the other to New York so that the collaterally extended family system remained intact and efficient in the new environment.

That system fosters security while discouraging change. The children who moved to New York all remain in working-class occupations, and with the exception of Rosa's moderate shift toward middle-class aspirations, are reasonably content. Even in Rosa's case, the impetus toward change did not come from within her family system, but came about because the family system was not working well for her; in her restructuring of values, the pull of the American value system made itself felt.

Resolution of the Problem

In one sense, the conflicts that had brought Mario raving to the hospital became clear to the investigators because those conflicts grew ever more open and more extreme as time went on. In another sense, however, the eventual unexpected resolution of conflict revealed most conclusively what the trouble had been. Both the worst and the best were yet to come for the Corosa family.

After Mario's psychotic episode, the couple seemed for a time to get along better. Mario was described as "listening" more to Rosa. In the autumn, however, Mario became increasingly intense, agitated, and grandiose. He also became increasingly attached to one of the investigators, Dr. Z., to whom he spoke passionately about his family, indicating that he was against them all. Rosa began to spend all day in the store, presumably because Mario's rudeness to customers was likely to discourage business.

In November, Mario had to be hospitalized again, an event that occurred while both observers were away at a meeting. The hospitalization was precipitated by what Rosa described as a harrowing episode. Mario crawled around the floor demanding that she leave. She went to get the police and returned to find that he had killed a pigeon and eaten its heart. He was very bloody and told the police that the pigeon was Rosa. He fought the police and had to be tied up in the hospital emergency room "like an animal" according to Rosa. Rosa was angry that she had had to cope with this alone while the interviewers were out of town and seemed pre-occupied with the thought that all of Mario's relatives had abandoned him.

Mario remained in the hospital three weeks. When he began to calm down, Rosa refused to believe that the psychotic episode was over. She was furious when Dr. Z. approved passes for Mario to visit at home and especially furious when her husband was discharged.

During December, Mario appeared depressed, defeated, and worried about business. He was taking Thorazine and was sleepy and quiet at the store, where Rosa more and more took over the management. Throughout the next three months, she showed a tendency to demonstrate Mario's incompetence and to maintain an image of him as seriously sick, even to the point of deceiving the investigators about his behavior. Mario complained that Rosa had put him in a position of no authority both at home and in the store. Business was desperately bad. He wrote to his sister Lotta for money, but she said she didn't have any. After an impulsive announcement that he would immigrate to Venezuela, Mario decided to sell the store and return to Puerto Rico. Rosa refused to comply. In mid-January, Mario admitted himself to Bellevue Hospital; he was kept overnight, then discharged, described as not psychotic or out of control. He seemed to want hospitalization as an alternative to pursuing his announced plan of returning to Puerto Rico.

In January, Mario was interviewed at the store. He was dressed and packed, ready to leave for Puerto Rico. He seemed calm but depressed. In an argument with Rosa, she had told him that she wanted him out of the house. Rosa reported that she had written to Lotta, who had refused to help Mario. Rosa complained to the female interviewer of Mario's sexual incompatibility—"He gets me all stirred up and then comes too fast." She was reserved but unrelenting in rejecting Mario.

After Mario's departure, Rosa said that she was planning to sell the store and follow her husband to Puerto Rico "if he wants me." At the same time, she expressed relief at his absence and a continued rejection of him. On March 14th, the interviewers discovered the store closed and in bankruptcy. Rosa had disappeared. Isabella claimed she did not know where Rosa was and that Rosa had moved because she was afraid of Mario.

In June, the observers were able to locate Rosa. She was living, with her children, in a common-law relation with a Mr. B. Mario had obtained a divorce in Puerto Rico. Although Rosa would not agree to an interview, the investigators dropped in one evening. After some initial stiffness, the couple were relaxed and friendly. Mr. B. had come to New York from Puerto Rico in 1948 and considered it his home; he had never returned to Puerto Rico for a visit. He was tall, heavily built, calm, and thoughtful, a striking contrast to Mario. He had worked himself up from porter to shipping clerk, and expressed his faith in education, preparing for the future, and personal determination. His mother and three sisters were living in the Bronx. He said he did not live too near them because families should live more on their own. He and Rosa regularly visited their mothers and Mr. B.'s children by a previous marriage. Although it is doubtful that Mr. B. and Rosa were legally married at the time of the interview, they appeared firmly established as a family.

An interviewer in Puerto Rico followed Mario closely after his arrival there in January. For the first four or five months, he was unemployed, living briefly with Alfonso before moving in with Lotta. He was totally dependent on Lotta, who treated him like an irresponsible burden. Mario did housework while Lotta worked. During this period, he asked his Aunt Cara to pierce his ear so that he could wear an ornament "like a pirate's earring." He drank a lot and was often intensely excited. Lotta argued with him frequently. The family blamed Mario's outbursts on alcohol rather than mental illness, but they considered Lotta "crazy."

After a few months, Mario got a job as a tourist guide and

began sending part of his salary to Rosa. He dated a secretary who lived next door to Alfonso. His family described the girl as better educated, lighter skinned, and prettier than Rosa. The investigators in New York had never realized how much Mario's family considered his marriage to Rosa as a marriage beneath him. Mario attributed his new calm to his return to Puerto Rico, adding that, in New York, he would have had to be hospitalized again because of his debts and Rosa's demands and arguments. The investigator sensed that Mario had renewed his ties with his family and had reasserted his male position. He was the oldest male of the family living in Puerto Rico. When he spoke of New York, he became excited in recalling how afraid of him his customers were; he said that he had had to show them he was boss; he talked of not being afraid of anyone, of being a man.

A serious struggle developed within the family over the house inherited from Catalina. She had been recognized as owner, even though the house was in Lotta's name. Lotta began to claim the house as her own. She sold it for $32,000 and persuaded each of her brothers to accept $1500 as a "donation" with the stipulation that they sign "donation papers." They all consented to this but were furious. All the family said she was like Sandor, with lots of houses and money. At the same time, their anger at her financial manipulation was tempered with concern about her mental state.

One year after the pigeon incident, Dr. Z. saw Mario in Puerto Rico. He had been promoted in his job but had broken off with his girlfriend or, probably, she with him. He appeared to be in a better state of mind than ever before in his contacts with Dr. Z. In another visit to Puerto Rico, roughly two years later, Dr. Z. found that Mario had been promoted again and was now a special guide for VIP tours. He was married to a woman strikingly different from Rosa in appearance and disposition. She was thoroughly naive, even-tempered and plain-looking, as characteristically a Puerto Rican in speech and manner as Rosa's Mr. B. was a New Yorker. She seemed to worship Mario.

The observers found it significant that little Cara had become a behavior problem in New York and that Rosa had written to ask whether Mario could have her to live with him and his new wife. The pattern of solving behavior problems by sending children back to Puerto Rico is not unfamiliar; what was striking in this instance was Rosa's implicit assumption that Mario was well and able to care for his daughter.

Analysis

Additional insight may be gained by considering the attitude of Mario and Rosa toward the investigators. For this purpose, bear in mind that the Corosa family incorrectly but firmly believed the investigators were acting as therapists.

As long as Rosa could believe that the observers would "cure" Mario's belligerent domineering as a part of his psychosis, she was able to cooperate. When she discovered that they would not take sides in the dispute and would not persuade Mario to conform to her wishes and values, she became actively resentful of their presence. For her, there was no middle ground; the observers were either for her or against her. Eventually she began to regard the observers' nonintervention as an active sanction of Mario's domineering behavior. At that point, her long struggle for her right to live with Mario on her terms was concluded. She gave up. Subsequently, all her efforts were directed toward undermining Mario in order to establish that he was not a man with whom she could live. In the end, her effort to separate fully and finally from her husband was successful.

Rosa's effort to separate was facilitated not only by her collateral relatives, but also by her having found a man whose value orientations and aspirations were more in line with her tentative steps toward an American middle-class value system. The Puerto Rican values were still evident in her willingness to live in consensual marriage with him. But, so far as the observers could determine, the relation was characterized by the determination of Rosa and her new "husband" to establish a small, independent, nuclear family with shared responsibility, educational aspirations for the children, and freedom from their collateral families.

For his part, when his psychosis failed to scare his wife into submission, Mario became depressed. His illness not only had failed to strengthen his position, but had further and fatally weakened it.

Now, even when he was symptom-free, Rosa was able to deflate his image of himself as macho by implying that any behavior of which she disapproved was a sign of imminent relapse and need for hospitalization. The emptiness of their marriage and the lack of hope for any viable compromise between Mario's and Rosa's values became brutally clear. The grocery store, the symbol and means of their earlier compromise, was in a state of ruin, with Mario in the position of its incompetent owner. Financially and emotionally bankrupt, he had no choice but to accept the separation he had so long been postponing and to retreat to Puerto Rico and his collateral relatives there.

In Puerto Rico, the restorative process that had eluded him in New York eventually began to operate. At first the reaction to the loss of his mother, wife, and children precipitated fresh regression. Slowly, however, with some help from his siblings, he was able to face these losses and to reconstruct his life in accordance with traditional Puerto Rican values. No longer undervalued by Rosa's expectations for a male role whose terms he did not understand and could not meet, the internal integrative process sealed over the memory of failure. He then became able to explore relations with women who were able to accept and appreciate the kind of male role he knew how to act. He was again respected, macho, able to master his everyday circumstances and to perform creditably.

To say that Mario's psychosis was caused by his marriage and cured by its dissolution is an oversimplification. It has been shown that considerable light can be thrown on his psychosis exclusively in terms of strains caused by discordant value orientations between him and his milieu as well as between him and Rosa within the nuclear family. In any case, the description of cultural and family strains is only the beginning of the diagnostic process. It approaches the background of the problems in the family, delineating normative expectations and departures from them. Health or pathology in interpersonal relations is perceived as based on these expectations and departures. Interpersonal, intrapsychic, and biological levels of integration must be explored for a full elucidation of any state of illness.

Even without an effort to collect data required for detailed analysis at these levels, however, the family case history as presented provides glimpses of the kinds of family interactions characteristic of Mario, Rosa and their children. The history supplies a picture of the interaction of Mario and Rosa when Mario's psychosis was at its height during the time of psychological testing. Mario's provoking, overassertive, and illogical behavior was evident in his relation to both Rosa and the tester; equally evident was Rosa's way of evading a direct challenge to Mario while subtly correcting him by revealing his errors. The subtle and not-so-subtle unmasking of Mario in the home by Rosa and the children is illustrated somewhat later in the case history along with the coalition of Rosa and the children and Mario's consequent isolation from the nuclear family.

The history gives evidence of the seesaw struggle between Mario and Rosa—he attempting to maintain face by "lording it" over his family and she, with the children, resisting through humor, mocking behavior, or pretenses to follow orders while actually disobeying. As the history progresses, Mario's violence is described as increasing periodically, such increases correlated with Rosa's efforts to distort the meaning of his behavior in her ever more vigorous attempt to undermine his position as the center of authority in the home. Interactions of this sort were a vicious circle from which husband and wife were unable to extricate themselves. The more Rosa directed, the more Mario defied and threatened her. The more he threatened her, the more she distorted. This process, as recounted in the history, led to fresh outbreaks of Mario's overt psychosis and to the ultimate collapse of his position in the extended family and in the community. With the final disintegration of his position as a person entitled to respect in the community, especially among his customers at the store, Mario became withdrawn and depressed. His interactions with Rosa and the children then became wholly concerned with disposing of the store and separating from his family.

It seems evident that these kinds of communications and interactions achieve their significance only within the framework of the cultural and extended family process already described. Why was it necessary for Rosa to distort and for Mario to threaten? Were they both innately evil? Or merely ignorant and stupid? Or so basically anxious and immature that they could not behave otherwise? Such explanations have been advanced in the past and have found acceptance. That they cannot be wholly accurate is indicated by the change in Mario and Rosa under other circumstances. Rosa turned out to be a nonmanipulative person when she found a husband whose values corresponded to her own; Mario became calm and nonthreatening when, in the context of his extended family in Puerto Rico, he found a woman who accepted him as macho. Nevertheless, there is a measure of truth in the imperfect explanations. The evil that is in men, that is, their hostile destructiveness, was maximally stimulated by the conflict in values between the spouses. They were ignorant not only of better ways to cope with the conflict, but even of the nature of the conflict dividing them. And they both displayed various defenses against anxiety that obscured the real nature of their problem and gave rise to remarkably maladaptive behavior. Over and above all these causes of their difficulties in interpersonal relations, however, were the cultural process and changing patterns in values and domestic roles in Puerto Rico, and the gulf between these values and middle-class values in the United States. Mario and Rosa were caught up in these contrasts, and they responded in increasingly divergent ways.

In our study we found it helpful to view Mario and Rosa in part as the ambassadors of extended families that were incompatible with each other. Hence a final word on this aspect of their relation is in order.

The transfer of Puerto Rican rural family patterns to the New York scene included, for Rosa's family, the preservation of some traditional marital instability. Francisco Garcia separated from his wife. Manuela divorced an alcoholic husband and remarried. Fidelio married a divorcee who deceived him about the number of children she had borne her previous husband. Jimmy separated from his wife and was living with his mother at the time of the investigation. Rosa's separation and subsequent divorce from Mario were, therefore, wholly in accord with her family's custom. Long-standing family customs, along with their supporting values, confer a peculiar sense of propriety upon the self-image of family members. To the family (Mario excepted), the casual, easy-going acceptance of lower-class status and marital instability shown by Rosa's family looked like unpardonable shiftlessness. They thought that Mario had married beneath himself, and they worked to extricate him from this error. To Rosa's family, Mario's relatives seemed excitable, quarrelsome, and pushy to the point of madness. They thought of them as a bunch of "crazy people." Though they tolerated Mario's "craziness" as they accepted many other mixtures of the good and the bad, they were not in the least impressed with his or his family's social standards. The lack of meshing between the two family self-images and the projective qualities of each, guaranteed an extended family conflict of nearly irreconcilable proportions. Mario's family members were unable to see the defects that Rosa's relatives saw in them, and vice versa. Nor could either family appreciate the strengths of the other. Therefore, contact between the two family systems tended to maximize the most disruptive features within each of them.

This point is of great importance to the microsociology of conflict in extended family systems. When two incompatible systems are required to establish transactions, each makes the other look worse than it actually is—that is, more irrational, more disruptive, more damaging to its constituent members. The apparent unreasonableness of interactions between the two families, their lack of effective ways of reducing conflict, cast an aura of bad faith and evil motivations on both camps. The resulting gloom and doom and the tendency to blame the other side gave rise to a spiral of hopelessness and impatience that could be terminated only by violence, exhaustion, or, as happened in this case, by total disengagement.

4

Contrasts in Italian and American Values

The unique features of the Italian family structure along with Italian cultural values created special problems of adaptation for Italians immigrating to the United States. In this chapter, we will examine these features and see how they affect second- and third-generation Italian-Americans.

In Table 5, the dominant values of southern Italian rural society are contrasted with those of American middle-class society. It is immediately evident that there is little congruity between the Italian and the American patterns. Southern Italians share first-order Being, Collateral, Present Time, and Subjugated-to-nature orientations with other agrarian cultures. The lot of the Italian peasant, however, was more harsh and difficult than that of many of his counterparts in other sections of Europe. At the turn of the century, and in fact to the present time, existence was marginal at best in the towns and villages from which the major wave of immigration to the United States originated. (For a description of southern Italian life, see Schermerhorn, 1949, and Banfield, 1958.) Most of the men were landless peasants or day laborers who were ex-

97

Table 5.

ITALIAN RURAL AND AMERICAN MIDDLE-CLASS VALUE
ORIENTATION PROFILES

Modalities	Italian Rural			American Middle-Class		
Activity	Be	>[a] BiB	> Do	Do	> Be	> BiB
Relational	Coll	> Lin	> Ind	Ind	> Coll	> Lin
Time	Pres	> Past	> Fut	Fut	> Pres	> Past
Man-nature	Sub	> With	> Over	Over	> Sub	> With
Human nature	Mixed	> Evil	> Good	Mixed	> Evil	> Good

Abbreviations: Be, BiB, Do stand for Being, Being-in-becoming, Doing; Lin, Coll, Ind stand for Lineal, Collateral, Individual; Past, Pres, Fut stand for Past, Present, Future; Sub, With, Over stand for Subjugation-to-nature, Harmony-with-nature, Mastery-over-nature.
[a] > indicates that the solution to the left is preferred to that on the right.

ploited by landowners, the middle class, and the nobility. Politicians
were viewed as natural enemies, on a par with the physical dis-
asters that often frustrated the farmer's valiant efforts to eke out a
living from the soil. The clergy tended to support the landowners,
the middle-class businessmen, and the nobility, and so they too became a part of the hostile and exploitative world (although the
ceremonial aspect of the church continued to be accepted).

Perhaps the best-known characteristic of Italian culture is
its family-centeredness. The origins of this characteristic are found
in sociohistorical experiences, especially the experience of the population of southern Italy, from which the overwhelming majority of
Italian-Americans are derived. A long succession of foreign invaders denied the native peoples a stable social order and a stable political system. The family, in the midst of this sociopolitical chaos,
emerged as the only social structure on which the southern Italian
farmer could depend and within which he could cope with the
vagaries of a marginal agrarian economy. Survival was founded on
the development of a strong interdependence among family mem-

bers; this interdependence permeated all spheres of human activity and was a bulwark against all those outside who were not blood relatives.

Because of this emphasis on the family we examine the ordering of relational values in Italian culture first. Development of a first-order Collaterality in the relational area suited survival needs, and it was limited wholly to the family. The extended family group commanded total and lifelong loyalty and commitment from each of its members. Interdependence among all members and across generations was evident in the occupational and social spheres of activity. Children were expected to work as soon as they were old enough, often with their parents, on the farms or in the other occupations their fathers engaged in, such as masonry. Schools were limited to the privileged classes, and, besides, education was not viewed as an activity that prepared men for the realities of their work-a-day world or that was a proper concern of women. Furthermore, social mobility through education was not a viable route for improving one's occupational status in southern Italy. Social life was centered around religious festivals, and social interaction was limited to blood relatives, including grandparents, great uncles and aunts, uncles, aunts, and cousins, and their families. Close friends were admitted to the family circle by becoming sponsors at weddings or godparents of children; in this way, they assumed a semi-familial status and were referred to as *compare*. The spouses and children of *compare* expanded the family unit even further. (For a graphic description of the Italian family, see Barzini, 1965, ch. 2.)

The second-order Lineality in the relational pattern is evidenced in the authoritarian position of the father in the southern Italian family, which, consequently, is often labeled *patriarchal*. While the father's patriarchal role is characteristic of a primarily Collateral family system, the Italian father does not function as the absolute head of the household on whom all family decisions are dependent. Though he is often the chief wage earner, the economic survival of the family rarely depends on him alone. This fact tends to dilute his authority within the family system. He is respected by his wife and children as the head of the household but not revered.

The lesser importance of Lineality is further evident in the constraints on respect paid to old people. Men do not ascend to a preferred position in the family by virtue of old age but instead must forfeit the prerogatives of their position as head of the family when they are no longer able to fulfill their responsibilities.

There is a sharp segregation of the husband and wife roles within the household. The husband is responsible for the general welfare of his family and is its main representative and spokesman in all dealings with the "outside world." His wife assumes a subordinate position in relation to him and is responsible for running the household, caring for the children, and keeping in contact with relatives. The husband is the main disciplinarian; he administers rewards and punishments (though often at the direction of his wife). The wife's power in the overall affairs of the family is often greater than her formally subordinate position reveals. In relation to the children, she comes closer to a revered position than her husband. The great reverence paid to the Madonna in Italian Catholicism is a reflection of the central importance of the mother in Italian culture.

Sex roles and age roles are also sharply segregated in southern Italian society. During regular social gatherings of the family, as well as during the working day, men tend to stay with men, women with women. Men are uncomfortable in the presence of women, and women who seek the company of men are, at best, suspect of bad intentions. Men and women are not expected to be able to control their sexual impulses. The virginity of daughters is the responsibility of their fathers and brothers, who are held accountable and who do not rest their vigilance until the girls are married.

Intergenerational separation is clearly demarcated, and there is little companionship between parents and children in non-work situations. Relatives of the same age tend to associate with each other, and close lifelong attachments are made that provide a continuing source of emotional support. In times of personal crisis, a man will turn to his brother or his cousin for help and, in most cases, help is freely given without regard to the sacrifice this might entail.

There are large numbers of children, and a man who does not have at least one son to carry on the family name is considered unfortunate indeed. Italians, however, have never been a child-centered culture in the American middle-class sense of that term. While they dote on their children, the children's needs do not in any way govern family goals and directions. Youngsters are viewed as sources of pleasure for the parents; they cannot be taken seriously since they are not expected to be able to make rational judgments about what is good for them. Thrashings are the preferred mode of punishing "bad" behavior—that is, behavior that involves disobedience to family norms. The good child learns early to suppress his individual strivings when these do not further family goals and aims.

Individualism is placed last in the Italian relational value orientation profile. Individualistic strivings in the southern Italian social structure would weaken the solidarity of the family system. Individual achievement in occupational and social spheres, by definition, would involve independence from the family unit. Since the family unit is the major system through whch the individual relates to the world, separation from it means a renunciation of the basic relations that sustain life and give it meaning. The price is clearly too high. The family cannot conceivably approve deviant behavior that threatens the major source of security for all its members. Furthermore, there is little opportunity for individual achievement-oriented activity in the Italian village.

Individuality, however, is another matter. Within the expansive family milieu one can express individuality and expect to be rewarded for it. Individuality usually takes the form of demonstrations of one's physical prowess, the fineness of one's clothes, the number of one's progeny, the beauty of one's daughters, and so on. One takes individual pride in one's reputation as an honest man, a hardworking and devoted mother, or a faithful and devoted son. These expressions of individuality reflect the preference for Being over Doing in the activity value orientation area. Since one cannot rely on individual achievements in the occupational area of activity, that is, on Doing, for enhancing the sense of personal worth, Being-oriented activities serve this function.

A festival in a southern Italian town provides an opportunity for families to show "who" they are. During a celebration, a promenade in the streets makes it possible to be seen in one's finery, to display one's sons and daughters, and to enjoy oneself fully. (For a delightful description of the central importance of "spectacle" in Italian life, see Barzini, 1965, ch. 4.)

Enjoyment is one of the major foci of southern Italian life; work is a means to make this possible and never an end in itself as in the American Doing-oriented core culture. It is here that the Being over Doing preference in the activity area becomes obvious. High value is placed on the expression of feeling. Living is enjoying—enjoying food and drink and music and most of all sharing these things with others. To be alone is a curse that even enemies would not wish on one. The main joy of life is to be with those one loves and to experience this joy in the present, not in some distant planned-for future.

The order of activity preferences is reflected in the ordering of time orientations, an ordering that Italians share with other agrarian societies. The emphasis on Being is reflected in the first-order Present time orientation. The Future orientation is weak in a society that is not technologically advanced. The second-order Past orientation in Italian culture, however, has special meaning that differentiates it from other agrarian societies. Italians are Past oriented to the extent that they value their heritage and are proud of their culture. The expression that this pride takes, however, is very much geared to the first-order Present orientation. Italian municipalities will expend large sums for the erection of statues and buildings to honor its famous men and heroes of the past. Every village has such a statue. But these monuments have a functional purpose —they justify celebrations and are the symbols around which celebrations are organized. They do not serve the function, as they do in other cultures, of renewing national consciousness. They are not intended to honor the sacrifices and accomplishments of past leaders in order to solidify the sense of ethnic identity and cohesiveness. Rather, they are a stimulus to present enjoyment.

The Catholic Church serves this same function in Italian rural culture. The numerous saints' days throughout the year are occasions for festivals, with parades through the village square in which families promenade in their best finery. Festivals interrupt the monotonous routine of village life and are cause for a spontaneous outpouring of joyous feeling.

Religion in Italy has never been used to preserve cultural traditions that helped maintain a strong sense of national identity. In Italy the family, not the "race," has been the major bulwark against the disorganizing effect of a succession of foreign invaders. Though Italians have manifested strong national feelings at different periods of their history, they have never been fiercely nationalistic in the same sense as other nations. They devised other ways of meeting threats to their survival and the family has proven to be the most effective.

In relation to man-nature orientations Italians again follow the pattern of other agrarian societies. They feel that there is little a peasant can do to combat the forces of nature that determine a good crop year from a bad one. A laborer cannot affect the amount or the frequency of the work he will be hired to do. Technologically advanced societies are Mastery-over-nature oriented for reasons that make functional sense—they have the capability of doing so.

The first-order Subjugated-to-nature orientation is reflected in fatalistic beliefs and practices that characterize the life of the Italian peasant. Illnesses and other misfortunes cannot be foreseen or prevented, and once they occur, they are accepted with resignation. Doctors are thought to be of little use, and their prescriptions are rarely followed. One either gets well, or one dies, because it was willed by God. Good fortune brings uneasiness with it—the evil eye, in the form of unforeseen catastrophe, is bound to be attracted and turn good fortune into bad. For example an attractive child is the object of envy, but the envy becomes a vehicle by which evil, in the form of an illness, can be imparted. (The Catholic Church has special prayers of exorcism through which the devil may be expelled from the body of the victim and the illness cured.) Peasants and laborers, in short, feel that one can do little to determine the course of individual destiny.

Southern Italians do not identify with the community that transcends the boundaries of the family. The notion of organizing themselves in order to improve their living conditions is an incomprehensible one. Collaterality, in the sense of cooperative and interdependent activity cannot be placed in the context of the broader community. Since Italians feel that they can exert little control over this aspect of their lives and thus have little interest in doing so, they do not concern themselves with political affairs. Politicians are expected to be corrupt and to enrich themselves at the expense of the electorate. At best one can hope for a personal favor in return for his ballot. This cynicism extends to the police and to other government officials, all of whom are viewed with suspicion and contempt. Nothing is expected of them. Wrongs committed against an individual are righted by members of his family; this matter cannot be entrusted to the police, and the sick are taken care of at home because hospitals cannot be entrusted with their care. Care-taking agencies, run on a charity basis at the turn of the century, were generally ignored as beneath the dignity of a family.

Italians carried this culture with them to the United States. The immigration of southern Italians to the United States represented a resettlement in the literal sense of a reconstitution of village life in this country. (For a comprehensive work on Italian emigration, see Forester, 1919; and for a book that describes an Italian-American community, see Gans, 1962.) This continuation of village life is perhaps the most distinctive aspect of the behavior of Italians in the United States. The cultural patterns described in the previous section were altered little, if at all. The central importance of the family remained essentially the same, and the life style was in most ways indistinguishable from that in southern Italy. Only the setting was different. (For a description of Italian life in New York City at the turn of the century, see Pisani, 1938 and 1957.)

The family was extended to encompass the neighborhood. Italian-Americans settled together in the less desirable sections of large cities; successive waves of immigration expanded these areas into distinct Italian communities, or "Little Italys," as they soon became known. Italian was spoken in the home, and Italian grocery stores provided an abundant supply of familiar foods. The transition to the new world, for the first generation, was comparatively easy.

Contact with the "outside" American society was limited to the work situation, and even there was often made through an intermediary. Italians, like the other immigrants, swelled the ranks of the laborers and factory workers that were absorbed by a burgeoning economy. They gravitated to the building trades where their immediate bosses were invariably Italian *padrone*. These were leaders who acted as intermediaries between the workers, who spoke little English, and the employers, who spoke little or no Italian. The employers were rarely encountered; like the absentee landowners in Italy, they were viewed from afar as exploiters and criminals who fed on the sweat and toil of the workers. The world beyond the borders of the neighborhood was viewed, as it was in Italy, as enemy territory, and "outsiders" were not trusted.

The efforts made by progressive members of the Italian-American community to organize their compatriots for the purpose of improving their social conditions in the new world got little support. Most of the original, first-generation immigrants planned to return to Italy as soon as possible. They were not interested in labor movements that would have improved their working conditions; they put their trust in the *padrone* through whom they obtained their jobs and who often exploited them. Also, they could not be persuaded to organize social welfare institutions to care for the needs of their compatriots, as did members of other ethnic groups. This, again, was the responsibility of the family.

The "American dream" was interpreted by the first-generation Italian immigrant in terms of the opportunity he received for obtaining steady work and providing food and shelter for his family. The values of individual achievement, planning for the future, and striving to improve his status in the American social system were irrelevant. The law that forced him to send his children to school when they could be working to contribute to the family finances was viewed as an unjust intrusion to be resisted as long as possible. The children carried these attitudes to school. They waited out the period of compulsory education and left when they could to go to work. The child who found himself drawn into the middle-class value system of his teachers and developed strong achievement drives found little support for these aspirations in the home. Career ambitions were shunned if they seemed to risk alienation from the family and loss of the broad base of social support provided by the expanded family unit. (See Covello, 1944.)

Second-generation Italian-Americans adapted the value orientations learned from their parents to the conditions prevailing in the cities in which they lived. The peer group took on real significance. (See Gans, 1962.) Though the same-generation pattern of interpersonal relations can be traced to village life in Italy, its function in the United States developed a special meaning. It provided for the expression of the Collaterality in which they were socialized in the home, while at the same time allowing them to escape the second-order Lineality that characterized the Italian family. The father's authoritarian position in the family could not be easily accepted in the United States. The Italian community could not insulate itself entirely from American egalitarian values and the corollary emphasis on Individualism. Italian-American youth, like their "native" American counterparts, felt the need to separate themselves from the family, and this they managed through a peer group society.

Their peer group relations, however, took on a distinctive Italian caste. The "street corner society," as Whyte labeled it, gave priority to Being, Present, and Subjugated-to-nature, as well as strong Collateral, orientations. (For a classic sociological study of Italian youth in a lower-class section of Boston, see Whyte, 1943.) Young men gathered informally in the neighborhood to have fun, to joke, to exchange stories about the day's activities, and to talk about girls. There was little organized activity, like baseball or other group competition, where one's individualism could be expressed, as there was among American middle-class adolescent groups. The peer group did not function as a medium for learning the competitive skills, interpersonal and otherwise, for adaptation to the broader society. It was Present oriented in that it functioned as a means for the ongoing gratification of its members. It was not a medium for the expression of Individualism in the American core value sense, but it did provide opportunity for the expression of one's individuality. It was here that the individual displayed himself and vied for status within the group. These expressions of individuality took the form of relating one's accomplishments, or engaging in verbal duels, or demonstrating one's physical strength. Skills were displayed to enhance one's position in the group structure and not to beat or humiliate a rival. Keeping competitive scores would tend to weaken intragroup cohesiveness and was avoided as much as possible.

Women were expressly excluded, and barriers between the

sexes remained strong. Sexual relations were limited to "loose" women who could not be considered as potential wives. "Good" girls were carefully watched over by their male relatives, and from among these, a wife would eventually be chosen. Marriage, however, did not affect the solidarity of the particular group or gang that a man belonged to. Relations formed by the young man or boy lasted throughout his life.

In the second generation, as in the first, upward social mobility and its corollary, residential mobility, meant separation not only from the family but from the peer group as well. It is not surprising, then, that relatively few ventured to enter careers that would have separated them from the Italian community. (For a comparison of Italian values and their relation to achievement motivation with those of other ethnic groups, see Strodtbeck's article in McClelland and others, 1958.) Those who succeeded economically through small businesses usually maintained their homes in the old neighborhoods even though they were in a position to move to the suburbs.

The age group pattern of their parents was also maintained by second-generation Italian-American society. A loosely knit group of brothers and sisters and their spouses, together with close friends who, as in the village, often became *compare,* godparents of their children, constituted the basis of social life. They frequently visited each other's homes for conversation and food, the men and the women congregating in different parts of the house.

Like their parents, second-generation Italian-Americans lived within a group, which they maintained to meet their personal needs for affiliation and not, like the American middle class, to achieve a group goal. Americans representative of the core culture live outside a group, entering it only to achieve objectives that cannot be accomplished individually. The contrasting American and Italian relational patterns are especially evident here. For Americans, Collaterality is secondary and serves to undergird Individualistic strivings; for Italians, Collaterality patterns the mode of interrelating itself. Collaterality, furthermore, is based on an egalitarian system of relations among the members of the peer group. There are no leaders who give it direction or toward whom its members look for support or help. One is strengthened by virtue of being an accepted member of an ingroup but does not want to rely on the group as a continuing source of help. This reliance would be considered a dependency that would violate his sense of personal dignity and place him in an inferior position in relation to the others. Members of the group freely help each other, but through a reciprocal exchange of favors. In times of crisis, help is given but is reciprocated as soon as possible lest the receiving member be left with a sense of obligation that would lower his status in the group.

The importance of holding equal status within the Italian-American peer group can be viewed as a reaction of the second generation to the second-order Lineality that patterned traditional relations in the Italian family. As the second-generation Italian-American grew older, he spent less and less time in the home and proportionately more time with his peer group. The control that his father had over his behavior was progressively weakened so that a clear intergenerational separation was evident when he married and formed his own family unit. Though emotional ties to the parental generation remained strong, the second-generation family was clearly a separate, independent system. "Blood" remained "blood," and a son would care for his parents and provide for them even at significant cost to his own family; but he would not be controlled or directed in any way by them. The second-generation family, in other words, was related Collaterally to the first-generation, and strong interdependent rather than dependent ties characterized their relations. These relations, like those within the peer group, were based on a mutual caring and helping, on trust, and on the continuous joy of being together.

The frenetic activity of native Americans to achieve goals, to "get ahead" personally, to solve problems, is seen by Italian-Americans as a violation of the human spirit. In their eyes, this activity reduces the individual to the level of an object to be used to achieve a goal and therefore demeans and dehumanizes him. It precludes the spontaneous interaction of individuals for the mutual enhancement of their sense of personal worth and dignity. Gans' distinction between person-oriented and object-oriented individualism is here especially apt. (See Gans, 1962, pp. 89–97.) He describes the Italian-Americans in the West End section of Boston that he studied as treating each other in person-oriented ways. They scrupulously avoided business transactions with friends lest they be seen as potentially exploiting them. Mutual trust was a basic ingredient in their relation, not to be jeopardized at any price. While middle-class Americans view the lack of interest in careers and professional advancement of many Italian-Americans as a deficiency in their characters, Italian-Americans view the achievement-oriented activity of middle-class Americans as disgracefully selfish.

Considering the contrasting value orientations, it is not difficult to see why acculturation to American core society is a slow process for Italian-Americans. The incongruence in values supports the traditional view of the world outside the Italian society as strange and inimical. The American political process continues to be viewed with the same cynicism as its counterpart in Italy. Politicians are viewed as insincere, untrustworthy, dishonest, and self-seeking individuals. American institutions are viewed as unable to care for or provide for the needs of citizens because the institutions are governed by corrupt individuals. These institutions, therefore, deserve to be ignored or, at best, regarded with contempt. A person obeys the law because he must, not because he respects it as a social institution designed to protect the rights of all individuals. One's loyalty is limited to those who deserve it—members of one's family and peer group. This attitude is the expression of "amoral familism" that Banfield describes in his study of southern Italian society. (See Banfield, 1958.) Moral values apply only in relation to members of one's family; those outside the family cannot expect the same moral code to apply to them. They are outsiders.

The deviant form of "amoral familism" is, of course, manifest in the Italian underworld which, while it constitutes a very small proportion of the Italian-American community, is the aspect of Italian-American life that most Americans are exposed to through television and the movies. The strong bonds of loyalty that bind members of the Mafia organization or "family" are the same as those that bind their compatriots in the rest of Italian-American society. Members of the Mafia in a particular city are often related either by blood or marriage, and initiation of new members is sealed with a rite where one's blood is literally mixed with those of his "brothers" in the "family" he joins. The leader maintains his power to the degree that he can maintain the loyalty and respect of the members of his "family." Those who attempt to impose their authority on a "family" by brute force invariably fail. Fights between gangs for the control of particular territories and illegal enterprises highlight in a macabre way the operation of "amoral familism." Execution of enemies is carried out with little or no feeling that an immoral act is being committed; these victims are outsiders and so beyond the protection of any moral code.

The inroads of middle-class American society on the culture of "Little Italy" is increasingly evident in the third generation, the grandchildren of the original immigrants. Intermarriage with non-Italians is more common, and the pathways to upward social mobility, principally education, are being taken by a greater number. Active participation in political life, especially in large cities like New York and Boston is increasingly evident. Movement to the suburbs and the adoption of a middle-class American style also reveals the accelerated acculturation process in this generation. Movement back to the Catholic Church is a further index. (See Glazer and Moynihan, 1963.) The first-generation Italian-American brought his distrust of all but the ceremonial aspect of the church with him. His children internalized this distrust, but his children's children, who are socially mobile upward, have embraced the church as appropriate for their middle-class status.

In spite of these changes, however, the pull of traditional value orientations remains strong for Italian-Americans, and it is not possible to foresee what course the acculturation process will take in the future.

5

Case Study of an
Italian-American Family

The unique problems of acculturation faced by members of Italian-American families in the United States are illustrated in the Tondi family case history. In presenting the Tondi family, we want to focus particularly on the relation of cultural values to the patterning of social roles in the family.

The Tondis, a nuclear family consisting of the parents and two small boys, were referred to a research project we were conducting for the treatment of moderately severe symptoms of psychological disturbance in both children. Mr. Tondi had initiated the diagnostic and treatment process. The youngest son suffered from chronic constipation with episodes of abdominal distress and severe pain on moving his bowels. He would go four, five, or six days with no bowel movement at all. The family doctor had ignored or minimized this condition. The father decided that his son should be seen by a specialist and brought the boy to an outpatient medical clinic for observation. There it was found that the boy had a moderately enlarged colon because of the retention of feces, but no organic cause could be found for the condition. The basic factor

was considered to be psychogenic, and a psychiatric diagnostic study
was recommended.

General Background

The family consisted of Antonio (Tony) Tondi, the husband, who was thirty-five years old; Celia, the wife, thirty-three;
Timothy (Timmie) age six; and Antonio, Jr. (Sonny) age five.
During the initial interviews it became evident that Sonny's constipation was not the only source of concern within the family. The
parents were also worried about Timmie. He was subject to severe
temper tantrums, stuttered badly, and could not go to sleep without
rocking in bed at a tempo that alarmed baby-sitters, relatives, and
friends. In addition, Timmie had great difficulty in separating from
his mother. If she left him at home to go shopping, for example, he
would become distressed, feeling that she would never return. Even
when she remained at home, which she did most of the time, he
could not play outside without returning to the house frequently to
make sure that she had not gone away.

At first both parents were in a state of near panic because
of Sonny's constipation, and, as a result, all other family problems
seemed to be secondary. By the third and fourth day of constipation, Sonny was obviously in pain and quite tense and irritable. He
also was clearly postponing going to the toilet because of fear, particularly fear of the pain that he experienced when he finally did
have a movement. The parents were beside themselves when, no
longer able to postpone the dread event, Sonny screamed and cried
during the evacuation. They were also repeatedly astonished at the
large size of the stool that Sonny produced.

Mr. and Mrs. Tondi were beset not only by the pity they
felt for their son and their inability to help him but also by the
tyranny that his symptom waged over the family. Family events had
to be timed to Sonny's abdominal state. If he had recently moved
his bowels, there was freedom to plan visits or other activities that
might take them out of the house. But when he was in the tension
phase of his constipation, it was necessary to stay at home. Sonny
was afraid of using any toilet but his own. In addition, the parents
were reluctant to expose him to anyone outside the immediate fam-

ily when he was tense and irritable. They were ashamed of his condition and of their possible responsibility for it.

Fortunately, the constipation yielded rather rapidly to treatment. Soon after treatment was initiated, a more temperate rhythm of bowel movements began to be established, and the anxiety of the parents began to abate. There then came into view a wider range of problems. Sonny also stuttered enough to cause the parents concern, although not as frequently or as severely as his brother. Mr. Tondi, it turned out, had stuttered severely in his youth and still stuttered whenever he became excited. He felt very badly about the stuttering of his two sons, for he was convinced that his own speech problem had been an obstacle to job advancement and economic improvement. He said repeatedly that stuttering can hold a person back. The idea of being held back because of inner defects and initial disadvantages was a theme frequently expressed by both parents.

Tony Tondi viewed himself as a person who had struggled hard all his life to overcome the disadvantages with which he was initially faced; that is, the large, impoverished, fatherless family in which he grew up, his stuttering as a youth, his shortness of stature, and his lack of educational opportunities. Though he sometimes wondered whether the struggle was worth the effort in view of the worries about the children, he usually maintained an air of optimism. His strenuous efforts to improve his circumstances had led, in his opinion, to a modest success. He was a skilled mechanic, and he believed that human problems, like mechanical ones, could be resolved through hard work and the application of the appropriate technology. This point of view had enabled him to hold a secure position for many years as an aircraft mechanic, to build a house for his family in an attractive suburban setting largely through his own efforts, and to give his children material satisfactions and personal attention that he had missed in his own childhood.

When the possibility of psychotherapy for the children and weekly interviews with the parents was suggested, the father immediately assimilated the procedure to his views on technical solutions to problems. He believed that he and his wife must be making serious errors in their handling of the children. If these errors could be located and corrected while the children were still young, then they would not have to suffer from unattractive traits of behavior that, he believed, would make life difficult for them. If his own participation would help correct the error and overcome the children's handicap, he was, as he said, "all for it." He asserted he had no complaints on his own account. He stated that his marriage was perfect. There were occasional domestic quarrels such as one finds in any family, but these, he felt, were of no consequence.

This relaxed, optimistic view of the marriage was not shared by his wife. She soon unburdened a multitude of complaints about herself, her husband, her children, her home, her relatives, and her life in general. All her life she had felt inferior to others because of her short stature, poor complexion, unattractive figure, and inability to express herself. Now she viewed herself as a failure both as a wife and a mother. Her husband, she said, was also short and unattractive physically and was a very ordinary man who needed to be pushed in order to achieve anything. She wished she could encourage him, but the difficulty was that she had never loved him; and now she was afraid that she was becoming the same kind of nagging, unpleasant, critical wife that her mother had always been. With two such handicapped parents, it was not surprising to her that the children had so many defects. Still, this outcome was not what she had wanted or hoped for. Like her husband, she had hoped to rise above the circumstances of her birth and to bring up children of whom she could be proud.

Almost all the attitudes which Celia Tondi expressed were marked with ambivalence and ambiguity. She was ashamed of her low estimation of her husband and had never directly told him how she felt about him. Nor did she want him ever to hear of her actual feelings about her marriage. Though she tended to consider Tony ineffective, childish, and unattractive, she knew that he was well liked by the neighbors and respected by his associates at work. She said she could appreciate him only through the eyes of other people. He tried hard to be a good father and husband. But he failed to meet her standards for these roles. He left too many family problems for her to handle. On the other hand, she knew that she compulsively criticized him so often for decisions he did make that it was no wonder he gave up trying to handle family affairs. Nevertheless, she secretly wished that he would overcome her tendency to dominate him; she wanted to be overruled and was happy when, on occasion, he would be firm and insist on having his own way, as he had about bringing Sonny to the clinic. She was even happier if his decision turned out to be correct and hers wrong. And, in a reversal of her usual, sour view of her marriage, she sometimes described with pleasure her feeling of accomplishment on the rare occasion when they had been able to resolve some problem in collaboration with each other. She said that, if the family were to be accepted for therapy, she hoped she could learn to be a better wife to her husband.

In her behavior toward her children, her usual ambivalence was complicated by nagging uncertainty. She felt that almost everything that she did with them was wrong; yet she did not know what was right. For example, for Sonny's toilet problem she had "tried everything" and "nothing worked." When Sonny threw rocks at other children in the neighborhood, she was especially upset. Unlike the Tondis, most of the parents in the community were college graduates, and their children were "well behaved." She was horrified at Sonny's behavior and appalled at what the neighbors must think of his parents. She also believed that a boy who throws rocks at age five will throw knives when he is older. In her imagination, Sonny was already a budding Italian gangster, fated to a career of crime like so many of the boys in Boston's North End Italian community in which she had grown up. The behavior had to be controlled, in fact, expunged. Whenever it occurred, she spanked him vigorously and confined him to his room for several hours. If she caught him in the act of transgression, she was likely to rush out of the house, collar him, and hit him in front of his friends, to show one and all that this behavior was discouraged by his parents. She told the interviewer of her serious doubt of the correctness of her method of discipline. But how could one and how should one handle such disturbing behavior?

Similar questions of what to do and when to do it plagued her relations with Timmie. She wanted to help him with his stuttering. Her husband's stuttering had been cured, for all practical purposes, when he was fourteen years old. A sympathetic, kindly teacher, an expert in speech problems, had devoted a great deal of time to his stuttering and had taught him how to breathe and speak rhythmically by pounding out a regular beat with his fist. They had tried this with Timmie, forcing him to count regularly, breathe in time, and speak slowly. It had not worked, and Timmie now cried if forced to persist. Most of the time he could not persist because Sonny kept interrupting and talking when Timmie was trying "the method." Timmie could not tolerate his brother's intrusion into his talking time. He would abandon the method and attempt to gush out words as fast as possible to compete with Sonny. When Celia tried to slow them both down or silence them, Timmie would have a temper tantrum and retreat to his room, leaving the floor to the victorious Sonny.

To members of the project staff who were conducting the diagnostic interviews, the appearance and behavior of members of the Tondi family did not correspond to the views of either of the parents. Tony did not seem the ineffectual person described by his wife nor the calm, purposeful husband and father that he appeared in his own eyes. He was a short (5′4″), compact, muscular man, of dark complexion, with large brown eyes and a round face. Always neat and well groomed, he usually dressed in sport or working clothes. He had a genial smile, an alert expression, and a friendly manner. Though superficially relaxed and mildly deferential, there was an underlying tension in his behavior, as if, though basically guarded and cautious, he labored to make himself accessible and to be cooperative. He was intelligent (I.Q. of 113) and responsive in interviews, but it was difficult for him to express openly any personal feelings about members of his family other than concern for his children's behavior. He seemed to show concealed pleasure in Sonny's rebelliousness when, with a smile on his face, he said that Sonny had his mother "wrapped around his finger" over his bowel movements.

Celia's behavior corresponded neither to the perfect wife and dedicated mother of Tony's description nor to the dismal failure of her own. She was short (5′2″) and stocky, with dark hair and eyes, neatly and conservatively dressed, and carefully made-up with lipstick and pancake powder. When at ease and cheerful, she had an attractive sparkle, but most of the time her facial expression was tense and her manner urgent. She had difficulty restraining her emotions. Her eyes often brimmed with tears as she told what a poor job she was doing as a mother. In the waiting room before and after the individual interviews, she seemed quite anxious about the behavior of the children, tensely correcting them, supplying the word that Timmie was stuttering on or commanding Sonny to be careful with toys belonging to the clinic. Yet, behind her obsessive concern about appearances, there was a hidden warmth and a buried interest in the needs and personalities of the children. In the interviews, she too was responsive and intelligent (I.Q. of 115) and eager to cooperate.

Six-year-old Timmie was of normal weight and height for his years. He had a thin, wiry build. His hair and complexion were lighter in color than other members of the family, and his movement was less heavy-footed. He was well coordinated and much interested in activities such as swimming, skating, building model airplanes, and modeling in clay. He stuttered so badly, distorting words, that it was often difficult to know what he was saying. Yet there were intervals when he could speak quite clearly. He was friendly and eager to please and rapidly formed a warm attachment to the female psychotherapist who interviewed him. His I.Q. was 103, representing average intellectual functioning. However, his vocabulary test score was low, and he was unable to admit not knowing the meaning of words. He made up fanciful definitions on the basis of clang associations.

Sonny was huskier and two inches shorter than his brother. He physically resembled his father, having the same large brown eyes, round face, and rosy, healthy appearance. There was a belligerence in his manner and an excitability of gesture that contrasted with Timmie's rather more shy and controlled conduct. He stuttered only occasionally, usually when he got into a talking contest with his brother in the waiting room. Despite a fleeting chip-on-the-shoulder attitude, he was friendly with the male psychotherapist who interviewed him. During interviews in the playroom, he alternated between exploring all the toys and other materials, examining them with great care, and gingerly putting everything back in place. He enjoyed painting and crayoning and was eager to display his products to his parents after the interview. His I.Q. was

87, but this score was considered to fall below his potential because of his inner conflicts. Both boys came to the interviews well dressed and immaculate.

In the course of the diagnostic procedure, both parents and children were given a variety of psychological tests. All the family members had considerable anxiety about the testing process. For both boys, the psychological tests revealed a greater impairment of ego functions than was evident in their relations with the interviewers. Sonny had difficulty attending to the test tasks. He frequently broke off, wandered around the room, opened drawers, and asked questions about what was contained in cabinets, paying little attention to the answers. He seemed both to be running away from the test and to be driven by an insatiable curiosity. He expressed the idea that the tests would reveal whether or not he could go to school, and he seemed confused about his age. There was suggestive evidence that this confusion resulted from an imperfect separation of his identity from that of his brother, who was about to enter the first grade. Stories he told indicated both a desire to destroy or mess up and a pronounced fear of the consequences of carrying out the desire. Considering his circumstances this fear was not unexpected. The defense against it, however, frequently consisted of a flight from reality or a distortion of reality. In the summary of the psychological test responses, Sonny was described as being in an active and somewhat aggressive flight from a painful reality in which he experienced a temptation to destroy and to mess and simultaneously feared that he would be destroyed as a result. Still, the possibility of other than regressive solutions to his anal-sadistic conflict were seen in his desire to go to school and his active curiosity. It was considered that treatment was indicated and that he had sufficient intelligence and capacity for relations with others to be able to profit from it.

During the testing procedure, Timmie was at first frightened, and at one point he was close to tears and asked for his mother. He was reassured by the tester that his mother was waiting for him, became calmer, and was able to complete the tests. Like Sonny, he had difficulty in paying attention to the test stimuli. The tests led him into a series of free associations and fantasies. The fantasies were repetitious, containing an endless sequence of bombs, black clouds, lightning, jet planes, and black storms. These apparently represented natural and man-made forces of destruction that frightened him, both for their actual and for their symbolic meaning. He told stories that involved a good deal of conflict between parents, in which he always chose to be on the father's side. In many stories he described an atmosphere of closeness between a father and son. (That this was a wish rather than an actuality was indicated by his fear of separation from his mother and by his father's statement that Timmie seemed to have little desire to be close to him.) In the summary analysis of the test responses, the psychologist stated that Timmie could be described as a phobic child with a tendency to autistic withdrawal under stress, particularly the stress of an unstructured situation. The boundary between reality and fantasy was indefinite and tended to disappear when his fears were evoked. However, there was also evidence of an attempt to turn back to reality through a counterphobic denial of fear. In consideration of his desire to master his fears and the warmth with which he could form relations, a good response to the therapy was anticipated.

Celia Tondi came to the testing sessions as a woman heavy with sorrow and guilt, the content of which was about to be revealed by the tests themselves. She sat primly, as before a judge, frequently readjusting her posture to an even more correct position. Anticipating exposure, she consistently interrupted the test procedures to make little confessions and excuses, perhaps in the hope of obtaining a lighter sentence. For example, she confessed to feeling guilty "to this day" for having somehow provoked "my gentle father into throwing a bottle at my mother which left a scar." Her responses revealed an excessive concern with what is proper and visible. In her TAT stories, women were portrayed in a dramatic, almost soap opera fashion, as suffering from deep hurts and injuries, longing for an unobtainable freedom. A preoccupation with being damaged or causing bodily damage ran through her productions, most heavily concentrated in her view of mother-child relations. In the alternation between attacking and being damaged, there was a tendency to seek relief through withdrawal to passivity and helplessness, "like a kitty who is quiet and fed and cuddled and doesn't destroy much." She showed doubts about the completeness of the female body. Arms, legs, heads, and hands were variously missing from her drawings and percepts. Cleanliness and neatness were also emphasized, usually in the context of a cold, unsympathetic mother being stern with a child. She saw herself and her own mother in this way. She talked about her own traumatic experiences as a child and her defective performance as a mother. Despite the conflict-laden material which was evoked, the tests did not reveal any serious distortions of reality or deficiencies in ego functioning. The diagnostic assessment was that of a neurotic character disturbance with hysterical and depressive features.

Tony Tondi was much less serious, more relaxed and matter-of-fact about the testing procedure than his wife. His anxiety was expressed in numerous digressions, jokes, and humorous attempts to disqualify himself: "I haven't done this since grammar school," and, in response to the TAT instructions, "I read nonfiction." In contrast to these disqualifications, he made known his competence in building houses, fixing cars, and sports. Unlike Celia, who spent a good deal of time defending and attacking herself before the tester, Tony was compliant in following instructions and sometimes asked for help. His productions were better organized than hers. In place of her pervading moralism, he displayed a practical common sense. However, he picked his words so carefully in the attempt to exhibit a sophisticated command of language that he often ended up with what sounded like a formal disquisition—for example, "This state going against his better judgment, he. . . ." (It was later discovered that a fear of being shown as possessing an inadequate vocabulary was endemic in the Tondi family.)

Tony's reactions revealed a pervading passivity and a restriction of aggression. For him the Rohrschach cards principally suggested butterflies, insects, birds, and various other animals with open mouths. In his TAT stories there was little assertion, either by men or women, but signs of concealed anger toward women appeared in the frequency with which he depicted them as sick or dying. Under a cover of conformity and compliance, he showed evidence of covert rebellion toward authorities. For example, when asked what sort of animal he would like to be, he said, "'A dog because it's friendly and people like dogs, although some people might say because it tears up the boss's garden." Because of his desire to control aggression, his productions in general lacked spontaneity. His ego-functioning, however, though constricted in some areas, was considered adequate.

These test procedures, plus the initial interviews, disclosed the Tondis as a family seriously entangled in emotional conflicts between each other and within themselves. All had sufficiently intact ego defenses and appropriate orientations to reality so as not to be gravely threatened with a psychosis or other mental illness too difficult to deal with in an outpatient setting. The diagnostic and behavioral data which we have presented so far are, of course, quite limited by the exclusion of material on the past history and development course of each family member. These facts were gathered in the course of the assessment in the usual way. But, since we are dealing with a family rather than an individual, we believe it desirable to organize the data of the past in a somewhat different fashion than is customary and to present them separately from this brief snapshot of the family's functioning. (See Figure 2.)

Tony and Celia Tondi were both second-generation Italian-American Roman Catholics. Their parents had been born in Italy and immigrated to this country in their teens. Tony and Celia were both born in Boston's North End Italian community though they had been unacquainted with each other until they met as young adults.

Tony was the youngest of ten children in his family. His father had died when Tony was three years old, leaving his mother essentially without funds or relatives to help her support the large family. Tony was full of admiration for his mother's valiant efforts to keep the family going without becoming dependent on public assistance agencies. She owned her own house, which was a large one, so that she was able to take in boarders. Thrifty and determined, she invested what she was able to save in real estate and eventually owned two other rooming houses. All the children were pressed into service in the maintenance and operation of these establishments, which were run like a small family business. Tony regarded her as a "pioneer woman" with a "good business head," and he attributed his desire to get ahead in life to the example that she set.

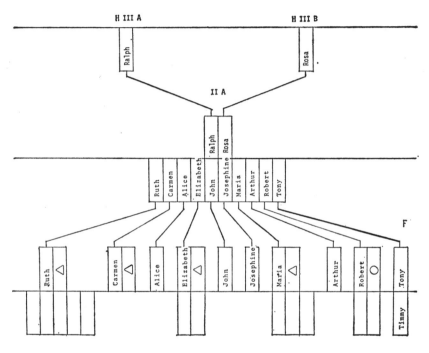

H III A

H III B

Ralph

Rosa

II A

Ruth
Carmen
Alice
Elizabeth
John Ralph
Josephine Rosa
Maria
Arthur
Robert
Tony

F

Ruth △

Carmen △

Alice

Elizabeth △

John

Josephine

Maria △

Arthur

Robert ○

Tony

Timmy

▬ Direct lines of ascent
▬ Indirect lines oi descent

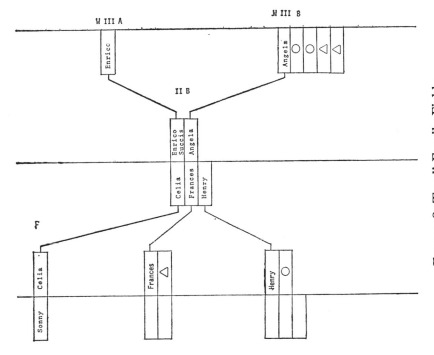

FIGURE 2. Tondi Family Fields

While the children were young and the mother alive, the closeness typical of the Collaterally-organized Italian family was maintained although there were some conflicts among family members that will be described later. After Tony's marriage, however, he and Celia took an apartment in the building owned by Celia's parents, and Tony's relations with his wife's family tended to take the place of the intimacy he had formerly maintained with his own. He continued to visit his mother dutifully every day, running little errands for her and talking over the day's happenings, but he saw his brothers and sisters less and less frequently.

Just before Timmie's birth, Tony's mother died. He was depressed for several months after her death and then angry about a controversy that broke out between the siblings over the distribution of the mother's estate. Thereafter, his relations with his brothers and sisters became even more attenuated. By the time we became acquainted with him, Tony's behavior toward his relatives was ambivalent. He maintained a formally correct attitude, paying visits on important occasions and avoiding outright rupture or conflict, but he was resentful that he had not received more help in times of stress, especially from his brothers. There were two sisters toward whom he still felt friendly. They exchanged visits frequently and sometimes served as baby-sitters for Tony and Celia. Tony felt he had little in common with the others.

As a result of Tony's attitude, there was no opportunity for project personnel to meet members of Tony's family, to see his personality through their eyes, or to determine, aside from Tony's and Celia's brief statements, what sort of people they were. Information about them is sparse. The eldest sibling, Ruth, was fifty-six years old at the time of first contact with the family. She was a widow with five children, living in a suburb remote from the Tondi's home. Her husband, a barber, had died several years before, leaving her in difficult financial straits. Tony had a special animosity toward this sister because, in his opinion, she had been disrespectful to his mother while demanding money from her because of her husband's difficulty in maintaining steady employment. The next born sibling, Carmen, was fifty-three years old. Her husband was a house painter. The couple had no children and lived in the North End of Boston, in the area in which the family had grown up. Arthur, age fifty-one, the oldest son, was unmarried. He was a chronic alcoholic whose behavior had troubled the family since Tony was a boy. Although a skilled mechanic, he was usually unemployed and dependent on his family for help. Currently he was living with his younger brother, Robert, in the North End of Boston. Elizabeth, fifty years old, a widow with two children, also lived in the North End, but nothing more was learned about her. Nor were any details gathered about the next sibling, John, other than the facts that he was single, worked as a printer, and still lived in the North End. Alice, age forty-four, was single, lived alone in the North End, and worked for a curtain manufacturer. Maria, age forty-two, was married and had three children. She and her husband, a machinist, lived in the North End. Maria and Alice were the two sisters with whom Tony still maintained friendly relations. The youngest sister, Josephine, was forty-one years old and unmarried. She lived alone in the North End, supporting herself through odd factory jobs. Finally, there was Robert, age forty, Tony's next oldest sibling. He had attended M.I.T. during the evenings while working as a machinist and had graduated with a degree in civil engineering. He was the only one of the children who had attained a college education. Married with two children, he also lived in the North End and was currently looking after Arthur, the unemployable, alcoholic brother. In spite of his superior education, his style of life apparently differed little from that of the other brothers and sisters who, unlike Tony, had never left the North End.

Under the matriarchal hand of the widow Tondi, functioning as both mother and father for her large brood, the emphasis on economic survival was heavy indeed. With work so demanding, there was little time or occasion for the recreational pleasures, the food and drink and gaiety, even for the maternal succor and solicitous supervision usually found in the Italian-American family. During his interviews, Tony often commented on the material deprivation and the stern tone of his childhood. There was no money for toys, and skates, bicycles, bats, and balls were nonexistent. Birthday celebrations and gift-exchanges were minimal. His mother was usually too busy and too hard-pressed financially to attend to such things. During most of his childhood, it was his sisters, Alice and Maria, those with whom he was still friendly, who had looked after him, not his mother. The mother functioned more as the commanding officer, making the important decisions and giving orders for child care but leaving the execution up to the older siblings.

With the family system engaged so much in work and sheer survival and so little in pleasure and gratification, the principle of maintaining close, collateral contacts inevitably suffered damage. There was insufficient emotional reward in it. Worse still was the effort made by the mother to maintain the prestige of the family in the extended Italian-American community by giving huge parties for friends and neighbors on important occasions, such as Easter, Thanksgiving, or local religious feastdays. That the money and the energy so hard to come by were used for this purpose gave rise to resentment among the children. As expressed by Tony, the children felt that, though a Rock of Gibraltar against catastrophe and devoted to keeping the family together, she was more interested in winning love and acclaim from others by performing services for them than in gaining love and affection from her own children by paying personal attention to their needs. Thus, a kind of isolated Collaterality developed, lacking the warm support of a fully Collateral group but nevertheless discouraging the children from seeking Individualistic or Lineal satisfactions instead.

As the youngest child, Tony felt that he had perhaps received the most attention and had suffered the least from this system of family life. Of all the children, he believed that he was the closest to his mother as he grew older, though she had been little in evidence during his earlier years. She had regarded him as the most reliable and stable of the sons and gave him a good deal of responsibility. Possibly on this account, he was the one who identified most with her desire for prestige and self-advancement. Under his mother's restrictive control, he chose his friends at school from among those boys who were ambitious and not likely to become juvenile delinquents and common laborers. Later, with his mother's encouragement and while working full-time in a garage, he attended night sessions at an aircraft technical school to be trained as an aircraft mechanic, the occupation which he then pursued up to the time of our contact with the family.

The key problem in Tony's growth and development—the

one, at any rate, of which he was most consciously aware—was his stuttering. The onset of the stuttering, which was quite severe, was also associated with a period of nervousness and self-consciousness that persisted throughout his adolescence. In his own mind, these problems were the result of family conflict occasioned by the behavior of his oldest sister, Ruth, and his oldest brother, Arthur. Ruth's disrespectful, hostile attitude toward his mother, together with her constant demands for money, distressed Tony. From the age of twelve on, he began to stand up to Ruth, demanding that she show a more respectful attitude. He was the only child to do this, and the mother seemed peculiarly vulnerable and helpless in the face of her daughter's emotional assaults. Something of the same nature occurred with respect to Arthur's alcoholic episodes. This oldest son had been the mother's favorite child, the one upon whom she had placed all her hopes for prestige and success in her offspring. When he became an alcoholic in his youth, she was utterly helpless and continued to favor him and protect him, even though the scenes he made when he arrived home drunk and abusive harassed the entire family. Again, Tony was the only child who was able to stand up to Arthur, attempting to control his wildness by threatening to call the police. On one occasion of particularly combative behavior, Tony did notify the police, and Arthur was jailed overnight. He recalled the episode with a combination of guilt, for having humiliated his brother, and pride, for having taken a step to relieve the family of a menacing situation. He was then eighteen years old, and, though the youngest son, found himself in many ways acting the role of the eldest son. Indeed, it was after this episode that his mother finally renounced all hope for Arthur's rehabilitation and transferred her expectation of success in a son to Tony.

Having partly relieved his stuttering, with the help of a sympathetic speech therapist, and having partly stabilized the family situation, through his domination of Arthur, Tony's attitude toward the mastery of problems and the wish for success was now crystalized. He was angry with his siblings for producing so much stress within the family, and he was left with a desire to get away from the family, to find some new, Collateral group that would be more satisfying. It was in this mood that he met Celia and her family and began a courtship that was to stretch over a six-year period.

At the time of therapeutic contact with the family, Celia's family, the Succis, consisted of her father, Enrico, age sixty-one; her mother, Angela, age fifty-three; her married older sister, Frances (Francesca), age thirty-six; and her married younger brother, Henry (Enrico, Jr.), age thirty-one. Her parents lived in the North End of Boston in a three-family house that they owned and in which the children had been brought up. Frances, her husband Joseph, and their two children lived in their own house in a suburb, while Henry, his wife, and their three children lived in an apartment in the North End, not far from his parents' home. Enrico, Sr., had been in the oil and ice business, making deliveries in the neighborhood in which they lived. Since he was ill with diabetes and partly retired, the business was now mainly in the hands of his son. Joseph ran a dry-cleaning establishment, and he and Frances lived on a somewhat higher economic plane than the others in the family.

In contrast to the polite but distant behavior existing among members of the extended Tondi family, the Succis were heavily involved with each other. Their social relations, however, were burdened with tension. Quarrels and flare-ups, acute and chronic resentments, reconciliations, restitutions for real or imaginary injuries, and constant exchanges of gifts, services, advice, and admonishment were the fabric of their family life. Both Celia and Tony participated, often painfully, in the volcanic eruption of her family's affairs, though Tony had made efforts to diminish his wife's and his own involvement. In fact, one of his main reasons for building the house in the suburbs was to be at least physically removed from her family. In the course of therapy, it soon became evident that helping the spouses either loosen these ties or make them more endurable would be an important aim of treatment.

The turbulence in the Succi family was usually precipitated by Angela, Celia's mother. She was a blonde, with a fair complexion, abundant energy, many skills, and a fiery temperament. According to Celia, she had been beautiful when younger and was renowned in the neighborhood for her hospitality and her excellent housekeeping and cooking. She was a competent midwife whose services had once been much in demand, though now the younger Italian-American mothers in the neighborhood preferred to deliver their babies in a hospital. In addition, she was active, throughout Celia's childhood and to the present, in caring for recent emigrants from Italy, housing, feeding, and grooming them for life in the United States. One of Celia's prominent complaints about her childhood was that her mother did more for others than she did for her own children, a feeling reminiscent of the resentment expressed in the Tondi family about their mother's exhibitionist hospitality.

Though Angela agreed that she gave much time and energy to doing things for persons outside her family, she also thought that she gave more than enough attention to her children. In any case, she was seldom happy with the outcome of her devotions, whether in or outside her family. No matter how much she did for people, they always managed to disappoint her. She was chronically critical of her husband, who, in her view, was passive, inffective, and unable to earn enough money to give her the social position in the community she would have liked. She believed that what status they had attained was wholly the result of her own efforts. She was bitterly disappointed in Henry, who had, in her judgment, all but ruined the reputation of the Succis by making what she insisted was a bad marriage to a woman of loose morals and unsavory family background. She had never expected much of Celia and took a dim view of Tony and the children. As for Tony's family, she regarded the Tondis as unstable, unrefined, and altogether beneath the social standing of the Succis. Even Frances, the favorite child and the one who had come the closest to satisfying Angela's wish for success through social advancement in her children, had lately been a disappointment. Frances had a poor relation with her children and quarreled with her husband, accusing him of not earning enough money. The couple were frequently on the point of separation. Angela felt let down by the domestic careers of all her children, as well as by her own.

According to Celia, her mother was incapable of believing that she had any responsibility for the many disappointments inflicted on her, and she did not regard her troubles as problems to be solved. They were deemed to come from bad luck, the innate wickedness and irresponsibility of others, or from evil magic—possibly from all three.

When her son fell in love with the girl of supposedly loose morals, whom he later married, he was in his early teens, and Angela was convinced that this girl's mother had administered a love potion to him. She and her friends consulted with each other about the most effective form of countermagic to dispel the influence of a love potion. Many things were tried—spells, incantations, and brews of various sorts—but the desired apotropaic effect never occurred. Angela was furious and stormed at her son, vilifying the girl and her family and forbidding him to continue seeing her. These emotional scenes also misfired; Henry only shouted back his defiance of his mother's opinions and orders. When, in spite of her efforts, the pair was married, Angela refused to attend and screamed blood-curdling curses on the newlyweds, the bride's family, their future progeny, and all who attended the ceremony when the procession passed in the street.

Angela's bad luck, it seemed, had begun in her village near Naples when, while she was in her early teens, the family suffered a business setback. As a result, her two brothers immigrated to the United States, and, somewhat later, a marriage was arranged by her family between Enrico Succi and the seventeen-year-old Angela. Enrico, then twenty-five years old, had immigrated at age sixteen to the United States, where he had worked on a railroad in the West. Now he had returned, briefly, to the region of Italy in which he had been born, to find a wife. Some weeks after the wedding, he returned to the United States alone with the intention of sending for his wife after he had found a better job and established a home. When, after a year and a half, he did send for her, the oldest child, Frances, had already been born.

Although Enrico had seemed enterprising and resourceful, even dashing, in Italy, in the new environment Angela soon discovered that he was good-natured but slow. Her sisters and parents were in Italy, her brothers somewhere in the Midwest, and she found life in the North End of Boston lonely and difficult. Only gradually did her beauty and talents establish a place for her in the community. Improvement of her social position would, without question, be up to her. And social status was, for Angela, the whole point of life.

It was in this atmosphere of social striving that Celia grew up. Her memories of childhood were stocked with examples of her mother's pushing behavior toward her children. The children were always being compared with other children in the neighborhood who were described as more attractive, competent, or intelligent. Although her mother displayed little physical warmth, such as cuddling and kissing, to any of the children, Celia always felt that her sister and brother received preferential treatment. Frances had her mother's beauty and talent, while Henry was an only son from whom great things were expected. Her father left the whole care and disciplining of the children in the mother's hands, and Celia recalled this with resentment. She felt that her mother's constant prodding and comparing them with others gave all the children the feeling that they were "no good." Her father was kind and gentle but could not be relied on for support because of his subservient position in the home. And it was Celia who needed his support the most, for her mother regarded her as the most inferior of the three children, almost as a lost cause.

During her childhood, Celia's greatest worries centered on her body and sex. Angela was constantly concerned about constipation. She herself suffered from constipation and was alert to its occurrence in her children. Celia recalled with distaste the many enemas she had received throughout her childhood. She regarded herself as the ugly duckling in the family. Her mother teased her about her unattractive nose and squat body. Fortunately she was well coordinated and good at sports. Her more beautiful sister, having had rheumatic fever in early childhood, was restricted in this area. Also, Celia was a good student and at least held her own with her sister and brother in school competitions. Sex was never discussed or mentioned in the home except as something bad; yet it was often on Celia's mind as a dirty and shameful aspect of human nature. Between the ages of nine and fourteen, an adolescent boy who lived across the street and was a brother of one of her best friends repeatedly made sexual advances to her. She fended him off but never spoke of the episodes to anyone, since she felt that they were caused by some unnatural impulse within her that this boy had sensed. The incidents made her feel sullied and degraded. Even before these incidents began, her mother had caught her reading a book about sex that had been given to her by a friend and she was soundly thrashed. On other occasions, a salesman who was often in the neighborhood exposed himself to her. All these preadolescent sexual contacts remained in her mind as traumatic events about which she felt ashamed.

During adolescence her guilt about sex and her anxiety about her competence in feminine skills increased. She developed facial acne and believed that this was somehow related to her sexual impulses. As her breasts developed, she was ashamed of them, and felt all the more that she was ugly and repulsive. She obtained no information about sex or menstruation from her mother and had to make the best sense she could about these matters from what she gleaned from her sister and in the street. Yet, her information was beclouded with the admixture of facts and fiction about childbirth related by her mother in the course of recounting her ministrations as a midwife. Compulsively clean, Angela always described "the mess" attendant to delivery of the baby and the afterbirth with a certain relish and in unnecessary detail. At the same time, her mother repeatedly scolded Celia for carelessness in carrying out housecleaning chores and incompetence in cooking and sewing, comparing her unfavorably to her more competent sister.

Celia recalled her adolescence as a time of unhappiness. She often had "black moods" during which she locked herself in the bathroom and daydreamed about running away from home in order to make everyone feel sorry. In high school she had few dates. Oddly, she found herself unwittingly encouraging a boy to make advances until the moment when he touched her. Thereupon she would feel a revulsion and shrink away. She also longed to have a romantic relation with a boy who was "tall, dark, and handsome" but somehow managed to avoid this possibility by dating only short men. Her explanation was that she felt too inferior and unattractive with tall men of her daydreams.

After high school and secretarial training, she worked in various business offices and encountered a surprising success. She was efficient and reliable and much liked by her coworkers and bosses. She blossomed under encouragement, feeling that she possessed more competence than she had been given credit for and that she understood the workings of a large commercial concern. Though her mother was not impressed, her father, for the first time, praised her, stating that she had a good head for business and that she "would always know how to make a dollar."

It was at this time of her life that Celia met Tony, who immediately took a liking to her. He saw in her the efficiency and knowledge, the family loyalty and trustworthiness that he wanted in a wife. She saw in him just another short man, not too exciting or promising. After a few dates, Tony insisted on meeting her family. Celia explained that this was impossible. Her parents were the Old World type who believed in arranged marriages. She was forbidden to bring any boy home unless it had already been settled that they were engaged. What she did not tell Tony was that her parents took no notice of what she did with her time outside the house, whereas they scrutinized her sister's and brother's behavior carefully, another discrimination that she resented. Either they trusted her completely or else they never considered her a risk, being too unattractive. In any event, she felt unprotected.

Paying no attention to her concern, Tony simply turned up at her parents' home and introduced himself as a suitor. For the next six years he continued to press his suit, interrupted only by a two-year stint in the Air Force during World War II. In the service, away from his family for the first time in his life and enjoying his work as an airplane mechanic overseas, he gained increased confidence in himself. Both before and after his absence, Celia, influenced by her mother's attitude, continued to postpone making a decision about his offers of marriage. Though Angela had no great liking for Tony, Celia's father became quite fond of him. Tony, in turn, liked the old man and responded to him as the father he had missed during his childhood. In fact, he adopted Celia's family as his own.

In the course of Tony's long wooing of Celia and her family, several events occurred that gradually tipped the balance in his favor. First, Frances was married. Celia had been telling Tony that she could not marry before her older sister was married. Actually, Celia was quite dependent on her sister and felt the loss keenly. Equally important to the change of atmosphere was the outbreak

of severe quarreling in the home precipitated by Henry's announcement that he intended to marry the girl his mother detested. Celia
was torn between sympathy for her brother and her mother and
wanted desperately to escape from the turbulent environment of
her home. Finally, when Angela, feeling pressed on all sides, irrita-
bly announced that Celia was not getting any younger and no more
promising suitor was in sight, Celia accepted his proposal.

For Tony, the marriage was a triumph, a victory after a
long campaign. His success was a neat compromise between the
Italian tradition of the arranged marriage and the American custom of an individualistic choice based on love. In effect, he had
arranged his own marriage, conducting the negotiations between
his family and Celia's with a skill that finally surmounted the obstacles on both sides.

For Celia, the marriage was a now-or-never affair. She still
longed for a "tall, dark and handsome" lover but had no faith in
her ability to capture the interest of such a man. In view of the
shortage of suitors, it seemed practical to marry Tony even though
she was ashamed of taking a husband whom she did not love. She
felt that he would probably be kind and considerate toward her and
a good father. Perhaps she could make something out of him if she
tried hard.

On returning from a brief honeymoon in Canada, Tony and
Celia took one of the apartments in the building owned by her parents. For the next two years they continued to live much as they
had in the past, Celia working as a secretary and Tony as an aircraft mechanic. They worked hard, and in the evenings, their lives
seemed to blend with those of the Succi family. There was not too
much communication between the young couple, but neither was
there any strife. Celia was disappointed that she could not experience any pleasure in their sexual relations. Since she said nothing
about it, Tony was not aware that Celia had such a problem and
thought that this part of their life was going smoothly. He and
Celia were both upset by the continuing fights between Angela,
Enrico, and Henry and his wife. Tony attempted to maintain neutrality and to function as a peacemaker, but his efforts met with
little success. Angela demanded total allegiance to her point of
view. She now had some new complaints against Tony—he did not

support her in her feud with her son, and, to make matters worse, he continued to be attentive and respectful toward his own mother, as if to highlight her miserable relation with her own son.

In their third year of marriage, Celia and Tony decided to have a baby. Despite the teachings of the Church, they had used contraceptives. Though they regarded themselves as good Catholics, they both believed that the position of the clergy on this matter was unreasonable, as did many of their friends. Accordingly, the pregnancy was carefully planned. When it occurred, Tony was exuberant. Celia was somewhat depressed but concealed her feelings from him. She was ashamed to tell her mother and her sister that she was "carrying Tony's child" and concealed the fact of her pregnancy as long as possible. Then Tony's mother died unexpectedly and he became mildly depressed for several months. The prenatal period was not a happy one for either of them.

Timmie was born in normal physical condition but only after a difficult, prolonged, wearing delivery. As soon as she set eyes on the baby, Celia thought that she saw all her suffering on his little face. He looked wrinkled and weak to her, as if worn out from the struggle of the delivery. Above all, he did not seem attractive or appealing. However he may have seemed, Celia was in no condition to pay attention to him. She told the interviewer that "for forty days and nights" thereafter, she experienced severe discomfort and pain from hemorrhoids and that the only thing she wanted was to die. Celia's expression was in keeping with an ancient tradition. Like the forty days of Musa Degh, the forty thieves of Ali Baba, the forty days that Jesus spent in the desert and Moses spent on Mount Zion, or the forty years of wandering of the Children of Israel, her forty days and nights of pain were not meant as an accurate count. For her, as for the folklore tradition, the number forty signified an impressive quantity of suffering or effort. During this period, the baby was in the care of her mother and sister.

The research staff, in discussing this phase of her life, debated whether Celia might not have been severely depressed immediately following the delivery. However, the episode was hazy in her memory; she was never able to be specific about the thoughts and feelings associated with it.

On recovering her physical health, Celia took charge of the

baby with many misgivings about her competence in child care. The idea of breast-feeding was repellent to her. Timmie was given a bottle propped up in the crib beside him. Holding and cuddling her baby was not something Celia could do spontaneously or easily. An even more difficult matter was what to do when the baby cried. Tony thought that Celia should pick up the infant and comfort him until he stopped crying. Angela labeled this as nonsense, in fact dangerous. The baby would soon be spoiled beyond all reason. Celia, having no firm opinion of her own, was torn between pleasing her mother and satisfying her husband. She vacillated, but most of the time accepted her mother's advice over her husband's. Still trying to keep peace with his wife's family, Tony did not veto their decisions, but he was not happy about them.

In the following months, Tony's discontent with his mother-in-law's rules and regulations and general behavior gradually increased until he and Celia were almost constantly arguing about his complaints. She tended to defend her mother or, at any rate, was unwilling to oppose her. Tony was angry because he felt that Angela did not give his wife enough help with the baby and what help she gave was wrong.

At first he was reluctant to voice his complaints too forcibly, because he wanted peace and Timmie seemed to be thriving. But when Timmie was six months old, the head-rocking in bed began, and shortly thereafter Timmie became "sickly." He ate poorly, had frequent colds and sore throats, and was underweight. Tony blamed the regime set up by Angela for Timmie's poor physical condition. Furthermore, Angela gave Celia practically no help at all with the diapering, washing, feeding, or general care of the baby. She was reluctant to look after the baby so that Celia and Tony could go out together to visit with friends. On the occasions when she did agree to baby-sit, Celia and Tony sometimes returned to find that Angela had gone downstairs to her own apartment, leaving Timmie alone.

Painfully, Tony had come to the conclusion that Angela was neglectful, not only of his son, but of his wife as well. As his disillusion and resentment mounted, he began to make plans to move his family out of the apartment, then out of the neighborhood and as far away as possible. He had heard that there was property available at inexpensive rates in a distant suburb, still partly rural and awaiting development. He became fascinated with the idea of buying some property and building his own house. To be a home-owner, to have a place in the country where his children could grow up away from the turmoil of city streets and family interference—this would come close to his dream of a better life. His savings were insufficient, but he could take extra jobs and borrow money to tide him over. Even Celia was impressed with his plan. Though she was not sure that she wanted to be so far away from her family, she too liked the idea of having her own house in the country. Unexpectedly, Angela fell in with the plan and offered to loan Tony part of the money needed to buy the land. The whole family drove out to inspect the property; it was found suitable by one and all, and the purchase was made.

Then, when Timmie was just nine months old, Celia discovered that she was pregnant again. This conception was unplanned. Celia felt that she had her hands full taking care of Timmie and was not pleased. Tony was delighted. When the baby was born, Celia was pleased. He seemed round and happy, "like a little butterball." She took note of his large brown eyes and admired his physique, saying to the nurse in attendance, "Just look at those shoulders!"

Now the trace of melancholy that had accompanied the newlyweds during their first years seemed to lift. Celia had no post-partum pain or discomfort and was in good spirits. Tony wanted the baby named after him, and she agreed, a notable concession considering her previous feelings about carrying his child. Everyone admired the new baby for his cuddlesome qualities. Celia picked him up and held him for display in a spontaneous manner that had been absent in her reaction to Timmie. Nevertheless, she again was unwilling to breast-feed him, and she used the propped-up bottle as she had previously. Recognizing the physical resemblance that the new baby bore to him, Tony had eyes for nothing else. He would rush into the apartment on returning from work, crying, "Where's my son? Where's my pal? Hi, Sonny!" The words "Hi, Sonny" were heard so often that "Sonny" almost automatically became the baby's nickname.

In the following months, the house-building project, the

symbol of social advancement and emotional harmony, continued to bolster the morale of the Tondi household. Discussing plans and solutions of problems together, he and Celia felt closer to each other than usual, though Celia was never confident that Tony was making the right decisions. She was also very busy caring for the two children. Timmie's poor health was a constant worry, but Sonny appeared to thrive. His appetite was good, he gained weight, slept well, and, somehow, the question of isolating him when he cried never arose as it had with Timmie, perhaps because he seldom cried and always seemed to capture the affectionate attention of those around him.

When Sonny was a year old, the problem of his toilet training emerged. He was soiling constantly, and her mother was complaining about the way he smelled. Celia had paid little attention, being so preoccupied with Timmie's health. She regarded Sonny as strong and healthy and had defined him as no problem. But when her mother, with characteristic impatience, said, "It's time that baby was trained!" Celia, fearing that she had been neglectful, switched the full force of her attention to Sonny's bowel functions. Abruptly and forcibly, she put him on the training-seat. He took an immediate dislike to it and struggled to get out. She then strapped him in. He screamed and refused to cooperate.

At eighteen months, Sonny had still made no progress and the situation was at a stalemate. Sonny seemed both to hate and to be frightened of a toilet. He would run away when he recognized signs of preparatory toilet-forcing in his mother's behavior. Then on one occasion, while a friend was visiting, Sonny appeared in pain and lay on the floor with his legs drawn up. The friend said that he must be constipated. In some anxiety, Celia got a syringe and administered an enema. The fear that Sonny suffered from a serious bowel disorder was from that time firmly implanted in her awareness. Angela, always concerned about constipation, tended to agree. And in fact, Sonny's withholding of his stools over a period of days dated from this incident.

As Sonny's constipation was in the process of becoming a firmly established pattern, the parents relied more and more on enemas to bring about a bowel movement. The family physician asserted that there was no obstruction in the lower bowel. He advised them to pay less attention to Sonny's bowels. Sonny reacted traumatically to the invasion of his rectum and promptly developed a fear of doctors. Furthermore, from this time on he seemed positively terrified of being given an enema. When he knew that an enema was about to be administered—and he developed a sixth sense about this—he would attempt to hide. Experiencing a distressing combination of fear, anger, and guilt, Celia would search for him, find him, and, with Tony's help, forcibly hold the child down on the floor while administering the enema. Sonny kicked and screamed like a wild animal during this process. Yet, afterwards, having delivered himself of a large stool, he would, to everyone's relief, relax and return to his usual, cheery, somewhat belligerent, good humor.

The house-building project was now nearing completion. Tony was working long hours on the house and was seldom at home. He attributed the symptoms and behavior problems that both his children had developed to the tension at home during this period. This inspired in him a frenzy of activity in order to finish the house sufficiently to move his family to the peace and quiet of the countryside. Celia felt increasingly burdened by her husband's absence from the home. She now had to make all the decisions and manage the affairs of the family under her mother's critical eye. Still, she continued to take heart at the idea of moving and even bragged a bit to her father and girl-friends about what a nice house they would have, implying that she would be better off than anyone else in the family. The making of such an overt bid for success, even triumph, was an unusual piece of behavior for Celia, and she almost immediately regretted it. What if her claims should prove false? Suppose the house should turn out to be inadequate, the children even more troublesome, and the neighbors cool or unpleasant? She would be the laughingstock of the whole family!

Timmie's "sickly" behavior at this time, when Celia felt so burdened, seemed to increase. His stuttering now came into evidence. But equally worrisome was his reaction to a short period of hospitalization for a tonsillectomy. He had awakened from the anesthesia to find his mother present, but shortly thereafter she was required to leave, by the rules of the hospital. Timmie believed he was being abandoned and was panic-stricken. When she returned the following day, Celia found him tearful and distrustful of her. She dated his clinging behavior and his chronic fear that she would desert him to this episode. Indeed, whenever he was asked why he was so afraid that his mother would not return from even a routine errand, he would cite his terrifying experience in the hospital.

Finally, after Tony had been working on the house for two years, the long-awaited move took place. The strain of preparation had been intense though relieved by the pleasure both spouses took in the prospect of fulfilling their wish for a better life. However, having taken up residence in her own house, furnished it, and set up her housekeeping routines, Celia did not find that bliss in suburban living that she and Tony had anticipated during moments of euphoria. If anything, her problems seemed to increase. She was often lonely, uncomfortable with the neighbors, and more conscious than ever of her husband's inferiority; and her children seemed determined to embarrass her in the community. There were times in the following two years when her anxiety and depression were so severe that she thought she might be losing her mind. Even Tony recognized her "nervousness," though as usual he blamed it on her mother's behavior. In general, however, and with his customary inclination to ignore difficulties with his wife if at all possible, he continued to regard Celia as a good wife and mother who was doing as competent a job as possible under the circumstances.

Family Role Conflicts

Concerning the Formal roles enacted by the Tondis, the presence of open or concealed complaints characterized much of their day-to-day behavior. For both Tony and Celia, actuality failed to live up to previous hopes and expectations. The ever-present note of disappointment had many sources but chief among them was the frustration they both experienced in regard to their hopes for a better life. In part, this frustration reflected their feeling of not being at home in the new community. In part, it reflected their disappointment in themselves, in each other, and in the children.

The switch from the values of native Italian culture to the values preferred in American urban culture is a difficult one, one not made in a short time. For different reasons connected with their families, both Tony and Celia were in a hurry; they were attempting to realize their hopes before they had made an adequate transition from Italian value patterns to the dominant American patterns. Their undersanding of each set of values, and thus of their worlds and of themselves, was imperfect and confused. In implementing their values, they were often at cross-purposes, though hoping to arrive at substantially the same goals. The value profile giving rise to their behaviors in their various roles is illustrated in Table 6, where each of their patterns is contrasted with native Italian and American patterns.

Table 6 reveals that Tony had actually moved much closer to dominant American middle-class values than had Celia. Although she had shifted some of the native Italian value choices in the second-order and third-order positions, her first-order preferences were still typical of the Italian group. Her view of the world, of rights and wrongs and of how people behaved, was pretty much that which her family had brought to this country from Italy. On the other hand, with the exception of his preferences in the relational orientation, Tony's value choices corresponded almost precisely to the American pattern, although his implementation of these patterns was not at all times in line with the avowed order of preferences. Facility at implementing a newly gained pattern of values takes a good deal of time, as well as freedom from internal conflict, a freedom that had not been available to Tony.

In many respects, Tony's reliance on his wife to help him obtain a better life was in error. He had mistaken her, and her mother's, sensitivity to social status for a knowledge of how to gain it. But her value patterns made her a poor helpmate for this purpose, all the more so because she had so little insight into the real nature of his or her strengths and weaknesses. In spite of his difficulty in recognizing the fact, Tony had a better knowledge of what was required for upward mobility than did his wife.

This poignant misunderstanding between the spouses consistently showed up in their interpersonal relations. In the time orientation, for example, Tony was able to visualize and plan for gradual change in the future. For Celia, if a desired change did not occur immediately and visibly, then it was never going to occur. And, if an undesirable change occurred, then she was likely to view it as a

Table 6.

DIFFERENTIAL TRANSITION OF HUSBAND AND WIFE FROM ITALIAN TO AMERICAN VALUE ORIENTATIONS

Modalities	American	Tony	Celia	Italian
Activity	Do >ᵃ Be > BiB	Do > Be > BiB	Be > Do > BiB	Be > BiB > Do
Relational	Ind > Coll > Lin	Coll > Ind > Lin	Coll > Lin > Ind	Coll > Lin > Ind
Time	Fut > Pres > Past	Fut > Pres > Past	Pres > Fut > Past	Pres > Past > Fut
Man-nature	Over > Sub > With	Over > Sub > With	Sub > Over > With	Sub > With > Over
Human nature	Neutral Mixed > Evil > Good	Mixed > Evil > Good	Evil > Mixed > Good	Mixed > Evil > Good

Abbreviations: Be, BiB, Do stand for Being, Being-in-becoming, Doing; Lin, Coll, Ind stand for Lineal, Collateral, Individual; Past, Pres, Fut stand for Past, Present, Future; Sub, With, Over stand for Subjugation-to-nature, Harmony-with-nature, Mastery-over-nature.

ᵃ > indicates that the solution to the left is preferable to that on the right.

permanent state of affairs. In the matter of undesired and undesirable change, especially where the children were concerned, other value preferences made cooperation between the spouses difficult. Tony's understanding of the Doing>Being>Being-in-becoming activity pattern led him in the first instance to judge desired or undesired behavior as an external performance that should be appraised on its merits. Celia's first-order emphasis on Being led her to view either desired or undesired behavior more as a reflection of the inner person and to become excessively emotional about it. Given her belief in a basically evil human nature, it is understandable that she should, at the same time, have regarded undesirable behavior in herself or others as a reflection of inner wickedness. Tony's view of human nature was Mixed and therefore closer to the first-order preference in the American pattern. He saw the potential for changing "bad" behavior to good through expert help. Thus, in the case of all her interpersonal relations, it was hard for her to decide whether the undesirable outcome—whatever it might be—was caused by the badness within herself or within the other person.

Lastly, her inclination to take a Subjugated view of the *man-nature* orientation was correlated with a sense of hopelessness or even of panic about the possibility of improving the situation. The forces that she was up against were too much for her. With her sense of hopelessness and her belief in her bad luck, it was almost impossible for Celia to convince herself that she could improve her way of handling matters. The upshot of these value interrelations was that she "tried" continuously but chaotically, always with the feeling that she was only making things worse.

Though it may sound paradoxical, this dismal view of herself and her world could be replaced on occasion with a more optimistic appraisal that was correlated with some of her second-order value choices. There were times, especially when she was not so depressed, during which she was able to believe in the Doing, Future, and Mastery-over-nature views advocated by her husband. It was during these times that she saw herself as able to help him, even to teach him how to succeed. And it was these moments of her interpersonal style that he took to represent her real self. This act of perception constituted partly a rationalization (it was what he wished her to be), partly a projection (they were his first-order values)', and partly a correct assessment (they were *her* second-order choices, and she was in conflict about moving them up into a first-order position). Tony was sure that problems between man and nature could be mastered and tended to take an optimistic view of difficulties. Accordingly, he did not regard the problems that he experienced either with his wife or with his children as resulting exclusively from a badness within them, but saw them as troubled individuals whose behavior could be corrected. As a result, it was easy, as well as convenient, for him to regard Celia's first-order preferences as a product of her "nervousness" rather than a representative of her "real" self.

What was most highly correlated with Tony's misperception of his wife's values was their agreement on the first-order choice in the relational orientation. They both consistently upheld Collaterality, though they differed on its application. They were in agreement that they should stick together and support each other as man and wife and that the nuclear family should function as a collateral group aligned with other collateral groups. They differed, however, on what groups to align with. Celia wanted to remain close to her family and relied heavily on her dependent relations with them. Tony wanted to get away from all extended family connections and find new collateral relations in the community to which they had moved. Because of his collateral views, Tony could not readily perceive his wife, or his children, as individuals, but tended to look at them as representatives of family needs and hopes. The same was true of Celia. Because of the Collateral emphasis in both of them, neither could view Tony's success strivings—nor their hopes for their children—as a matter of achievement for the sake of the individual concerned. Success in the new environment was needed and demanded as a sign of the family's prestige, almost as if it were a matter of removing a stain on the Tondi family name. In this fashion, the American achievement pattern was largely torn loose from its Individualistic moorings and assimilated to the ancient Italian wish to keep the family honor bright and its reputation free of blemish—fighting issues in Italy from time immemorial.

The agreement on this issue between Tony and Celia was so solid that it might well be regarded as the pivot around which all other matters of interpersonal behavior rotated. It accounted for the solidity of the marriage itself; Tony and Celia and the children would stick together in spite of mutual disappointments, in the shame of failure, in the tragedy of defeat, and in the joy of success if ever it should arrive.

In contrast to the agreement on the first-order preference in relational orientation, their divergence on second- and third-order choices in this category gave rise to considerable strain. When Tony was faced with conflicts within the family that disturbed its Collateral base of operations—for example, disciplinary problems in the children—he was inclined to deal with them on an Individual basis. Celia's second-order Lineality clashed forcibly with this method of procedure. Faced with a conflict of wills or expectations, she became authoritarian and asserted her dominance. Where the children were concerned, she tended to accuse Tony of spoiling them. She would reproach and goad him until, his wish to individualize the problem undermined, he would lose his temper and yell at the disobedient child or hit him or threaten some dire punishment. Then she would accuse him of having gone too far, implying that, in spite of her wish for him to take charge, she understood these matters better and they had best remain in her hands. Yet, because of her belief in her bad luck and the evil nature of her basic impulses, she was never able to maintain sufficient self-confidence to carry through a consistent program of disciplining for the children. Sooner or later, she would resume her plea to Tony to take charge when there was an infraction of her hastily composed rules and regulations, only to undermine his handling of it all over again.

The question of who was in charge of decision-making in the family was thus seriously confused and subject to seesaw struggles. Responding from his Individualistic orientation—imperfect as his understanding of it was—Tony wanted to find out how his wife felt about the issue, which needed deciding, and to arrive by discussion at a mutual decision. Regarding the same matter from the viewpoint of her hierarchical, Lineal orientation, Celia took Tony's outlook as a sign of weakness. She thought he could not make up his mind. Since any decision was something of an emergency for her, she felt that what was required was a firm decision, almost any decision would do so long as the question was resolved quickly. It was difficult for her to communicate to him her inner feelings on any subject and often impossible for her to know how she really felt. Accordingly, discussion and the airing of problems was beyond her. Besides, she believed that it was the responsibility of a man to make the difficult decisions. Having interpreted Tony's procedure as a sign of weakness, she usually ended by feeling that she had to make the decision. Celia would abruptly make decisions and take action only to feel, after some time had passed, that she had been wrong and that Tony, in his bumbling way, had probably been right. It was then that she would feel reproachful toward him, believing that he should have asserted himself and overruled her in the first place. The net effect of such to-and-fro swings was that though Celia won most of the short-term decisions, any line of action proposed by Tony usually won out in the long run.

We are now in a position to see how the congruent and divergent aspects of the values held by the spouses introduced complementarity or conflict into the manner in which they took their formal roles. Starting with the biological roles of age, sex, and body management as enacted by the husband and wife, we immediately observe the effects of a value discrepancy, that is, the partial conversion, under stress, of Formal roles into Informal or Fictive roles. For example, the disagreement between Tony and Celia about how decisions were to be made affected, as we have seen, both their ability to relate harmoniously to each other and their perception of the role ascribed to the role partner. Celia could not adapt her need for a quick decision to Tony's more deliberate and thoughtful approach. The complementarity of the roles, as taken, was very low, and Celia responded with a role induction maneuver: she coerced, forcing a decision by contemptuously criticizing his views. At the same time, considering Tony indecisive and vacillating, she assigned him a set of distorted age and sex roles. She perceived him as immature and unmanly. Having reduced his age to that of a child, she then adopted a role that, to her mind, would be complementary to the Informal role she had assigned him. She became the protective parent who had to criticize and take care of her dependent child-husband. She often told the interviewer that she had not two but three children on her hands. Since Tony appeared to go along with her procedure, the Informal role she had assigned him was confirmed, and he had accepted it, as far as she was concerned.

On his side, of course, Tony knew that he had done nothing of the kind. If his wife had to be so critical, bossy, and protective as to treat him like a child, it was due to impatience caused by her "nervousness." There was no point, as far as he could see, in directly attacking her, that is, in showing countercoercion. One does not attack a person who is in a disturbed state. By assigning her a quite different Informal role from that which she had assigned him, that of a sick or harried person, he managed to dodge the issue. He also managed thereby to conceal from himself the anger he felt because of her depreciation of him. What became of this unconscious resentment we will consider in a moment. It is enough, for the present, to note that the Informal, transitional, sick role he had assigned to her required of him only that he adopt an Informal complementary role that would not upset her further. He attempted to mollify her by becoming the patient teacher or advisor, waiting for her to recognize her error and to accept his recommendations.

These undercover Informal roles were introduced into their transactions with each other as a way of avoiding further strain and its associated anxiety. Communication by indirection, however, is no adequate substitute for a thorough airing and discussion of underlying issues. In this case, the conversion of the Formal age and sex roles between husband and wife into distorted and implicit informal roles was reenacted, but now revengefully, in the arena of parent-child roles.

Before examining these displaced effects, we wish to point out that Celia shared a problem in body tempo, or psychobiological rhythms, as related to distance in contact with others. Celia's rhythms were characteristically fast, sometimes explosive; Tony's slower, more deliberate. However, he exhibited an underlying tension which gave observers the impression that he was holding in and controlling himself. Most of the time he sat quietly, in forced self-possession. On rare occasions, however, the excitation would burst through, and he would, in interviews, wave his arms around, gesticulating forcibly and talking rapidly. Because of this contrast between them, Celia considered her husband slow, while he considered her impatient or nervous. With respect to physical distance, the contrast between them was equally vivid. Tony wanted to be physically close, almost literally in touch with his role partners.

Walking toward the interviewing room with his male therapist, he tended to touch or bump into him somehow, not quite deliberately but not by accident either. He stayed in physical contact with his children, especially with Sonny, enjoying the acts of touching, holding, putting his arms around them, or even manipulating them in the course of demonstrating some activity. Celia remained at a greater distance from everyone. She frequently drew herself up as if shrinking from contact. This posture produced a strained, unrelaxed effect, certain nuances of which could easily be interpreted as guardedness, that is, feeling defensive and ill at ease, while other nuances gave the impression of unspoken disapproval.

From their varying positions vis-à-vis their role partners, however, both of them engaged in a similar pattern of sudden intervention, either physically or verbally. To the observers, these rapid intrusions were more easily detected in behavior with the children than between each other, but they occurred in both situations. Celia, from her withdrawn position, would suddenly insert herself into an ongoing activity of Sonny or Timmie, breaking it up and taking control of it. For example, in an early clinic contact, the family was assembled in a waiting room equipped with a blackboard. Timmie, the center of attention for the moment, was showing off his newly acquired skill in printing words on the blackboard. Celia had remained in the background, looking tense as usual. When he misspelled a few words, Celia could no longer contain herself. She dashed to the blackboard, seized an eraser and rubbed out the misspelled words, snatched the chalk from Timmie's hand, and printed the words correctly, all the while verbally expressing criticism and distress at Timmie's inability to spell correctly. Timmie responded with a temper tantrum, screaming and protesting at being interfered with.

There was always an element of the surprise attack in such interventions. But whether anticipated or not, they were forcible enough to disorganize whatever behavior was in process unless the object of the intervention was remarkably resistant. Among the research staff, these episodes received the label of *the interruption pattern*. Indeed, interruption, as an interpersonal style, seemed to characterize all family members. Tony erupted into unexpected activity when his children annoyed him or Celia goaded him out of what she considered to be his passivity. From his closer physical distance, he would turn on one of his sons or his wife, suddenly imposing a line of action or a punishment that no one had expected. To the observers, the interruption pattern was highly correlated with the uncertainty of behavior and the tendency to stutter among the family members. Celia and Tony interrupted each other, the children, even themselves, to the extent that it was sometimes hard to hear what was going on. When Timmie had the floor, Sonny interrupted him. When Timmie stuttered, Tony tried to slow him down, while Celia attempted to speed him up, both maneuvers having the identical aim of getting the message out. When Sonny was the center of attention, Timmie had a temper tantrum or withdrew with an angry outburst.

The effect of such interferences with biological rhythms was to block the integration of a behavior process within the ego of the child. This effect was most noticeable in the case of Timmie's rocking in bed to put himself to sleep and in Sonny's constipation. In each case, a biological rhythm that required sensitive handling on the part of a caretaker had been ignored. What Celia did—often under pressure from her mother—was to attempt to coerce the child or to provoke him into emitting the desired behavior. When Timmie was an infant, it had been decided that he should learn to stop crying and go to sleep in a room by himself. Any physiological or psychological process that may have been interfering with his sleep-wake patterns was thus simply ignored. When it had been decided that Sonny should learn to evacuate into a toilet, he was made to sit and was spanked if he did not produce; but the sitting and spanking were not timed to coincide with a peristalic process in Sonny's colon. From the standpoint of the most naive principles of learning, to say nothing of the most sophisticated, such maladroit training practices could not be expected to lead to a good result. What, then, prompted them?

The chief, but not the sole, instigator of such coercive training was the aspiration within the Tondi family for higher social status, an aspiration that led to the scrambling of Italian and American value orientations. Celia, like her mother, wished her husband and her children to exhibit behavior consistent with the American success pattern. Every bit of behavior was judged—on misguided lines, to be sure—as to whether it fit or did not fit this pattern. Since it had been learned that American children are supposed to be self-reliant at an early age, the Italian pattern of close, warm, emotional attention to infants and children was simply reversed. Timmie was taught to rely on himself by being given no attention at all in going to sleep. It was understood that American children, unlike Italian children, learn to be clean and neat and to go to the toilet by themselves, at an early age. Ergo, Sonny must rapidly acquire these habits. What was not understood was that middle-class American parents did not expect their children to complete the acquisition of body management roles so early or so quickly. Nor was it understood that middle-class American parents handle the training process on an individualistic basis, studying the particular child to determine his needs. Rather, the Tondis assimilated the new training procedure, but joined it to the Italian relational orientation. For the sake of the family's honor, the correct habits must be acquired; if any resistance crops up, then authoritarian handling is in order.

This widespread confusion in two areas of child training illustrates the significance of the connection between cultural value orientations and cognitive issues. Celia literally did not understand what was required. In her interviews, she constantly asked her therapist for instruction in the care and training of the children and for confirmation that what she was doing was right or wrong, depending on how guilty she was feeling at the moment. She could not construct a sensible plan for child training—whatever her unconscious motives—because she had lost the coherent cultural orientations on the basis of which such plans are built.

Our purpose is to trace further the relations between the patterns of values in the family and the prospects for complementarity of roles, both Formal and Informal. It is this prospect that governs the organization and integration of the family considered as a whole. And it is the fate of the integrations and conflicts in the family as a group that we wish to describe. While pursuing this end, however, we shall also pay attention to the fact that Formal and Informal roles inevitably reveal the motivations of the persons involved in them.

The purely biological roles in the family, age, sex, and body management, were so distorted and chaotic as to preclude a smooth gearing-in of behavior among the family members. We have attributed the lack of harmony to ill-fits between the value orientation patterns. Furthermore, the presence of compensatory mechanisms through the elaboration of Informal roles has been cited as one way in which Formal role strains were temporarily neutralized. It was suggested, however, that implicit suppression of the strains, and the formation of compensatory mechanisms, was not the best way to handle them. Explicit communication would have been preferable but it was not available. Therefore one could expect the strains to produce effects in other role systems.

The underlying strains did indeed show up in other domestic roles and in the relation between them and roles in the various behavior spheres. Let us consider, first, the fate of the strains in the body management roles on intrafamily relations. The interruption pattern had led to the development in Timmie's behavior of bed-rocking, temper tantrums, stuttering, and a regressive tendency to cling to his mother like a much younger child. In Sonny, it was correlated with constipation and a degree of defiant belligerence. But these responses were not simple products of the strain in the body management roles. They were gradually inserted into Informal character roles to which the children were assigned on the basis of the wider strains in the biological roles as a whole. We noted above that, although Tony consciously adopted the Informal roles of teacher, advisor, or therapist when his wife treated him as an effeminate boy, he still experienced an unexpressed feeling of injury and resentment for being made to look so dependent and weak. And, we asked, what happened to this sense of resentment, where did its energies go?

Injury, injustice, and the resentment to which they give rise are very easily incorporated into a set of three Informal character roles that are logically related to each other: the Victim, the Oppressor, and the Protector. A variant of the Oppressor is the Persecutor (he is more vicious), and a variant of the Protector is the Rescuer (he must act faster). Tony took his revenge for his sense of injustice and injury by a skillful but displaced manipulation and assignment of these roles. Almost from the moment of birth, Tony had identified Sonny with himself, calling him "my pal" and "my son" and showing him attentions he did not give to Timmie. Timmie responded with increased clinging. Regarding Timmie as hopeless and, in any event, inseparable from his mother, Tony took Sonny with him when he visited his relatives or went fishing or to a ball game—never Timmie. Similarly, if Celia went shopping or visited her relatives, she took Timmie because he would not be left behind, but seldom took Sonny with her. Even on the face of it, Tony had become Sonny's protector, mentor, and companion, while Celia had the same roles toward Timmie. But why?

The explanation lies in the complementary, assigned roles. Tony had implicitly assigned to both of his sons the role of the Victim, the victim of their mother's (and grandmother's) poorly disguised hostility toward men and of their erroneous notions of child care. By taking Sonny under his wing, he was sending an unacknowledged message to his wife. He was saying in effect, "It's too late to rescue Timmie from the ill effects of your attitudes toward men (toward me), but I'll do my best to protect Sonny. Timmie will therefore represent the failure and injustice of your ideas, while Sonny will stand for the rightness and fairness of mine."

In this fashion, Tony made Timmie the symbol of injustice endured, Sonny the symbol of injustice defied. Both were projections of his own attitudes. In acting out these contradictory attitudes indirectly and in dividing them between his sons, he achieved several goals at once. He relieved himself of the internal pressure of feelings that he could neither wholly repress nor express directly. Thus, by keeping the opposed attitudes apart he avoided the pathogenic consequences of an internal conflict. In addition, his revenge was accurately aimed at its target. For Celia did indeed feel guilty and responsible for Timmie's troubles and experienced them as a burden which, in all fairness, she alone should carry. As a result, the defiance Tony indirectly encouraged in Sonny provoked her alternately to violent attacks and fits of remorse, deepening her concept of herself as a mother who had failed.

It is important to emphasize that these arrangements were made outside of conscious awareness. When the therapists first picked up the clues regarding the Tony-Sonny, Celia-Timmie partnerships and called them to the attention of the parents, they expressed surprise and indignation. They had attributed the arrangement entirely to Timmie's clinging to his mother and did not think of it as something that they might be fostering. As, under the continued probing of the therapists, they began to consider this a real possibility, they soon made attempts to alter the arrangement. Tony made a greater effort to show interest in Timmie and invited him with increased conviction to come along when he and Sonny went out on an expedition. Celia began to control her feeling of anxious responsibility for Timmie and urged him to join his father and brother. This new tolerance for threesomes in the family, however, sat badly with Sonny. Dethroned as crown prince in his father's eyes, he became more openly rivalrous toward his brother and, like a miniature Iago, employed various stratagems to put Timmie in the wrong with his parents.

While this account of the effects of a therapeutic intervention takes us ahead of our story, it nevertheless throws light on an important issue: the consequences of disturbing a pathological equilibrium that has been set up in a family. A pathological equilibrium is an unrealistic and hostile balance of forces within a family that is unconscious for the key members involved, unmodifiable (without external intervention) because it is not susceptible to reality testing or new learning, and conducive to psychopathology in family members because of the role distortions of which it is composed and the improbability of their taking effective action about the matter. Under the influence of their incongruent value orientations and the associated strains in their Formal roles, Celia and Tony had become entangled in such a pathological equilibrium. What was out of balance in the area of Formal roles was made up for in the category of Informal roles. While Tony had permitted himself to be put down formally as an incompetent husband by Celia, he arranged, through the children, and with her help, to put his wife down as an inadequate and oppressive mother.

This tit-for-tat arrangement had certain advantages and certain penalties for all concerned, though its disadvantages outweighed its benefits. Celia could continue to gain sympathy from her mother for being married, as her mother was, to an ineffective man. But she also had to accept the shame of losing out in her rivalry with her sister who, from this view, was married to a more successful man. The guilt that she experienced through being defined by Tony (and herself) as an inadequate, oppressive mother was neutralized during visits to Angela, who blamed Tony for the problems with the children. Angela claimed that the children were disturbed because all the Tondis were disturbed; it was in their blood! It had nothing to do, according to Angela, with Celia's capacity as a mother.

The pathological equilibrium served to give the others a similar mixture of pain and pleasure. Though severely hurt by his wife's attitude, Tony was pleased with his more rational (and modern) approach to her problems. Although unaware of it for the most part, he derived pleasure from his revengeful maneuvers and was only occasionally pained when, provoked by Celia, he was brought down to her level through an explosive outburst against the children. Timmie's role as Victim, while painful enough, entitled him to more attention from his mother than anyone else in the family. Considering Celia's tendency to pull away from contacts with the children, this was a triumph in itself. Meanwhile, Sonny, ensconced as his father's deputy, lorded it over Timmie, though he had to put up with his mother's disapproval.

Given the intricate, unconsciously established patterns of a pathological equilibrium, it is not surprising that any change caused by therapy releases protest somewhere. In fact, it is surprising that change can occur at all. But change does happen because the system is out of balance and only seems to have been stabilized. If relations are founded on a set of strains, any external impingement that dislodges the secondary compensations will tend to bring the primary imbalance into prominence. For the same reason, the secondary compensations tend to be endlessly ramified. We will discuss only a few important behavior spheres into which the pathological equilibrium had spread.

One area was that of the Tondis' relations in the neighborhood and the wider community of the suburb in which they lived. Since Tony had made friends with his neighbors while he was building the house, he had a head start, so to speak, over Celia and the children. His easy-going manner, his technical facility in fixing cars and equipment of all sorts, and his willingness to do favors for people in anticipation of deferred returns all made him an accepted member of the local neighborhood community. He took a good deal of pleasure in this neighborly setting, regarding it as a network of collateral relations that could well function as a substitute for the extended family relations he had rejected. He was pleased with the idea of introducing his wife and children into the local network so that his immediate family could feel at home in their new surroundings.

But he had not reckoned with the effects of the pathological equilibrium on Celia and the children. Soon after the move to the suburb, Celia began to miss the daily contacts with her mother and sister and other family members. She required the contacts because her Collateral > Lineal > Individual pattern was not easily realized in the new community. Also, she needed the compensatory reassurance (that she was superior to Tony) and criticism (that she had not achieved as much prestige as her sister) that her mother always offered her. Her extended family was actually the only agency that would satisfy her desire for the constant, dependent relations that her previous experiences and her psychological makeup had prepared her for. Accordingly, she felt tied down in her new home, confined in cramped quarters with troublesome children and little adult company. Since Tony used the car to go to work, it was difficult for her to go to town to shop or to see the family.

Tony's solution for the problem was simple. He thought that Celia ought gradually to loosen her reliance on her family while she busied herself with making friends and becoming involved in activities in the community, in the classic suburban pattern. Though she half-heartedly agreed, she was unable to carry out such a program. In addition to the strong pull exerted by her relatives in town, the chief obstacle was her sense of inferiority vis-à-vis the neighbors. She tried to justify her feelings of inferiority in accordance with her mother's views that her husband had not obtained the prestige that would qualify him as a successful American, but his manifest acceptance by the community made this disqualification increasingly difficult to maintain. Furthermore, it was undermined by a growing awareness of presumed disqualifications that she thought she shared with her husband but that did not inhibit him. Celia was acutely conscious of being a Catholic Italian-American from the working class and of being surrounded by better-educated Protestants of muted national origins. On request, she would prepare Italian dishes for neighboring housewives; but, instead of being able to take justifiable pleasure in this activity, she felt that it set her apart and called attention to her marginal position. So far as the research team could determine, there was no evidence of ethnic or class prejudice in the neighborhood, at least not in relation to Italian-Americans. In this area, her Lineal beliefs served her particularly ill, as she always had to place herself on a vertical scale of social importance, usually in its nether regions.

But the core of her inferiority feelings in the neighborhood centered on the behavior of her children and the reflections that she thought they cast on her qualities as a mother. We have already referred to Sonny's belligerent behavior with other children as one of the complaints Celia brought to the diagnostic interviews. Episodes of this sort usually began with scraps between Timmie and other children in the neighborhood. If Sonny thought that Timmie was getting the worst of it, he would become Timmie's protector, acting out the role his father took toward himself. Stormy, threatening to hit or kill Timmie's assailants, he sometimes grabbed a rock and threw it at the head of the offender, all the while screaming oaths and curses in words that he had heard from older children in the city streets. Celia, who believed (perhaps correctly) that the neighborhood children were unused to such language and behavior, would become horrified. What would the parents of these children think of her and her family?

On one occasion Sonny heaved a rock with such accuracy that it lacerated the forehead of a boy who lived next door. The boy ran home to his mother, streaming with blood. That evening the boy's father spoke angrily to Celia about controlling Sonny's aggressiveness in the future. Though she was terribly upset, she managed to blurt out that she knew Sonny's behavior was inexcusable but that she was taking him to a psychiatric clinic to have it corrected. The next day the man apologized profusely. He felt badly for having shown such anger toward a "disturbed child" whose parents were doing their best to help him. His change of heart was small comfort to Celia. To have an emotionally disturbed child was almost as bad as having a delinquent one; in either case, the family was responsible. She feared that all the neighbors would hear of this and look down upon her. Although the neighbor and his wife tried their best to be hospitable and friendly thereafter, Celia was unable to feel comfortable in their presence until near the end of her therapy. Tony, on the other hand, saw nothing in Sonny's behavior beyond the ordinary and thought Celia's reaction was part of her general difficulty in adjusting to the neighborhood. Privately, he was pleased that Sonny would stand up and fight for his brother.

The determinants of such behavior obviously had their roots in the pathological equilibrium. Having been inducted into the role of Victim at home, Timmie was prepared to find his Persecutor abroad. And, while Sonny was willing enough to be Timmie's Oppressor indoors, outside the house he enjoyed being his Protector and Rescuer, making himself a hero in his father's eyes, an embarrassment in his mother's. Whether he was defined as hero or scoundrel depended on the perception of the Formal roles from which these Informal roles derived. According to Tony, Sonny was defending the masculine honor of the collateral family in the neighborhood; according to Celia, he was dramatizing the ethnic and class inferiority of the Collateral family. Given the choice between the aggressive activity his father wished him to present in public on behalf of manliness and the passivity or self-control his mother wanted enacted in the interests of good manners, Sonny naturally sided with his benefactor and ally, his father.

Once a pathological equilibrium has become established in a family, it acts like a magnet; the most diverse aspects of the biographies of the individual family members become aligned within its field of forces. For example, the cluster of Informal roles that Tony was encouraging his children to enact resulted in a reversal of age roles among the two boys. Sonny behaved like the older, stronger brother, Timmie like the younger, weaker one. The role exchange served Tony well in his unconscious plotting to pay Celia back for the wrongs she had inflicted on him. They demonstrated plainly enough (to his mind) that his principles of child care and his notions of competent masculinity were more correct than hers, since Sonny was his child, while Timmie was hers. But, there was another motive for Tony's secret pleasure in the role exchange. Like Sonny, Tony had been a youngest son. He, too, had struggled to catch up with and overthrow a weaker, older brother, the alcoholic Arthur, becoming the hero of the family. In encouraging Sonny's behavior he was repeating a piece of his own life history. But he would not have needed to act out this fragment of his past had he not become involved in the hidden power struggle with his wife that was the nucleus of the pathological equilibrium.

From her side of the arrangement, Celia accepted the age role reversal as part and parcel of the unconscious bargains within the pathological equilibrium. If Tony wanted to make her responsible for Timmie's weaknesses, let him. She was prepared to agree that she was guilty of faulty motherhood, as long as Tony accepted her version of his failures as a husband, a man, and an American. The bargain required that she also accept Sonny's domination of Timmie at home. But she could not accept Sonny's belligerence outside the home, since it stood, in her mind, for the ethnic and class inferiority for which she reproached her husband. However, there was another reason for the anxiety Sonny's aggressiveness and rebelliousness stirred up in her. It revived memories of her brother's rebelliousness and hostility toward her mother and the shame he had brought on the family within the neighborhood. Thus, in attacking the aggressiveness in Sonny, she was repeating her mother's behavior toward her brother, the boy who had been the light of Angela's eyes, as Sonny was of Tony's.

Redefinition and Change

Psychotherapy of the family is inevitably directed at both individual and group processes.

Even during the first diagnostic contacts, the Tondis began to expose and to explore the nature of the pathological equilibrium in which they felt trapped. Celia treated her therapist, a middle-aged, female social worker, as a confessor, a confidante, and a teacher. In her initial interviews she poured out the details of her life history—her resentments against her mother, her envy of her sister and brother, her feelings of inferiority as a woman, and her shame over the shortcomings of her husband and children—with considerable emotion. These were feelings of which she was perfectly aware but that she had never openly communicated to anyone. The experience of talking to someone who listened sympathetically and uncritically, with an eye to being helpful, was new to her. After the second interview, she spontaneously attempted to carry over, in talks with her mother and her husband, this newfound freedom to express herself. Tony was surprised to learn for the first time of her intense, long-standing inferiority feelings. As usual, he blamed her mother for them, while expressing sympathy toward her problem. By the time Celia saw her mother, the previously suppressed resentment for past injustices was strong. As Celia brought out complaints of ancient wrongs, Angela flew into a rage, denied everything, blamed Tony and his "crazy family" for all of Celia's shortcomings, and then elaborated on them in great detail. Celia left in tears; she was depressed and apathetic for days afterwards. During this period, Sonny went through severe cycles of constipation.

These events constituted a symptomatic episode, that is, a clear and dramatic picture of some aspects of the basic conflict in the family. Such episodes always contain an important message for the therapeutic team. In this instance, although it was too early in the treatment process for the full significance to be appreciated, the symptomatic episode was understood as showing the desire on Celia's part for an Individualistic definition of her behavior and feelings as opposed to the Collateral > Lineal definition that so much of her training had emphasized. It was as if she were saying to her mother, "Look at me as an individual rather than a cog in the family machinery or a representative of the family's interests. Pay attention to my feelings." This wish, which had been evoked by the therapist's receptive attitude, was interwoven with feelings of guilt over the unacceptable desires that might attain expression were her personal feelings to be credited. Therefore, at the same time that she indirectly conveyed to her mother the sense of how she would like to have been treated, she exposed herself to her mother's predictable wrath and received her expected punishment. In the following days, she was depressed, withdrawn, irritable toward her children's demands for attention, and antagonistic toward her husband. Having put herself in a position with her own mother where she could be defined as the disloyal, unloving, disobedient child, she subsequently assigned a similar set of Informal roles to her own children, especially to Sonny, who became chief villain in the family because of his attempts to deceive her about his bowel movements. This projection of the sense of wrongdoing undoubtedly relieved Celia's internal burden of guilt feeling and remorse. However, it increased her external difficulties. Sonny was willing enough to adopt the job of Protector-Persecutor toward Timmie and of mischief-maker in general. But he could not bear the isolation and anxious accusations that were part of his role as villain-in-chief. In revenge, he extracted from his mother the pity, anger, and horror that always accompanied a withholding of bowel movements. And the shared anxiety in the household was raised to a nearly intolerable level.

That Sonny's behavior was quite explicitly governed by motives of revenge and counterattack was revealed by Celia in the following interview. She told how on a previous occasion, when he had been punished for some misbehavior by being deprived of a toy, he threatened never to have a bowel movement again in his whole life unless the toy was restored to him. To be sure, Sonny's threat on this occasion was more indicative of the secondary gains he derived from his symptom than of its primary determinants. Nevertheless, the circular transactions—from Celia's pleasure at the Individualistic reception of her complaints by her therapist, through her masochistic request for similar treatment by her mother, to her subsequent provoking of the constipation behavior in Sonny—provided the therapeutic team with a clue for the initial management of the symptom, in terms of the family process.

It will be recalled that Individualism was in the third-order position in Celia's relational orientation. The events of the symptomatic episode showed that this last-in-rank position was a locus of intense emotional conflict. To oversimplify a complex matter, Celia unconsciously longed to shift Individualism from its third-order position to at least a second-, if not a first-order position. The desire for the shift was governed by complex considerations, among which may be included her perception of the importance of Individualism in American culture and her feeling that she had been exploited by the Collateral > Lineal orientations so deftly deployed by her mother. But this desire was strenuously opposed, also unconsciously, by the guilt and the associated anxiety that attached to any expression of Individualism. The fantasies of revenge to which a possible Individualistic reorientation gave rise were too frightening. Yet, therapeutic encounter could not avoid dealing with this problem. It centered directly on her handling of her relations with her mother and her children; and it was directly at issue in the transference situation. The lesson emerging from all these considerations seemed to be that Celia's striving for an Individualistic reorientation was to be encouraged, but always within the constraints of a Collateral definition of the therapeutic relation. The constraint and the control exercised by the therapist would constitute a protection against premature and self-punishing releases of Individualistic self-assertion, especially aggression. The therapist, in other words, was best advised to function for Celia partly as a mother—but a mother who, this time around, would honor Celia's individualism (and her competence) while exercising some controls over her behavior.

In view of the end result of the symptomatic episode, it seemed wise to center this strategy squarely around Sonny's symptom, which was, in any event, the focus of Celia's and Tony's interest. They both repeatedly requested advice on how to handle it, and Celia, in addition, constantly voiced her fear that Sonny had managed to damage himself in some irremedial fashion. These fears were understood by the therapist as indicating the nature of Celia's unconscious sadistic wishes toward Sonny. She had already been told by several physicians that Sonny's constipation was functional and that there was no sign of organic damage. Therefore, every time Celia expressed such fears, the therapist assured her that no harm had been done and sympathized with her concern. When Celia asked for explicit directions for managing Sonny's behavior, the therapist asked her what thoughts she had on the subject. This action was taken not for the sake of maintaining neutrality or with a view toward eliciting material for interpretation. Rather, its purpose was to establish a collaborative relationship. Celia reviewed various possibilities that had occurred to her, and then she and the therapist discussed the wisdom of one versus another of these possibilities. Among the variety of suggestions brought up by Celia, one seemed particularly promising. This was the possibility of Celia's offering to sit with Sonny whenever he felt like having a bowel movement, staying in the bathroom with him and distracting him from his discomfort in some way.

To everyone's surprise, Celia negotiated this arrangement with considerable adroitness. Sonny was caught off guard by the offer and immediately took it up. As it turned out, he was ready to accept almost any offer of attention from his mother, especially one proffered in good faith. And Celia was enthusiastic about her experiment. She sat on a chair opposite Sonny on the toilet, reading to him or singing or playing some game. He did not always have a movement; nor did he always draw her attention to the times when he had a spontaneous urge. There were repetitions of the constipation pattern; but these repetitions of the old pattern were increasingly punctuated by stretches of smooth sailing in which the reciprocal behavior of mother and child led to a successful and comfortable evacuation. Eventually, toward the midpoint of the therapeutic process, Celia told Sonny that she thought he had reached the point where he could go to the toilet by himself and that perhaps he would not need to tell her every time he wanted to go. Although concern over constipation had long since evaporated, the symptom was now officially a thing of the past.

It would be an error to conclude that Sonny's symptom disappeared exclusively as a result of this one maneuver. Other changes were occurring around the family at the same time. Meanwhile, in his own therapy, Sonny experimented with the manifold possibilities of making a mess. Policed at home, he gloried at the clinic in squeezing and pounding clay, smearing water colors, chalk, and crayon on receptive surfaces, exploding a ping-pong rifle at the therapist, and teasing him with riddles ("Guess what I'm thinking!"). At first Sonny's experimenting was abruptly concluded with scrupulous cleaning-up and putting-in-order, restoration on a grand scale. Later, with the help of the therapist, he was able to define his play less as offensive messing and more as investigating or making. His role gradually changed from that of the little-slob-in-the-parlor to that of the little-explorer-in-the-playroom. It was impossible to determine what factor played exactly what part in his improved bowel control. The fact, however, that the improvement set in so early and, apparently, in response to a solution conceived by

Celia with the help of her therapist put the whole therapeutic enterprise in good standing with the Tondis.

While Celia and Sonny were learning to sort out their impulses and feelings with the help of their therapists, Tony took a different stance in his treatment. He defined the relation as purely a matter of technical or pedagogical instruction, as if he were back in school. He asked for information about what caused his children's symptoms and directions for solving the problem. He took the position that mistakes had been made in child care and training that could easily be corrected in exactly the same manner as he corrected faulty equipment in an airplane. He was immensely pleased with Sonny's prompt response to Celia's handling of the toilet-training situation and expected all the other problems in the family to vanish with equal dispatch, once the key had been found.

It had never occurred to him that his personal feelings and impulses, as well as his own childhood experiences, were a part of the problem. Although his therapist often asked him how he felt about various events in the present or past, Tony was able to give only the most meagre response. Sometimes he was "happy," at other times "disgusted," depending on how the children were behaving or what past event was under discussion. Where Celia's behavior was concerned, he was always satisfied that she was doing her best under difficult circumstances. He could not understand why the therapist wanted him to talk at greater length about something so irrelevant as his own feelings. Aside from the problems of the children, he presented himself as entirely content with his lot in life. And even in regard to the children he was mostly concerned with the significance of their present problems for their success and happiness in the future. If he could have convinced himself that they would ultimately outgrow their behavior problems of their own accord, he would have rejected treatment altogether. It was only the slender thread of his anxiety about the children's future that attached him to the family therapy program.

It seemed evident that the therapeutic problem presented by Tony was that of a technological defense against inner anxiety, something roughly parallel to an intellectual defense in a more highly educated person. The denial of affect was intense, and it was rationalized and justified by his view of the almost mechanical per-

fectibility of human conduct. In his experience, he had found un-
wanted behavior correctable if the right person came along with
the right method, as had happened in the case of his own stuttering. To be sure, every defense has its adaptive aspects. Tony's technical approach made him optimistic of success. He was willing to
try any rational method, and he tried hard to understand and cooperate with the method of psychotherapy. He delivered long, completely neutral accounts of the latest happenings in his family or at
work. Still, as long as the defensive side of his behavior kept his
feelings so rigidly out of the therapeutic relation, little insight into
his motivations could be obtained. And, without insight, not much
progress could be expected.

Frustrating and confusing as the therapeutic problem was,
one thing was crystal clear: Tony was not going to change his position on the expression of emotion as a result of encouragement or
interpretation. After six months of the therapist's probing for feelings he once said, "Oh, I see. You're interested in how *I* feel about
this!" But the illumination was not a prelude to change; he kept
right on with his denials that he was much affected, one way or
the other, by family events, and, as usual, he asked for a prescrip-
tion for handling the particular incident. On the principle that "if
you can't lick 'em, join 'em," it was tempting to yield to Tony's
requests for specific direction and advice. The difficulty with this
strategy was that, without a better understanding of the meaning
to him of any particular behavior, it was impossible to know what
advice to give. With Celia the problem was simpler because she
revealed her feelings and her fantasies without much urging. Tony
wanted to know, for example, how he should handle Timmie's
temper tantrums. Should Timmie be punished? If so, how? Should
he ignore the outbursts? Was there some other method for putting
a stop to this behavior? What caused it in the first place? And what
about the rocking in bed? The therapist responded to all such
queries with the statement that the answers were not yet known,
that psychotherapy consisted of a long process in which one studied
and worked with the children in order to discover the solutions. In
the meantime, it was important to know how the parents felt
about it.

A potential therapeutic stalemate of this sort is often—

though by no means always and never exclusively—the result of an imperfect comprehension of the value orientations and role relations of the patient. The therapist's procedure would have been appropriate had Tony displayed a dominant American middle-class value orientation. The hitch occurred because Tony seemed in some ways a typical American; he had adopted all but one of the first-order American value choices. Certainly he had moved a considerable distance from the native Italian-American value profile. His doubly atypical values, conforming neither to the American nor to the Italian patterns, underscored the problem of how to proceed therapeutically. It also raised the interesting question of the relation between value orientation and intrapsychic defense in a particularly pertinent context.

Had Tony's value orientations conformed more exactly to the American, middle-class pattern, his resistance to therapeutic exploration would have taken a different form. Because of long-standing repression reinforced by various character defenses, he might have had just as much difficulty in revealing his feelings. But he would have understood this difficulty as an obstacle to therapy, would have become interested in it and willing to inquire into its meaning. The key to the difference lies in the first-order emphasis on Individualism. The American would have been more inclined to ask himself such questions as "Why do *I* have so much trouble showing my feelings?" and "What is *my* relation to my family, apart from what others expect of me?" Tony's first-order emphasis on Collaterality tended to make such questions irrelevant. In his own mind, his personality was not well distinguished from that of others in his family, and the choices and decisions about actions had not seemed to be so definitely in his own hands. True, he had moved Individualism into a second-order position. But this happened partly in response to his perception of the importance of Individualism everywhere in American culture and partly because the Lineality of his own family systems, which had been the second-order choice of his childhood training, had led to so much anxiety and disappointment. Individualism, accordingly, had been installed in the second-order position as a reaction-formation against the anxiety and the sense of shame that accompanied the Lineal choices. Behind the defense, therefore, lurked the hidden desire for the devalued Lineal satisfactions—to be told what to do, to have an assured place in an hierarchy, to be loved for his obedience by a more powerful person. This desire was the problem that got him into difficulties with his wife and that produced the hitch in therapy.

When a switch in value patterning is the result of a defensive reaction-formation in a single value orientation category, even one as sensitive as the relational orientation, it can usually be isolated and brought under the scrutiny of the therapeutic process. In Tony's case, however, switches in other categories were also the result of reaction-formations. The first-order position of Doing, for example, was held in place by the not always successful repression of Being, while the primacy of his Mastery-over-nature position was barely maintained against strong pressure for the fatalistic acceptance of the Subjugation-to-nature position. It was the defensive combination of these positions that gave his technical approach to problem solving its mechanical and unrealistic optimism.

A pattern of values that is rank-ordered along such defensive lines, quite obviously, is difficult to modify; in addition, a precipitous alteration risks severe personality disruption. It must be handled with care. Therapeutic interventions must be carried out within the pattern structure rather than in opposition to it. In Tony's case, an added problem was that the very character of the defense made its elucidation difficult. It was not until many months had passed that the pathological equilibrium previously described came into view. Only then was it possible to see how the feelings that he kept out of the therapeutic interviews were expressed in action, how the Formal roles in the family had been distorted through the segregation of the family into two subgroups, and how, in this fashion and in other ways, the tensions in the family had been transferred to a set of inappropriate Informal roles. Once the significance of the role segregation was understood, it became clear that this was an area in which Tony's desire for human engineering could be satisfied along adaptive lines, thus putting only a small strain on his defensive systems.

Tony was asked why the family always did everything in twos rather than in threes or with the whole family together. The question startled him, and, although he gave an indignant justification, he was not entirely convinced of its truth. His behavior now looked to him like a violation of his first-order Collateral orientation. He took immediate action. He began to invite Timmie along on various excursions with Sonny and to take the whole family on outings. At first, Timmie resisted, displaying his phobic pattern of inseparability from his mother. When his behavior was discussed by Celia with her therapist, she was able to see that she was aiding and abetting Timmie's avoidance of his father by her overcautious attitude. She then understood that she wished to keep control over Timmie because she felt so guilty and responsible for him. With this insight established, she was able to insist that Timmie accompany his father and brother, and the pattern of avoidance was broken.

If a pathological equilibrium is loosened, the feelings formerly used to solder it in place begin to appear in verbal communications and in protest reactions, as stated above. It was now that Tony began to verbalize his envy of his children, to whom he gave so much and with whom he tried so hard. Such expressions of feeling were, however, quite brief, and he was completely unable to admit that they had anything to do with his actions. It was also at this time that Sonny, having lost his exclusive position with his father, became more aggressive toward Timmie, attempting constantly to put him in the wrong. And Timmie, having been pried away from his mother and not yet feeling secure with his father, seemed only too willing to be put in the wrong. He, rather than Sonny, now became the chief family problem.

One might have expected that with the elimination of the distortion in age and sex roles formerly imposed upon him, Timmie would have blossomed; in some ways, this is what happened. In activities concerned with physical coordination, in sports and games, he developed quite impressive skills. But other problems that had been hidden behind his phobic behavior now came to the fore. One of these was a tendency to tell tall stories in which he figured either as hero or victim. Timmie usually told these tales with such a mixture of excitement and stuttering that it was difficult to hear exactly what he was saying. More difficult was the problem of distinguishing fact from fiction in these adventures, the greatest part of which was fantasy. Many of his accounts were so preposterous that they raised the question of his ability to discriminate fantasy from reality. For example, he called himself "Sky King," a role borrowed from a television show, and related his adventures in outer space and his dramatic rescues of earthbound creatures. He told his therapist many tales of his working on planes at the airport with his father, of planes that he had piloted, and of underwater adventures in submarines in which he had participated. At other times he depicted himself falling out of trees into ponds and having to be rescued from the threatened attacks of underwater monsters. However, his role as Victim or Rescuer was unstable; in the same story he might alternate several times between these two roles.

Timmie's behavior represented a fascinating, psychosocial problem. The unconscious determinants of the manifest content of his fantasies were fairly easy to interpret. Quite obviously, he was satisfying a wish to reverse his lowly status in reality as the weak, rather effeminate, mother-bound child by assuming dramatically masculine roles in fantasy, in which his association—indeed his identification—with the father from whom he was so distant was clearly portrayed. The fantasies also incorporated punishments for seeking to gratify the wish—the fall from glory and the reversion to the Victim's role. The person he most often rescued in the stories was either his brother or some symbolic substitute for him. But the chief behavioral problem was not the content of the fantasies or the unconscious wishes which gave rise to them. Rather, the significant questions were: Why did Timmie tell these stories? Did he really expect others to believe them? Was he aware of the distortion of reality?

The answer to these questions was contained in the status of Fictive roles in the Tondi family. Fictive roles are elaborated within all societies, as well as in persistent small groups, to allow the individual some escape from reality with its often grim necessities. Where children are concerned, each culture elaborates a set of Fictive roles that the child can assume in play. Within a particular culture, these roles vary with the age of the child, younger children usually being permitted more inventiveness and freedom in the choice of Fictive roles; between cultures, variation proceeds along different dimensions. But the two most significant variations are the differences in the choice of role for same aged children and differences in the cues exchanged between adults and children (or between children and their playmates) when Fictive roles are being assumed. These are subtle matters that have not been systematically studied in the context of cross-cultural comparison. For families undergoing acculturation to new customs, the cues often become confused and ill understood. This is what had occurred in the Tondi family.

In the native Italian culture, Fictive roles, especially in the sexual or aggressive areas, are well understood and expected behavior. Bragging, dramatic impersonation either by impromptu acting or by telling long, circumstantial tales, and histrionic exaggeration are part of everyday behavior. In Italy and in Italian-American communities, life would seem colorless without these touches of the *commedia dell' arte* and of theatrical display in general. The behavior of Angela, for example, when she delivered her "mother's curse" while viewing the wedding procession of her son could have been taken from the libretto of an Italian opera. The key to the assumption of Fictive roles in Italian culture is ambiguity. The observer, or participator, should be left in a certain doubt as to whether the role is really a Fictive one; otherwise the display is no fun. Part of the entertainment consists of calculating and gossiping about what part of the behavior is serious and what part merely for the sake of putting on a good show. To make such discriminations requires experience with the culture in general, the local group in particular, and the indivdual himself, since the cues are almost indefinable.

The behavior of the Italian in assuming Fictive roles is guided by the preference for Being in the activity orientation, supported by the general configuration of values in Italian culture. For the middle-class American, Fictive roles have an entirely different status, one confined to particular recreational or informal occasions that deemphasize successful performance of a job. The cues, in these circumstances, are much more definite, and the observer or participator wants to know "for sure" whether or not the behavior is serious or in jest. When children play, it is considered "good for their development"; when adults joke or play, their fun is believed to have been "earned" because they have worked so hard. The hard-and-fast distinction between work and play leaves no room for ambiguity. This much of the American approach to Fictive roles both Celia and Tony had learned. But they had not learned how to place their children's behavior within these rules. They did not know how to determine when the boys were showing behavior that ought to be taken "seriously" and when the behavior could be taken "lightly," as childlike or amusing byplay.

When Timmie embarked on one of his epic tales, for example, Celia would listen, unbelieving, yet fascinated by the excesses of his youthful imagination. As he became more and more wound up in the dramatic effect he was creating, she would make a great effort to control herself while experiencing a sense of panic about how to control him. Self-control, the calm, urbane behavior exhibited by the families surrounding her in the neighborhood, was what she desperately wanted for herself and her children. Yet self-control somehow always eluded her. Goaded to distraction by what seemed a deliberate confabulation, she would end up screaming at Timmie: "Stop telling lies!" Deflated, Timmie would retire in a confusion of stuttering and ineffective protest. Still, there had occurred that subtle, mutual participation in a dramatic encounter, a catharsis, that both mother and child had unwittingly enjoyed and to which they would both return.

We can now see why Timmie told his farfetched stories. He was a poet, indulging in hyperbole and poetic license. Although he made up tales out of phallic exhibitionistic materials that were of the greatest importance to him psychodynamically, he told them for the sake of their effect upon an audience. He was not interested in their accuracy but in their ability to generate interest. In the presence of his mother, he received the accolade most desired by a poet—attention and appreciation, even though the appreciation had to be concealed behind an admonition.

The problem for psychotherapy, then, was how to deal with Timmie's muse, the internalized mother image. The therapist decided that it was a question of establishing ground rules for the appreciation of fantasy. She listened patiently and with unfeigned pleasure while Timmie displayed his dramatic talents. For he was almost irresistible in the role of bard. He twinkled with mischief, glowed with courage, and shuddered with terror while staging his minature spectaculars. After he had finished, she reviewed the account with him piece by piece, to discover what was fact and what fiction. At first Timmie had little patience with this procedure. What he wanted was an effect on an audience, not an analysis of his performance. Gradually, however, he fell in with the practice, as if to say that he liked her and, if this interested her, he would try to cooperate. Later the therapist attempted to explore the conent of his stories and offered some interpretations. Timmie never seemed to respond to this sort of probing. His interest turned to making and doing, especially to making model airplanes. As he became more involved in this activity, in active mastery of his physical environment, his fantastic stories both at home and in the therapy diminished in quantity and stayed closer to reality, though they never completely lost the aura of the fable.

Unfortunately, Timmie's status as the family problem was not confined to his feats of myth-making. As this problem behavior subsided, another took its place. His school reports began to show unsatisfactory progress in reading and spelling. Again, this was something that neither Celia nor Tony could take lightly. To them it meant one more injury to the family's reputation. If Timmie was an incompetent student, then his parents were also intellectually inferior. They responded with a flurry of home instruction. Timmie was made to read aloud to his parents, who alternated between correcting his reading and correcting his stuttering while reading. Meanwhile they both brought the problem to their therapists, asking how to handle Timmie's learning difficulty.

The question that this newest piece of symptomatic behavior posed for the therapists was how to determine the actual severity of Timmie's learning defect. They had the impression that the anxiety of the parents was wholly out of proportion to the seriousness of the problem. Normally, this would have been established by a conference between Celia and Timmie's teacher. But Celia was terrified of a meeting with the teacher. She made and canceled appointment after appointment. On one occasion, when she thought that she saw the school principal walking down the street toward her house, she hid in the bathroom and refused to answer the doorbell.

It was clear that Celia's fear of teachers could not be resolved in therapy in time to discover the nature of Timmie's reading and spelling difficulty. The information could be obtained only by direct contact between the therapists and the school. With Celia's permission, the therapists talked to both the principal of the school and Timmie's teacher, as well as the teacher of remedial reading with whom he had begun to work. He was regarded as somewhat slow but not gravely deficient. The teaching staff was unaware of the parents' anxiety, and they believed that the home instruction was unnecessary and possibly harmful. All the teachers commented on the charm of Timmie's personality and said that, although his stuttering was occasionally noticeable, it was not a serious problem. As a result of the visit, however, they promised to pay more attention to his individual needs.

Armed with this information, the therapists advised the parents to discontinue home instruction. In addition, summoning up all their credentials of authority, the therapists told Celia and Tony that Timmie was not a backward or stupid child and should not be treated as one. Furthermore, they said that Timmie should not be put under constant pressure to achieve better grades in school since, in the normal course of events, the teachers expected him to perform adequately and saw no reason why he should not be promoted at the end of the year.

This maneuver did relieve Timmie of some of the parental pressure, though he was not immediately released from his role as family problem. After all, the authoritatively delivered advice did nothing to alter the pathological equilibrium in the family but only diluted some of its force. Though they were reassured, Tony and Celia continued to await the school's next report on Timmie with fear and trepidation. Timmie still occupied the role that symbolized the parents' projected inferiority and marginality in their middle-class community. The path toward further loosening of the pathological equilibrium was not yet available.

Now two events occurred that prepared the way for a more effective exposure of the pathological equilibrium. One concerned Tony and the other Celia. Tony had, from the beginning, mentioned in therapy the problems he experienced in his job. The problems concerned his lack of promotion after so many years of working for the same company. He was still a line mechanic; although younger and newer people had been promoted to the position of foreman, he had remained stationary. For a long time he attributed his lack of advancement to factors completely beyond his control, such as the constantly growing complexity and increasing impersonality of the airline company, the cliques that formed within the line personnel, and the personalities of various foremen with whom he did not get along. Gradually, his therapist was able to show him that some of the factors that blocked his progress were within himself. They mainly concerned his first-order Collateral value preferences. Tony actually could not push himself forward as an individual or fight a competitive struggle for self-advancement. He felt that people who pushed were selfish and unfair to the company, caring only about their own benefits, while he always had the interests of the airline, the whole organization, at heart.

It was clear that Tony's relational orientation was not well suited to the American occupational setting, which places so much emphasis on Individualism. Since values are incorporated into the superego, he felt ashamed at the idea of pushing himself forward and could not include such acts in his concept of his occupational role. He treated the airline company as if it should be, ideally, one, big, happy, collateral family. Even the anticipation of becoming a foreman caused him some anxiety because a foreman was a boss, the head of a Lineal chain of command. Lineality was last in Tony's hierarchy of values.

As these matters were discussed in therapy, Tony began to see that, in his job at least, he was not a typical American. He also began to understand that Celia's constant pressure on him to obtain a job promotion was not simply a matter of her "nervousness." As a result of the slight change in his self-concept and in his concept of others, he was able to make demands on the company's management personnel for an improved job status. We have already described Tony's weak Individualistic preferences as the result of a reaction-formation. Therefore it was no surprise that he experienced much anxiety when he had his talk with the personnel supervisor. He had rehearsed what he would say for days, using Celia as an audience. On her side, she did her best to be uncritical and supportive. Still, Tony was afraid that he would begin to stutter or that he would forget what he had intended to say. The result was not an overwhelming improvement in his career, he was not promoted to the position of foreman. But he was given a great deal more consideration and recognition on the job. He was sent to London to obtain training in the use and maintenance of a new piece of equipment. Then he was sent to New York and Florida to train others in the necessary procedures. As a consequence, his pay checks were larger, and his status in the company, in his family, and in the neighborhood was higher.

The further removal of Celia from her involvement in the pathological equilibrium was brought about through the therapist's cooperation with a sudden insight that she achieved. She had been repeatedly discussing her conflicts about visiting her family or having them visit her. She wanted to see her mother or her sister on Tony's day off, when he could look after the children at home. She regarded this arrangement as a vacation from child care, as well as one of the simple courtesies to one's relatives that are expected in an Italian family. Tony objected to these weekly excursions, both because she took the car in order to cover the long distance to the city and because he wanted her to be home on his day off. But Celia became aware that there was more to this situation than an external conflict with her husband. She had begun to realize that she herself was not of one mind about her obligations to her extended family. Visits to her mother usually ended in some sort of unpleasant disagreement, while seeing her sister made her feel envious and dependent. She had reached the intellectual insight that there was no longer any reason for feeling inferior to her sister, who was experiencing even more severe domestic problems than Celia herself. However, she was unable to shed the longstanding though now unreasonable feeling of inferiority. She had also recognized that her mother was helpless against an inner need to deprecate the persons and things closest to her.

While struggling with this quandry, looking for a way out of the traditional Lineal compulsions within her behavior, Celia one day had a brilliant idea. She proffered the idea that Angela's unpleasant behavior had grown worse over the years as she had increasingly been separated from her children and her activities in the Italian community. There was no longer any need for her services as a midwife and little call for her talents as a hostess, entertainer, and trainer of the newly arrived Italian immigrant. Perhaps, thought Celia, her mother was suffering from unemployment. Having been impressed with the effectiveness of the therapists' intervention in the school situation, Celia wondered if something could be done to provide her mother with a job.

Celia's therapist, a social worker, thought the idea well worth considering. She asked Celia whether her mother would enjoy the job of homemaker or housekeeper in families troubled by illness or absence of the mother. Celia proposed this possibility to her mother. Angela was at first surprised, then uncertain, and finally offered to try out such a job if she did not have to travel a long distance. Celia reported Angela's response to her therapist, and her therapist reported to the research team, whose members enthusiastically endorsed the plan. A position was soon found for Angela, and, to everyone's relief, she took pleasure in it. She liked taking care of a house and the small children in the family; she enjoyed being in control of the situation; and above all, she was pleased to feel useful and to be earning money again.

A definite change in Angela's moods and behavior now took place, an alteration which reverberated throughout the extended family system. She was more cheerful, had fewer criticisms of her husband, children, and grandchildren, and made fewer demands on them. It seemed clear that a longstanding but clinically masked depression had been partially relieved through her involvement in an activity that was in accord with her ego ideals and that satisfied her need for contact with and control over others. As a result of the change in Angela's mood, family gatherings became less harassing. Celia reported with amazement and delight that a get-together for a Thanksgiving meal had taken place in an atmosphere of harmony for a change. Furthermore, since Angela now had less need for contact with her own children, Celia was freed of the responsibility for ritual visiting.

The unexpected loosening of the Lineal bond between Angela and Celia now put Celia in a position to spend more time with her husband in collateral activities. They began to plan together for the completion of the unfinished rooms in the house. Not only did they plan together, they actually discovered how to work together in the building process. There were still seesaw struggles for dominance between Tony and Celia, with Tony exhibiting patience while Celia learned, to her dismay, that she had been wrong about a structural detail; but as the rooms took shape, Celia began to feel somewhat more comfortable about her house and its overcrowded feeling. Now that her pride in her house was partly restored, she was able to feel a bit more relaxed in the neighborhood. And feeling more acceptable, she was able to be more active in the community. In fact, the most striking change in the Tondi family was increased participation in community activities. Celia joined the P.T.A. and discovered that she had some organizational ability; this reflected her tendency to be bossy like her mother. Tony, having had a head start in the community, now indulged his desire to join as many organizations as he had time for. Collaterality, which had always been Tony's first-order relational preference, became dominant for Celia, bringing their domestic and community roles into better consonance with each other.

Though still not completely resolved, the loosening of the pathological equilibrium, which now took place, resulted in a considerable increase in the level of mutual appreciation and self-satisfaction in the nuclear family. Tony, feeling that he was "beginning to live for the first time," bought himself new clothes to celebrate his rebirth as a suburbanite. Celia appreciated his dressed-up look. She went on a diet, lost ten pounds, and was quite pleased with herself. The new look was also shared by the children, who began to do better in school, fought less with each other, and seemed to feel more comfortable with playmates in the neighborhood. Above all, the parents and the children were able to give up the need to put someone in the role of family scapegoat or problem. The problems were still there, but they tended more and more to be defined as family problems rather than as the result of the undesirable behavior of one or another member.

The easing of tension in interpersonal relations was so noticeable that both the parents and the therapists began now to talk of the possibility of terminating the therapeutic work. As one might expect, the prospect of severing the dependent relations and the collaborative teamwork so painfully established in the course of therapy brought about a recrudescence of family tension. Symptomatic episodes reappeared as a probable date for termination was agreed upon. What was interesting, and different, was that the conflicts remained visibly embedded in the Formal roles of the family without being displaced to distorted Informal or Fictive roles. As a part of this new mode of conflict resolution, Celia and Tony were better able to discuss the emerging problems with each other, with persons in the community, and with the therapists.

For example, a typical conflict developed over the purchase of a new car. The family's old second-hand car was constantly breaking down and required extensive nursing. Tony was embarrassed because its deficiencies seemed to reflect on his mechanical aptitudes. No matter how much he fussed with it, the car refused to remain in good running order. Celia was embarrassed because its shabby appearance made an unpleasant contrast with the shiny, well-cared for cars of the neighbors and seemed, thus, to symbolize not-making-the-grade-with-the-neighborhood. She wanted Tony to buy a new car. Tony, his eye on the state of the family finances, wanted to buy another secondhand car. To bolster her position, Celia told Tony about her mother's teasing description of Tony as a man who always gave his family second-hand things. Tony was wounded by the kernel of truth in this remark and decided, in desperation, to buy a new car. Whereupon Celia reproached him, as usual, for not sticking by his guns, essentially, for not being a man.

There was much in this family interaction that reflected the old cultural value disorders—Celia's inability to plan for the future versus Tony's emphasis on caution and careful planning; Celia's emphasis on appearances and symbolic representation versus Tony's interest in functional mastery at the expense of externals; Celia's equating of masculinity with dominance versus Tony's notion that decisions should be made mutually. But, instead of the dissociation of Formal roles that these value discrepancies would have produced in the past, Celia and Tony argued the matter out with each other and actually did reach a mutual decision—that it would be best to buy a good second-hand car, shiny enough to please Celia and cheap enough to satisfy Tony. The compromise attained by confrontation and explicit communication was reached soon enough to avoid having the children become involved in a displaced role conflict.

The ability to cope with conflict through discussion was steadily maintained in the final weeks of therapy. Individual gains in performance and insight were also recovered. Celia held steadfastly to the difficult insight that her dissatisfaction with her husband and her children was colored by her dissatisfaction with herself. This insight enabled her to be more content with them, on the one hand, and more direct and less emotional about disagreements, on the other. As she gained self-confidence, she began to see Tony's good points for herself rather than through the eyes of others. Feeling encouraged, Tony accepted a job promotion that had given him considerable anxiety when it was first proposed. He became a company man, a teacher of advanced mechanical techniques. The position demanded that he give lectures to trainees, an activity that evoked his fear of stuttering in an intense fashion. Nevertheless, he mastered his fear, worked very hard, and eventually felt proud of his promotion, as did Celia. At the point of termination, they both expressed satisfaction with the gains achieved in therapy; they also expressed keen awareness of the problems that they had not been able to resolve. But they thought that they would prefer to work on these problems by themselves. Celia expressed their attitude in the words, "I can see now that there is no magic to solve our problems; it's up to us." Although they had been told that they could get in touch with the therapists at a later time if they wished for more therapeutic consultations, they did not do so. A follow-up inquiry several months after termination revealed that the mutual satisfactions were being maintained.

6

Contrasts in Greek and
American Values

In order to understand the special problems of acculturation faced by Greeks living in the United States, it is necessary to examine the agrarian culture from which they emerged. In Table 7 the dominant values of rural Greek society are contrasted with those of the American middle-class culture. Principally, the value patterns are those of other agrarian societies. There is a first-order preference for the Being orientation in the activity area, the Subjugated-to-nature orientation in the man-nature area, the Present orientation in the time area and the Mixed alternative in the Human nature area. Most Greeks live in small villages and engage in farming and sheepherding with primitive implements on small family-owned tracts of land. In general, only a marginal existence can be extracted from these small farms, a condition that has always made the Greek farmer especially open to opportunities for emigration.

The features that Puerto Rican, Italian, and Greek families have in common tend to obscure important differences. An examination of the relational value orientation area in the Greek profile

Table 7.

GREEK RURAL AND AMERICAN MIDDLE-CLASS VALUE
ORIENTATION PROFILES

Modalities	American Middle-Class			Greek Rural		
Activity	Do $>^a$ Be	>	BiB	Be > Do	>	BiB
Relational	Ind > Coll	>	Lin	Lin > Ind	>	Coll
Time	Fut > Pres	>	Past	Pres > Past	>	Fut
Man-nature	Over > Sub	>	With	Sub > With	>	Over
Human nature	Neutral Mixed > Evil	>	Good	Mixed > Evil	>	Good

Abbreviations: Be, BiB, Do stand for Being, Being-in-becoming, Doing; Lin, Coll, Ind stand for Lineal, Collateral, Individual; Past, Pres,
Fut stand for Past, Present, Future; Sub, With, Over stand for Subjugation-to-nature, Harmony-with-nature, Mastery-over-nature.
^{a} > indicates that the solution to the left is preferable to that on the
right.

on the one hand and the Puerto Rican and Italian profiles on the
other reveals the essence of these differences. The Greeks are characterized by a Lineal > Individual > Collateral pattern, while
both the Puerto Ricans and Italians are characterized by a Collateral > Lineal > Individual pattern. In Italian and Puerto Rican
families primary emphasis is placed on the interdependence of
family members who work collaboratively for the maintenance of
the family unit. This emphasis is manifest in both occupational
and recreational spheres of activity. In their villages they often
work together on their farms, and in the towns and cities they may
operate small family businesses where all members who are able
take part. Even when they work in different occupations, this pattern is maintained in that the earnings of individual family members constitute a part of a total family budget. When the children
marry, their interests and welfare continue to be interrelated with
those of their parents and siblings.

In the recreational sphere, Italian and Puerto Rican family
members, including the children, participate in the festivities ac-

companying saints' days and other religious holidays. Among Italian-Americans, vacation trips, usually to visit relatives, are participated in by all the family members. (See Chapter Seven.) The Lineal authoritarian position of the father is secondary to this primary Collaterality. He is head of the household, and he is expected to intervene in crisis situations and to provide an integrating and stabilizing influence on the other family members. He is not, however, necessarily the major wage earner in the family; nor is he looked to as the only source of emotional support and guidance by his children. The mother, older brothers and sisters, grandparents, uncles, aunts, and assorted cousins also provide a broad base on which children can lean for all kinds of resources. The patriarchal nature of the father's role is, therefore, tempered by the broad extended family structure in which it is embedded.

The third-order positioning of Individualism in Italian and Puerto Rican families means that individual aspirations and motivations do not count for much unless they are consonant with those of the family group. The continuing support of other family members is predicated on the individual's gearing his aspirations to those of the total family. The decision to pursue a career or a business venture based on the individual's own preferences must meet with the approval of the family. Otherwise, the individual will be viewed as disloyal and ungrateful by those he leaves behind. More critically, support, both emotional and financial, can be withdrawn. For a family where interdependence is an internalized orientation to the world, this can be indeed a devastating outcome. However, the support of the family in the pursuit of individualistic goals can be an important source of continuing strength for their realization.

In Greek families, the Lineal preference definitively orders the relations among family members. After the father, the eldest son is next in line for authority, with the younger sons holding positions according to their order of birth. (See Sanders, 1962.) The father is the final authority; the first-order Lineal preference places him in a singularly dominant relation to the other members of the family. He is responsible for the economic welfare of his family, and his wife and children work for him, not with him, on the family plots of land around the village. The father makes unilateral decisions regarding the aims and goals of his family, and his wife and children look almost entirely to him for economic and emotional support. When younger children receive support, either financial or emotional, from their older brothers and sisters, it is only with the full knowledge and sanction of their father. To do otherwise would be to challenge his authority, an act of great disrespect that is met with a threat of rejection that can be devastating and complete. The approval of the father, therefore, must be maintained at all costs.

The Greek father, as guardian of the family's reputation, is responsible for the behavior of his children. Because of this, he takes personal pride in their successes and feels a personal responsibility for their failures. His relation to them is characterized by a formality that belies the close emotional attachment that binds them. This formality shapes and stylizes even physical expressions of love such as embracing and kissing. Generational separations are sharp, and a son in his forties relates to his father with the same manifestations of respect expected of him as a child.

Formality is also maintained by a Greek husband in his relation with his wife. (See Sanders, 1962, p. 191.) Open expression of affection, especially in the presence of children, is deemed inappropriate. A wife is expected to support her husband's decisions in all matters and to take a secondary role in the management of family affairs. She is her husband's representative in the broader community and is expected to function as such. This role precludes publicly criticizing him or his decisions on any matter, even though she may disagree. His ineptitudes and personal failings cannot be revealed to those outside the family, and she will go to great lengths to protect him from the criticism of others. The family's good name is, for the wife also, a sacred trust that must be protected from outsiders. (For a description of the physical design and positioning of houses in the village of Vasilika to ensure the privacy of each family unit and to discourage prying from outsiders, see Friedl, 1962, p. 14.)

The Greek male traditionally takes great pride in his individualism, and this is a highly-idealized value in Greek culture.[1]

[1] The theme of individualism is a central one in ancient Greek mythology and literature. See esepcially Homer's *Iliad* and Xenophon's *Ana-*

Though Individualism is the second-order preference in relational orientation, Greeks consciously view themselves as primarily individualistic in their interpersonal relations. A considerable amount of folklore reinforces this perception, and Greeks often jokingly refer to self-importance as a Greek national trait. (For a discussion of the contemporary Greek's view of his individualism, see Saloutos, 1964, p. 19.) The Greek relational profile captures the endemic strain that characterizes interpersonal relations in Greek society. Strong independent Individualistic strivings conflict with a first-order orientation to Lineality and make collaborative efforts, in the form of Collaterality, a weak alternative.

This point needs to be elaborated further because it is central to understanding the special problems of acculturation faced by Greeks in the United States. The Greek male is expected to honor and respect the authoritarian position of his father. He also identifies, however, with a father who prides himself on independence from other men. His father tills his own land, does not work for others, and is not indebted to others (since borrowing money is viewed as bordering on sin). (For a discussion of the contemporary Greek attitude toward land, see Sanders, 1962, pp. 59–74.) Although the peasant father's existence, from an economic point of view, may be marginal, it is not appreciably different from the position of other men in the village. Furthermore, the traditional father feels free at all times to criticize the government, dishonest politicians, the church, with its dishonest priests and bishops, and foreign powers that continually exploit his mother country, Greece. In other words, a son can identify with the individualism and independence of his father who is able to displace his own conflict with authoritarianism to authority figures and symbols outside his immediate family. The cycle is of course repeated, and the son is able to honor and respect his father within the family while resisting authority outside the family.

The son is, in fact, encouraged to express independence and individualism outside his family. This training is reinforced by the village school and the Greek Orthodox Church, which are the main

---

basis, which are epic narratives of Greek resourcefulness, endurance, and ingenuity in the face of overwhelming obstacles.

socializing agencies outside the family. (See Sanders, 1962, chs. 13 and 14.) The monumental achievement of the Greeks and their contribution to Western civilization constitute a basic foundation on which all the teaching in the schools is based. Ancient Greek history is taught with a primary emphasis on the individual achievements of Socrates, Aristotle, and other great men of history. The war of independence against the Turks and the accomplishments of the heroes of that era are extolled. The development of a strong, pervasive national consciousness is a salient feature of modern Greek culture. The church, for historical reasons, is closely identified with this national consciousness. (See Papadopoulos, 1952.) During the Turkish occupation of Greece, it was the church that became the major vehicle for the survival of Greek culture and Greek identity.

The Greek villager need not proceed very far in school before the sense of national consciousness and identity becomes an integral part of his perception of and relation to the world. The drive to improve his individual position is a natural corollary of his cultural identity, and it is with this orientation that he decides to emigrate to the new world. The village provides little opportunity for him to realize his individual aspirations and those of his children. The United States, on the other hand, is the "land of opportunity," and he comes to it with a determination to realize the hopes and aspirations that were nurtured in his native country. (See Saloutos, 1964, ch. 2.)

The major immigration of Greeks to the United States occurred between 1900 and 1920. The typical pattern was for the male to immigrate first by himself. When he had gotten a job, he would send money back to Greece for passage for the wife and children. An unmarried man would make a return trip to obtain a bride or would arrange a marriage through relatives still in Greece to a local village woman, who would then join him in the United States for the ceremony. Marriages were almost always arranged with little or no courtship.

At first it was the intention of many Greek men to remain in the United States only until they earned enough money to return to Greece with sufficient financial resources to improve their living conditions there. Some did, but the majority remained.

They got jobs through relatives who had preceded them in the nonskilled occupations that were plentiful during that period. On the East coast where most landed, they got jobs in the factories. Some moved West with the railroads as laborers laying track, and many settled finally in that region of the country. Others worked as dishwashers in restaurants and did other menial tasks required in such jobs.

They rented flats in low-income areas of the cities, and as soon as enough of them were concentrated in a particular area, they founded Greek community centers with a Greek Orthodox Church as its nub. Typically they raised enough funds to build or buy an appropriate structure and then sent passage money to Greece to import a village priest for the new church.

The priest was expected to be also a school teacher. The Greek afternoon language school became an integral part of the Greek community. It was the principal socializing agency for the teaching of Greek culture to children of the immigrants. The perpetuation of Greek ideals with a primary emphasis on freedom and individual excellence along with the safeguarding of the sense of Greek national consciousness became the major objectives of the Greek school. In serving these objectives the Greek Orthodox priest was in the role that he has traditionally filled from the period of the Turkish occupation of Greece. (See Papadopoulos, 1952.)

The Greek community center served another critically important function for the immigrant himself. It provided a buffer between him and the American society to which he was pressured to adapt. It was here that he could reaffirm his Greek identity and draw resources from his heritage. Here he was respected for who he was, as had been the case in the Greek village, and not for what he did, that is, his occupation, as in American society.

Working for others, however, not a "natural" state for the Greeks in their native villages, was not so in the United States either. The Greek man would tolerate this condition for a while, but he felt he must find the psychological equivalent of his own plot of land. The Being orientation Greeks brought with them was rapidly abandoned for a Doing orientation, and their strong individualistic drives asserted themselves. The more resourceful accumulated money and started their own businesses as soon as they were able. As dishwashers, busboys, and waiters, they managed to learn the restaurant business and then opened their own establishments. Others bought small grocery stores or florist shops and managed to learn the ways of American entrepreneurship. They entered a broad range of enterprises where they could get started with a small initial capital outlay, where overhead was low, and where profits were high. Their enterprises invariably involved long hours of work, but these the Greek was more than willing to give. (For a detailed description of business activity among Greeks in the United States, see Saloutos, 1964, pp. 258–273.) He was determined to be successful, to become wealthy, and, even more important, to make it possible for his children to live a better life than he had. This resolve meant that the children would enjoy a good education, a profession, and the social status and high income that went with them. The dream he brought with him from the village could be fully realized only in his children, and he was determined, through hard work, to see that this dream became a reality.

Before reviewing the special issues of acculturation faced by the second generation, the children of the Greek immigrants, it is important to make explicit what the Greek immigrants' adaptation to the American social system and to its underlying value orientations implies. In contrasting the traditional Greek and the core American value orientations, we see that although a Being orientation was the only one that made cultural sense in the village, the American first-order Doing orientation suited the Greek's position in America. Hard work with the goal of personal advancement was the enthusiastic choice of many Greek immigrants. Some realized this goal in the form of a successful business, and furthered it by providing the means for individual achievement by their sons and daughters. Others remained in their factory jobs and realized their ambitions principally through their children. They saved as much as they could from their small wages and put it aside for their children's education.

Either way, Doing, not Being, became the guiding value in the United States although a Being orientation could be enjoyed in the Greek community on Sundays and at the frequent religious or Greek national celebrations. On these occasions, Greek-Americans could enjoy themselves and allow themselves to experience the spontaneous outpouring of feeling that they were accustomed to. Their actions took the form of reaffirming their pride in their origins mainly through patriotic speeches, but it also meant revitalizing friendships, dancing Greek dances, and listening to Greek music. On Monday, however, it was back to Doing, with a serious determination.

The American pattern in the relational area was easily accommodated to the traditional Greek one. First, even though Lineality is in theory relegated to the third-order position in American culture, lineal practices are tacitly tolerated. Americans abhor authoritarian personalities, and child-rearing practices accent permissiveness as a basis for the development of independent individualistic traits. Yet, as the youth of this country have recently impressed on us, our institutions are structured in a lineal, hierarchical manner. For this reason, Lineality, that is, authoritarianism, did not get the Greek entrepreneur into much difficulty in the United States. He was positively reinforced for achievement, and his insistence on being his own boss, running his own show, was an acceptable means to this end.

It was the weak, third-order Collaterality preference that impeded the Greek's adaptation to the American social system in the beginning. This preference emerged as a problem in different spheres of activity. The ability to collaborate with others in the work situation is an important factor for success in the American business world. Though Lineality may covertly operate to a greater extent than is often acknowledged, it is also true that survival in the economic sphere is predicated in part on collaborative relations. Vested interests in various occupations and businesses are protected through professional associations, unions, and other formal organizations.

Greeks had difficulty at first in implementing this orientation even though there are clear indications that they understood its importance. In the wake of the nativism that swept the country in the first decade of the twentieth century, Greek businessmen organized to protect their rights. Restaurant men and men in the confectionery business formed national associations in reaction to discriminatory threats by competitors. They also attempted, in the process, to form loose kinds of corporations in order to pool their resources and be better able to meet competition. These efforts quickly deteriorated, however, through the inevitable emergence of intragroup rivalries and bitter struggles for power within the organizations. The notion of sharing power through an elected decision-making body rather than through a strong individual leader was one that was difficult for Greeks to internalize. (For a discussion of the abortive effort of Greek confectioners to unite in a common economic front, see Saloutos, 1964, p. 264.)

Their strong Lineality also presented difficulties in managing their own businesses. Delegating responsibility and treating employees as equals, both implicit in American Collaterality, were difficult for the Greek businessman. Also, in his dealings with the broader American business community, he tended to ignore possibilities for collaborative arrangements that would have enhanced his own position and furthered the success of his own enterprise.

It was in relation to his children, however, that this strong Lineality produced the most strain. In the public schools these children were absorbing American values. The American relational pattern, with its strong emphasis on early independence training, its extolling of democratic values, and egalitarianism—that is, Collaterality—as the preferred mode of relating, was internalized by the immigrants' children. It mattered little that the covert Individual > Lineal > Collateral pattern in fact permeated the organizational structure of the school and that independence was sharply restricted by the hierarchical ordering of relations in the school systems' power structure. The fact that the school overtly taught the importance of self-reliance, self-sufficiency, and independent decision-making clashed with what was being transmitted in the Greek home.

There the preferred pattern translated into unilateral decision-making by the father and dependence on him in all matters. What was reinforced in the Greek home was obedience and respect for the father and a reliance on him to indicate what was right and what was wrong. Independent thinking, when it conflicted with the father's, was labeled rebellion and summarily punished.

The Greek child saw that his peers related differently to their parents. Americans played together, and children shared their thoughts and feelings with their parents. The distance that separated Greek children from their parents was now painfully perceived. The authoritarianism of the father was resented as the child grew older, and adolescence became an even more difficult period of adjustment.[2] In matters relating to sexual behavior the position of the Greek parents was both clear and adamant. Girls could not date or, for that matter, be alone with boys. They were not expected to be able to control their sexual impulses. It was the parents' responsibility to see to it that their daughters did not get into trouble and disgrace them. With boys there was considerably more permissiveness in this area. Boys could get into trouble too, but if they did, the major portion of the blame had to be borne by the girls' parents. Nevertheless, compared with many of their schoolmates, Greek-American boys were "under surveillance."

Greek parents expected their children to marry Greeks. One could count on Greek women, so the saying went, to be moral and loyal. This was not an assumption that could safely be made about non-Greek, "American" women. Furthermore (and this factor was more often than not covertly operative), how could a Greek-born mother-in-law relate to an American daughter-in-law? Greek men, according to the same lore, could be counted on to be industrious and "family-minded." One could never be sure about "American" men. Religion was often given as the reason why intermarriage was undesirable, but its importance was often exaggerated as it was used to cover other motivations. In a strange land, it was important to parents to maintain bonds with their children, who were being continually drawn into ways of thinking, feeling, and acting that were foreign to the older generation.

Maintaining strong Greek bonds, however, became increasingly difficult. The Greek afternoon school that all children were expected to attend served to reinforce the importance of Greek culture and Greek identity, which were inculcated in the home. But the socialization in the public school was more pervasive and the internalization of American value orientations by Greek children inevitable. The strains between the generations, increased

---

[2] The novels of Harry Mark Petrakis, a Greek-American writer, have captured the drama of this intergenerational conflict. (See especially Petrakis, 1963.)

with the length of time in the United States. The Greek father's authority was increasingly challenged by his children, and the way in which the resultant stress was managed made a difference to the mental health of family members. The degree of cultural change that the father was capable of making in his own relational orientations was the factor that determined the severity and duration of intergenerational conflict.

In addition to cultural adaptation, another important factor helped mitigate the rigid adherence to Lineality by the Greek father—his absence from the home for a large part of the day. His total dedication to work involved his spending long hours in his place of business. The village pattern of having his family around him continually was no longer relevant (with the exception, of course, of small family businesses). He was no longer in a position to exercise control over his children as he had in his traditional culture; he found he had to delegate this function in part to his wife. It became her responsibility to discipline the children although he remained the ultimate but distant authority and disciplinarian. To the wife also fell the major responsibility for transmitting Greek culture to her children. She saw to it that they spoke Greek in the home (primarily because her own English was limited) and that (despite their frequent protests) they attended Greek school regularly. She attended church regularly with the children, while her husband more often than not was too exhausted by Sunday to go anywhere at all.

The husband's relation to his wife underwent subtle but important changes in the United States. The necessity to rely on her to assume new responsibilities in relation to their children and to become in the process the major representative of the family in the Greek community led to the structuring of a more egalitarian relation between them. Very often the balance of power shifted imperceptibly in the wife's direction regarding the major decision-making for the family. Decisions about where to live, how to allocate their financial resources, whether a daughter's suitor was acceptable, and with what other families to socialize often became the domain of the wife. The cautious Greek woman saw to it, however, that this shift never became too obvious. She continued, as she had in the village, to present herself as her husband's representative in the wider community and never contradicted him in the presence of their children. She continued to regard him as the head of the household and probably was only dimly aware of the shift herself.

The hierarchical structure of relations among the children also began to change with the passage of time in the United States. The eldest son, who was assigned a dominant role in relation to his younger brothers and sisters by his parents, exercised it, if at all, with a great deal of ambivalence. The egalitarian values of the American school and community were having their effect. Besides, his siblings, for the same reason, were not responsive to his efforts to be dominant. Only in times of crisis, such as illness or death of the father, would they submit to him in decisions affecting the entire family.

Because of the importance of hard work, children were taught how to work from an early age. They were assigned duties around the home and were expected to get jobs outside (the experience being valued even when money was not needed), and to work diligently at their studies. School was especially important since education led to a better future. There was no question that they would go to college. Saloutos sums up this theme succinctly: "They were told in clear and often blunt language that their principal purpose in life was not to have fun, but to work, take advantage of the opportunities denied their parents, assume responsibilities, make a success of themselves, see their sisters happily married, and provide for their parents in their old age" (1964, p. 311).

The achievements of fellow Greek-Americans were a constant subject of conversation among the parents. The more successful Greeks became leaders in the formal organizations of the Greek community and were held up as examples to their children. The Doing orientation began to compete with the Being orientation in the evaluation of individual worth in the Greek-American community. A man could still be respected because he was honest, sincere, and a good family man. Gradually, however, values shifted so that a man lacking these Being-oriented virtues could still be admired because he made a lot of money. The Greek child was being well prepared for achievement in American core-culture terms. The Protestant ethic would seem a familiar one, although he might think of it as the Greek cultural ethic.

It becomes evident from the above that there were areas of congruence as well as areas of incongruence between the traditional Greek and core American cultural patternings. In some value orientation areas, the fit between Greek and American profiles was good, while in other areas it was not. (For a discussion of the "goodness of fit" concept, see F. Kluckhohn and Strodtbeck, 1961.) The Greek child was being well prepared for achievement in American terms through the focus on Individualism in the relational area and through training in the corollary attitudes toward work, that is, in the Doing activity area. Furthermore, the traditional solidarity of the Greek home (divorce was rare) and the child-centeredness of the family made for an emotionally supportive environment, especially during early childhood years.

The Lineal structure of relations, however, was a continual source of strain. In girls, this often took the form of rebellion against the mother. The issues invariably revolved around control and were often focused on the prohibition against dating. Contact with boys was formally limited to church dances and other Greek community affairs with the mother or older sister or brother present. The practice of dating in early adolescence by "American" girls was viewed as an invitation to tragedy. Supposedly, girls simply could not control themselves in the wrong circumstances. Though this attitude of the Greek mother was accepted by her daughter in the Greek village, it was viewed as old-fashioned by her counterpart in the United States. Idealized "American" mothers, trim and assertive, were the appealing models against which Greek mothers were compared. Traditional views were seen as constrictions and the recalcitrance of a misinformed woman from another world. The resultant strain that this caused could be deep and lasting.

In boys, rebellion took a variety of forms directed against the father. For the son, the father's absence from the home exacerbated the problems of identification with him and made his authoritarianism more deeply felt. In the village in Greece the son worked closely with the father in agricultural activities and could identify with his self-reliance and individualism while maintaining a submissive position in relation to him. In the United States the son was confronted with conflicting models in the persons of his American friends' fathers as well as teachers and other men with whom he came into contact. He could not avoid comparisons between their permissiveness and egalitarianism and his father's authoritarianism. Furthermore, the mechanism employed by Greek sons in the Greek village to resolve the inconsistency between dependence on the father and independence outside the home was not as easily applied in the United States.

In Greece, one's individualism outside the family system was expressed in a Lineal context, that is, one tried to achieve a higher position in an hierarchically ordered social structure. He or she approached this effort as an individual representative of the family. The intention was always to rise to a more dominant position in the system in order to have power over those who were lower on the scale and in more submissive positions. Therefore, one did not expect help from those with whom he competed and over whom, by virtue of his success, he would be placed.

In American society, individualism and independence outside the home were exercised in the context of Collaterality, that is, competitiveness was sanctioned within group collaborative efforts. The ground rules were quite different. The American child of the middle and upper strata was socialized into attitudes of fair play, respect for the individuality of the one with whom he competed, and the ability to be a good loser. Above all, he was socialized to respect always the rights of others. Success was explained to him as a matter of individual excellence and hard work. In the official version, it did not give him the right to dominate others. He was expected to show strong qualities of leadership, but had to treat others as equals, even though they may not have been.

This latter point was an additional source of confusion to the Greek-American child as he attempted to deal with the American social structure. He sensed the covert Individual > Lineal > Collateral profile that patterned American institutions. He saw that authoritarianism was a reality on the American scene, but he was confused by the reluctance to accept it.

Training in Lineality served the Greek-American child well in one respect. He adjusted well to the American school system.

He was obedient and took to instruction easily. In general he did what he was told. He also pleased the teachers by being constantly respectful. These attitudes coupled with his high motivation for individual achievement and his experience in working made for success. (For a study of the high educational and vocational aspirations of Greek-Americans and the achievement values that are corollary to these compared to other ethnic groups, see Rosen, 1959, pp. 47–60. For a study documenting the upward social mobility of Greeks in "Yankee City" in the mid-1930s, see Warner and Srole, 1945.)

It is in relations with peers that things can get difficult. Like his father, he did not always do well in collaborative efforts; he had found it difficult to work with others and he made fine distinctions as to when a submissive position was proper or improper.

Lineality, therefore, is very important to any understanding of the problems of adaptation faced by Greeks. In the following chapter, this and other traditional values, will be described with reference to these problems in the second generation.

So far this chapter has consisted of a descriptive analysis, within the framework of value orientation theory, of the acculturation process undergone by Greeks in the United States. We decided to test the relevance of our observations empirically through a systematic study of value orientations in a group of first- and second-generation Greek-Americans living in the Boston area. We did this testing as part of a larger research project on mental health and illness among members of this ethnic group. (For a report of a subanalysis of the data obtained in this study on the second-generation portion of the sample only, see Papajohn and Spiegel, 1971, pp. 257–272.)

This research was designed to test the hypothesis that acculturation stress, defined as conflict in value orientations, is related transactionally to social-role conflict in the family and to psychological disorder in individual family members. We therefore selected a group of Greek-American families in each of which a member was hospitalized with a psychotic disorder, and we compared them with families free from a history of psychopathology. From a transactional, theoretical perspective we predicted that in families in which an individual manifested serious personality disorganization, severe family disequilibrium and acute culture conflict would also be present. Within this theoretical framework it was also possible to examine the acculturation process in families that, in the absence of evidence of mental illness, were able to manage the problems of culture change in adaptive ways. We hypothesized that culture change would be associated with stress even in families free from manifest psychopathology. This stress, however, was expected to be less and to be correlated with a smoother, that is, more adaptive, value orientation change. It was precisely the nature of the value orientation change that concerned us in empirically testing this parameter in our Greek-American study.

We studied thirty-four families headed by parents who were born and spent their formative years in Greece and nearly all of whose children were born and raised in the Boston area. One-half the sample of families was selected on the basis of a diagnosed psychotic reaction in a second-generation son or daughter. The other seventeen families were matched with the first group for relevant sociological variables but were free from a history of psychopathology in any member. The total sample was 144 individuals. The seventeen families with patients had thirteen first-generation parents (three fathers and ten mothers) and fifty second-generation American-born sons and daughters (twenty-one sons and twenty-nine daughters). The seventeen families without patients had twenty-five first-generation parents (eleven fathers and fourteen mothers) and fifty-six second-generation sons and daughters (thirty-five sons and twenty-one daughters). The average age of the first-generation subjects was sixty-six, while the second-generation subjects had an average age of forty. (See Papajohn, 1974.)

We administered the Value Orientation Schedule to each of the 144 individuals included in the study. This schedule has twenty-two items, each of which describes a situation in which a problem lends itself to three solutions; these solutions reflect three alternative value orientations. The subject is asked to make first and second choices from among the three solutions, and rank ordering of value preferences for each item is thereby determined.

The twenty-two items are grouped into four areas representing the four modalities of human experience as formulated by Kluckhohn: activity, relational, time, and man-nature (see

F. Kluckhohn, 1953). (Those items that fall into the activity area lend themselves to two alternative choices, not three as in the case of the other modalities.) Here is an example of an item from the relational area (Kluckhohn and Strodtbeck, 1961, p. 82):

> I'm going to tell you about three different ways families can arrange work. These families are related and they live close together.
>
> C (Ind): In some groups (or communities) it is usually expected that each of the separate families (by which we mean just husband, wife, and children) will look after its own business separate from all others and not be responsible for the other.
>
> B (Coll): In some groups (or communities) it is usually expected that the close relatives in the families work together and talk among themselves about the way to take care of whatever problems come up. When a boss is needed, they usually choose (get) one person, not necessarily the oldest able person, to manage things.
>
> A (Lin): In some groups (or communities) it is usually expected that the families which are closely related to each other will work together and have the oldest able person (*hermano mayor* or father) be responsible and take charge of most important things.
>
> Which of these ways do you think is usually best in most cases?
>
> Which of the other two ways do you think is better?
>
> Which of the ways do you think most other persons in ——— would think is usually best?

An example of an item from the time area (Kluckhohn and Strodtbeck, 1961, p. 84):

> Three young people were talking about what they thought their families would have one day as compared with their fathers and mothers. They each said different things.
>
> C (Fut): The first said: I expect my family to be better off in the future than the family of my father and mother or relatives if we work hard and plan right. Things in this country *usually* get better for people who really try.

B (Pres): The second one said: I don't know whether my family will be better off, or worse off than the family of my father and mother or relatives. Things always go up and down *even if* people do work hard. So one can never really tell how things will be.

C (Past): The third one said: I expect my family to be about the same as the family of my father and mother or relatives. The best way is to work hard and plan ways to keep things as they have been in the past.

Which of these people do you think had the best idea?

Which of the other two persons had the better idea?

Which of these three people would most other ———— your age think had the best idea?

The schedule was administered individually to each subject in his home or place of business by a trained social worker. Because most first-generation subjects spoke and understood Greek better than they did English, the schedule was translated into Greek and administered by a Greek-speaking social worker to these subjects.

In Table 8 the summary patterns that were obtained for the four subject groups, first generation with patient, first generation without patient, second generation with patient, and second generation without patient, are provided. The dominant traditional Greek and core American hypothesized value orientation profiles are also provided in this table for purposes of comparisons with the patterns actually obtained from our sample. The interpretation of these empirically derived profiles occupies the remainder of this chapter.

In interpreting Table 8 it is important to keep one statistical consideration in mind. An asterisk between two value preferences in a profile indicates that the choice of the first over the second alternative was made consistently by members of that group and therefore is statistically significant. For example, Ind* > Coll > Lin indicates that Individualism was chosen in preference to Collaterality consistently by members of a group in responding to items in the relational area. Also, an asterisk after the third, or last, value orientation in a summary pattern—for example, Ind >

Table 8.

RESULTS OF THE BINOMIAL ANALYSES OF THE VALUE
ORIENTATION DATA

Modalities	Rural Greek Profile	First generation with patient	Second generation with patient
Activity	Be >Do	Be > Do	Do >*Be
Relational	Lin >Ind >Coll	Coll>*Lin > Ind	Ind > Coll >*Lin*
Time	Pres>Past >Fut	Pres>*Fut >*Past*	Pres >*Fut >*Past*
Man-nature	Sub>With>Over	Sub > With >*Over	Over>*With> Sub*

Modalities	First generation without patient	Second generation without patient	American core culture profile
Activity	Do >*Be	Do >*Be	Do >Be
Relational	Ind > Coll >*Lin	Ind >*Coll>*Lin*	Ind >Coll >Lin
Time	Past>*Pres > Fut	Fut >*Pres>*Past*	Fut >Pres >Past
Man-nature	Sub>*Over> With	With>*Sub > Over	Over>With>Sub

* Paired comparison significantly different at the 0.05 level.
Abbreviations: Be, Do stand for Being, Doing; Lin, Ind, Coll stand
for Lineal, Individual, Collateral; Pres, Past, Fut stand for Present,
Past, Future; Sub, With, Over stand for Subjugation-to-nature, Harmony-with-nature, Mastery-over nature.

Coll > Lin*—indicates that it was significantly preferred to the
first orientation in the paired comparison of these two alternatives.
The absence of an asterisk between two value preferences in a profile indicates that, although a value was chosen more often than
the one that follows it in the profile, consistency was not high
enough to produce a statistically significant result in the compared
analysis. There was not, in other words, sufficient consensus among
the members in that group in their preference for the one over the
other value. Absence of asterisks reflects ambiguity among the
members of the group. This ambiguity, in turn, indicates conflict
in value choices and is attributed to a transitional stage in the acculturation process. In our sample, ambiguity, or lack of consensus

among members of a group, relates to the conflict of the dominant traditional Greek and core American value orientation profiles.

With this consideration in mind let us now examine the obtained summary value orientation profiles in Table 8. Let us focus first on the patterns produced by the two first-generation parental groups. In the with-patient first-generation group the parents, after forty odd years of residence in the United States, still adhere remarkably closely to the traditional value orientations that they brought with them. The summary patterns they produced indicate little shift from the traditional Greek to the American direction. In the activity and man-nature areas the patterns produced are identical with the traditional Greek ones. The pattern in the relational area, Coll* > Lin > Ind, is clearly closer to the traditional Greek than to the American pattern. The first-order Lineal orientation of the traditional profile has moved to the second position, while Individualism has moved from second to third position. Since Individualism is the first-order position in the American profile, the obtained pattern, in fact, reflects a movement away from the dominant American profile. In the time area, a statistically significant one, Pres >* Fut >* Past* was obtained. This pattern, too, is closer to the Greek than to the American profile. Some shift in the American direction is evident in the preference for Future in the second-order position since Future is the third choice in the traditional Greek profile.

The first-generation parents in the without-patient group evidence considerably more change toward the American value orientations than do their counterparts in the with-patient group. In the activity and relational areas the obtained patterns, Do >* Be and Ind > Coll >* Lin, are the American ones. The pattern produced in the activity area is a statistically significant one indicating a strong preference for Doing over Being. In the relational area, however, while Collaterality is preferred significantly to Lineality, the obtained pattern in general does not reflect a decisive shift, pointing to the ambiguity natural to the transitional stage of culture change in which these individuals find themselves. Movement in the American direction is evident, but the ambiguous nature of this trend is also clear. This ambiguity is further supported by the patterns produced in the time and man-nature areas. Here the pat-

terns Past >* Pres > Fut and Sub >* Over > With* are clearly
closer to the traditional Greek than to the core American profiles.

The differences in the patterns produced by our two first-
generation parental groups reveal something about the acculturation process iteself. Namely, movement in the American direction
is associated with the absence of psychopathology in Greek families,
while rigidity, in the form of total adherence to traditional Greek
orientations, is associated with the presence of psychopathology.

This finding supports the inferred character of the culture
change that was outlined in the descriptive analysis in the first part
of this chapter. We hypothesized that individualism was a consciously held value in Greek culture which could be accommodated
to the American first-order preference in the relational area. The
parents in the families free from manifest psychopathology, in fact,
show a preference for Individualism in the first-order position and
choose Lineality as a third alternative. In the time area they prefer the Past alternative, a statistically significant choice. At first
glance this preference would appear to reflect an inconsistency regarding movement in the direction of adopting American value
orientations because the Past alternative is the least preferred in the
American profile. This outcome is consistent, however, with the importance of the Past orientation in traditional Greek culture. Its
adaptive utility in mitigating the shock of acculturation was described in this chapter. A reaffirmation of the past achievements of
Greek cultural heroes also is a resource from which to draw in
socializing children to the ways of American individualism. For
Greek-Americans, then, the Past orientation is not inconsistent with
a first-order Individualism, and in fact it constitutes a supportive
base for the implementation of individualism.

This interpretation is supported by the results obtained in
the analysis of the value orientation patterns produced by the second-generation, American-born children in the without-patient
families. It can be seen in Table 8 that, with the exception of the
man-nature area, the obtained patterns for this group are the core
American ones. Also, these patterns are statistically significant ones;
the preferences for the American patterns were made unequivocally.
Thus, the culture change process begun by the parents is completed
by their sons and daughters.

The intergenerational patterns in the with-patient families are quite different. The second-generation children in this group have moved toward the adoption of American value orientations in a less decisive manner. Since this movement nevertheless reflects, with the exception of the time area, a sharp divergence from the value orientations maintained by their parents, the very lack of decisiveness may make the transition especially wearing.

Let us consider these interpretive points further in relation to the patterns produced in the five value orientation areas by the second generation. In the activity area the with-patient second-generation produces a statistically significant American Do >* Be pattern while their parents maintain, albeit ambiguously, the Greek Be >Do profile. In the relational area the pattern obtained by the children is Ind > Coll >* Lin*, the American one. Individualism is chosen in the first-order position but by a statistically negligible margin. In this crucial area, which patterns interpersonal relationships, the acculturation process is not complete in this group in contrast to the decisive Ind >* Coll >* Lin* pattern produced by their second-generation counterparts in the without-patient group. The inability of the parents in the first-generation with-patient group to shift in the American direction in the relational area suggests that the ability of their offspring to do so is also slowed down.

Furthermore, the Coll >* Lin > Ind pattern produced by the parents in these with-patient families is a compromise between the Greek Lin > Ind > Coll and the American Ind > Coll > Lin cultural profiles. The primary emphasis on Collaterality in the first position in the parental group reflects the pulling in and pulling together of members in these families in an effort to meet the complex stresses being confronted in the United States. The emphasis on Lineality characteristic of Greek families is given up, but in contrast to the pattern in the without-patient group Individualism does not take its place in the manner described above. The authority of the father is relegated to the second-order (Lineal) position, and the primary emphasis now is put on a collaborative effort by all members of the family to work together to meet the economic and social realities of the new world. (This point is elaborated further in Chapter Seven.)

This interpretation is further supported in the patterns of the with-patient families in the time area. For the parents in the with-patient group the critically important Past orientation is relegated to the third position (Pres >* Fut >* Past*). In other words, Greek tradition and all that it implies in its undergirding of Individualism as a resource for adaptation to American middle-class core society has low valence in the first-generation with-patient group. And their children also have adopted the identical pattern in the time area. Furthermore, the Pres >* Fut >* Past* pattern, with its primary emphasis on the Present, is a poor supportive orientation for the first-order Doing in the activity area and the first-order Individualism chosen by the second-generation with-patient group. The fit, in other words, between the patterns produced in the different value orientation areas is not a good one. This discord also applies to the man-nature area, where the second generation produced the American Over >* With > Sub* pattern in contrast to the traditional Greek Sub > With >* Over produced by their parents. Planning for the future is an essential component for an achievement orientation in American society. Its absence, in the presence of the first-order Doing, Individualism, and Over-nature orientations, points to an endemic strain that can be a continuing source of frustration and failure in efforts to achieve occupational goals in the American social system.

Let us finally return to the without-patient group in order to focus on the man-nature area, where an apparent inconsistency emerges in the interpretive analysis we have made up to this point. Table 8 indicates that the parents produced a Sub >* Over > With* pattern in this area, which is closer to the traditional Greek Sub > With > Over than to the core American Over > With > Sub profile. There is evidence of some movement in the American direction in that the Over-nature alternative appears in the second position in the obtained pattern. This would be characterized as "slow" change, however, in contrast to the shifts to the American poles evident in the activity and relational areas in this parental group.

In order to understand this inconsistency we must look again to traditional Greek cultural themes. Rural Greeks share with their counterparts in other countries a Subjugated-to-nature orientation. An Over orientation is irrelevant in this technologically undeveloped country, where farming is still carried on with primitive tools. A salient feature of this orientation in Greece, however, is the primary emphasis placed on the concept of fate (*mira*). This theme is an ever-present one in ancient Greek literature and drama. One's ultimate destiny is in the hands of the gods. One may plan rationally and strive to achieve goals, but in the last analysis the outcome is in the hands of greater powers. (For a discussion of the Greek villager's perception of God as part of the Subjugated-to-nature orientation, see Friedl, 1962, pp. 77–78.) The outcome becomes a matter of chance, of good luck or bad luck (*tihi*). One is not, therefore, totally responsible for failure, and one's pride in success is tempered by the realization that a man or woman has been graced by good fortune.

This theme can be a salutary one for Greeks entering the highly competitive economic sphere of activity in the United States. It can provide an emotional buffer to the failure that many endure in their efforts to achieve occupational success. Their sense of personal worth and dignity can be preserved in the face of potential as well as actual failure. Failure is not perceived as an indication of personal inadequacy, as it is in American culture. One can, therefore, accept the importance and value of achievement while allowing for the contingency of failure. As in the time orientation, then, an adherence to traditional value orientations in the man-nature area undergirds and supports the adoption of American value orientations in the activity (Doing) and in the relational (Individualism) areas.

The sons and daughters of first-generation parents in the without-patient group have not shifted in the American direction in this area. This, in fact, is the only area where the second-generation without-patient group did not produce the American profile. They appear to have been influenced by the direction taken by their parents in this area. The obtained pattern, With >* Sub > Over, is a resolution of the conflicting pull of the Greek parental and American dominant patterns. The first-order With orientation provides a viable alternative to the Greek first-order Subjugated and American first-order Over preferences. It represents the effort to tune in, to come to terms with the American societal forces the second generation faces in its effort at adaptation. They cannot feel subjugated to these forces in their parents' manner, but neither can they accept totally the Over position, which would leave them vulnerable to the impact of failure should these efforts not succeed.

In the with-patient families, by contrast, the second-generation sons and daughters have accepted the dominant American pattern in the man-nature area, Over* > With > Sub*. Parents and children are at opposite poles in this area. For the second-generation children, then, in the with-patient families movement to the American pole again is a radical and therefore potentially stressful shift. They are fully exposed, furthermore, to the demands of the dominant Over orientation of the American core society, with its emphasis on overcoming obstacles to achievement, and they do not have an alternative that can mitigate and buffer the force of the resultant stress as do their counterparts in the without-patient group.

The empirical findings obtained in the analysis of the value orientation data support the observations made about the acculturation process for Greek-American families in the first part of this chapter. These data also provide a microscopic view of culture change itself and help to clarify the particular intergenerational variations in value orientations that differentiate those Greek-American families characterized by conflict and severe personality disorganization in a second-generation member. In the next chapter we undertake an in-depth analysis of one of the seventeen with-patient families, the Constantine family, which formed part of the sample from which the data reported above were derived. Transactional analysis of this family makes it possible to illustrate the passage from conflict in value orientations among family members in the acculturation process to social-role conflict within the family accompanied by interpersonal disturbance and finally to intrapsychic disorder in individual family members.

The in-depth analysis of the Constantine family serves another important function. The empirical data reported above are summary patterns of value orientations of the with-patient group and therefore obscure the particular variations in the acculturation process that characterize individual families. These variations are important to consider since they illustrate the fact that both "healthy" and "unhealthy" features of the acculturation characterize the organization of individual families. The "healthy" features, many of which become evident in the description of the Constantine family, are lost in the general findings provided by the summary data. By the same token, the without-patient families included in our sample were not found to be totally free of acculturation stress. The culture change process was neither as smooth nor as conflict-free as our summary of the patterns would indicate. There were variations in the "unhealthy" direction in these families as well, as evidenced in social-role conflict among famly members as well as in individual emotional disturbance. This disequilibrium, however, was neither as pervasive nor as severe as it was in the with-patient families.

Case Study of a Greek-American Family

On August 25, 1966, Ann Constantine, a 39-year-old suburban housewife and mother of two children, was transferred to a state hospital located in the Boston area from a private psychiatric hospital in the area where she had been admitted five weeks earlier in an acute psychotic condition. Shortly after, our research unit at Harvard was informed by members of the state hospital that Ann met the criteria for inclusion in a study of Greek-American families currently underway there. Ann was a second-generation Greek-American who was born and reared in the Greater Boston area and was hospitalized with a psychotic diagnosis. Her father, George Nicholopoulos, was alive, and her siblings, two brothers and three sisters, were living in the area; all were available for study.

General Background

Mrs. Constantine's hospitalization, her first, was precipitated five weeks earlier when she ran to a neighbor's house in the middle

206

of the night in a panic convinced that her husband was planning to poison her. This episode culminated a period of several months in which she had been tense and withdrawn. She had, during this period, become increasingly convinced that people were talking about her behind her back and, principally, accusing her of having extramarital affairs. Her feeling of people talking about her first started at her husband's tennis club at the beginning of the previous summer when she had gone there to play tennis. These feelings coincided with the belief that her husband was being unfaithful to her.

Michael Constantine's immediate reaction to his wife's illness, when he fully comprehended the nature of the crisis that confronted him, was to call Ann's older sister, Thalia. He did not think much about why, and later at the Emergency Ward of the general hospital in the area when Thalia suggested that the rest of Ann's family be notified of her situation, he adamantly refused to do this. He was angered at the thought of her whole "crazy" clan—Ann's brothers and sisters—descending on him. They had never been of any help in the past for any reason, he protested, and Ann's father was too old. Ann was *his* wife. Later Michael relented when the psychiatrist informed him that Ann was acutely ill and that she needed to be hospitalized for an indeterminate period of time. In fact, he now was comforted by the thought of being able to share the burden with them. Michael made arrangements to have his wife transferred from the psychiatric ward of the general hospital to the private hospital a few days later. The latter is a private psychiatric hospital providing high-quality care and serving mostly an upper-income clientele. Michael insisted that his wife would be happy in this environment. Under no circumstances did he want her to go to a state hospital, and he indicated he was prepared to sustain the financial hardship that this decision entailed.

However, Ann never felt completely comfortable at the private facility. As at the tennis club, she believed herself thrown among people with whom she felt she had little in common. Her stay there lasted only five weeks. The Social Service Depeartment helped Michael realize that he could not sustain the financial drain beyond that period of time.

The paranoid behavior symptoms she had manifested sub-

sided in a short period of time but returned during the last week of
her stay at the private hospital just prior to her transfer to the state
hospital. She again felt her husband was planning to kill her. He
was tampering with her medication at the hospital and would
finish her off when she got out.

Her mood during her hospitalization at the private facility
was depressed. Although this depression lifted from time to time,
she remained withdrawn and never related to other patients.

Individual psychotherapy never got started—she was suspicious of her therapist and admonished him constantly "not to get too
close."

A psychiatrist at the private hospital was able to complete
twelve interviews during her stay, however. The following is a summary of the main features of his report based on these interviews.
Two events precipitating her present illness were isolated. The
first was the death of her mother a year earlier; Ann had become
progressively more depressed since that time. The second was the
onset of menopause that had also occurred during the past year.
The cumulative effect of these two major sources of stress strained
an already frail ego structure.

Her developmental history pointed to primary emotional
deprivation in relation to a mother who was chronically depressed,
who lived in constant conflict with her husband (Ann's father),
and who, when the patient was nine years old, worked outside the
home to support the family.

On admission to the state hospital, Ann's condition markedly
improved. She no longer manifested delusional thinking. She remained somewhat withdrawn and depressed, however. She reported
that she was confused about what directions to take in her life, and
specifically about whether or not to divorce her husband. She had
difficulty in making decisions in general. Her adjustment to the state
hospital, a public institution, was remarkably smooth. She made
friends easily with the other patients and felt very comfortable in
this environment, in contrast to the private hospital. She felt the
patients were more "down to earth" people like herself.

She was assigned a psychotherapist who saw her on a weekly
basis. Her therapy did not progress. She remained tense throughout
the sessions with long silences punctuating the hour. Her therapist

felt he could not get through to her to establish a psychotherapeutic relation. He welcomed, therefore, the involvement of the Harvard research team in the hope of obtaining a better understanding, from a cultural perspective, of what was happening with his patient.

Ann was interviewed jointly by a social worker on the team and a Greek-American psychologist. Given the history from the hospital, the interviewers were both surprised by the impression she made on them in the initial interview. She was attractive, of medium height, and carried herself with dignity, projecting an image of cold aloofness, but underneath seemed to lie an element of sensuousness. The suit she wore was well tailored and obviously of high-quality fabric. It was the discrepancy between the projected image of worldliness, self-sufficiency, and sexual openness, on the one hand, and her history of limited coping capability, on the other hand, that particularly struck the interviewers. At first, she was reserved and not sure that she wanted to participate in the study. Her husband, she was sure, would not be interested in collaborating. After the interviewers reviewed in detail the purposes of the research and the methods planned to obtain information, she relaxed perceptibily, and by the time the interview session was completed, she agreed to participate in the research.

The social worker project staff member interviewed her husband later that same day. Michael was described as the prototype of the "man in the gray flannel suit," above average height, handsome square features, and an athletic build. He was well groomed and dressed in a well-tailored suit. He moved quickly and dynamically and seemed to be restraining himself in sitting still for the hour the interview took. In fact, he got up several times during the interview and walked around the room, all the time talking and gesticulating. On one occasion he excused himself, saying he just remembered an urgent business call he had to make. When he came back, he expressed relief that his wife seemed to be getting better. He hoped that she might now be cured once and for all. She really had been ill for a long time, he said. He had begun to realize that she was not well about eight years before, after the birth of their son, Sam. In order to relieve his wife during the recovery period, he had taken their first child to his sister's house for a few days. His wife became very agitated about this and expressed the fear that his sister would poison their child. She had always been "hostile" and "paranoid" during their married life together. She wanted him home promptly at five o'clock. He could not get her to entertain his business associates, or persuade her to participate with him in the many recreational activities he engaged in. He loved to ski, bowl, and go dancing with their friends, but she was reluctant to take part in any of these activities. She just wanted to stay home, according to him.

Ann Nicholopoulos Constantine was born in the Roxbury section of Boston, the youngest of six children (see Figure 3). Roxbury was a multiethnic, working-class neighborhood of Boston during the 1920s when Ann was growing up, inhabited principally by Irish and Jewish immigrants. She had three older sisters, Christine, Angela, and Thalia, and two older brothers, Gregory and James.

Her father, George, had immigrated to the United States in 1912, accompanied by two friends from the same village in rural Greece. He had been married to Ann's mother, Antonia, for two years prior to his immigration to the United States and had two children, Christine and Angela. Her father was the village priest and had disapproved of his daughter's marriage to George, who was considered to be of lower social status in the village. George's father had been a farmer and a shepherd. Although George provided comparatively well for his family by the standards of the village at that time, they had a marginal status. His decision to immigrate to the United States was motivated by a desire to improve the financial situation of his new family and to "become somebody." This motivation was shared with many of his compatriots who immigrated during this period. Antonia's parents never relented in their disapproval of George. The young couple had finally eloped. This was certainly deviant behavior in a Greek village during this period. (The information about the elopement of Ann's parents was revealed by Christine as a dark family secret, and the matter could not be pursued for more details.)

Antonia remained in the village with her two daughters, at the home of her parents, when her husband departed. On his arrival in the United States, George worked as a laborer in a cotton mill in Maine where he had gone because he had the address of a man from his village who was living there. He subsequently moved to

Boston, worked in a restaurant owned by another Greek, and sent money back to Greece so that his wife could join him. Antonia joined her husband in Boston three years after he had come to the United States. She brought her daughter Christine with her but left Angela in Greece. The reason given for this was that she could not afford to bring both daughters, and, furthermore, she was concerned about the health of the younger child. Angela in fact remained in Greece for an additional twelve years. When she rejoined her family as a teenager, she had a deep resentment toward her parents for leaving her behind. Her subsequent relation to her parents was colored by this event and continued to be a source of strain between them until her own marriage four years later.

The information about the circumstances of George's immigration to the United States was obtained directly from him. He was eighty years old at the time of the interview, a tall, lean, spry man who conversed in a warm and easy manner. His warmth increased markedly when the interviewer spoke to him in Greek. He laughed often as he related the circumstances of his immigration to the United States. In response to the question, "Why did you decide to immigrate to the United States?" he responded, "Because we were very rich in Greece." He underscored his sarcasm by throwing back his head and in a subtle but clear way through his facial expressions, asking the interviewer to share the comedy of this statement with him.

During the interview, George had difficulty in understanding questions that dealt with work issues. He hesitated in responding to these questions, asking that they be repeated, and so on. Christine Demetriou, who remained in the room, a kind of protector and aide to her father during the interviewing, intervened to excuse him, explaining that he had difficulty hearing at times. It became evident later, however, that the issue of work was a very loaded one for him.

In a subsequent interview with Mrs. Demetriou, we learned about George's role as wage earner in the family. Its central importance in understanding the dynamics of the extended Nicholopoulos family, and specifically Ann's development, will become evident.

Christine's account of her father's work history was corroborated in the interviews we held with her brothers and sisters. When he first arrived in Boston from Maine, and before his wife

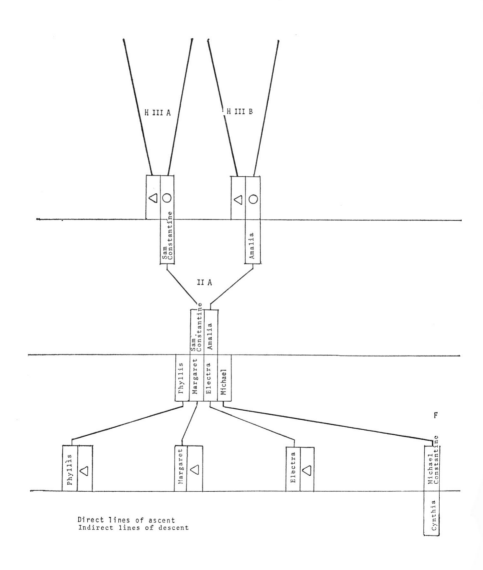

H III A   H III B

Sam Constantine   Amalia

II A

Sam Constantine
Amalia

Phyllis   Margaret   Electra   Michael

F

Phyllis   Margaret   Electra   Michael Constantine

Cynthia

Direct lines of ascent
Indirect lines of descent

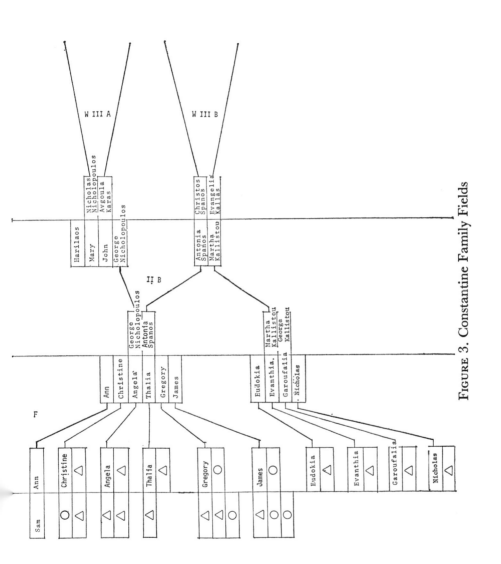

FIGURE 3. Constantine Family Fields

arrived with Christine from Greece (the exact time sequence here could not be determined), he got a job in a restaurant owned by a Greek compatriot. At first, he worked as a dishwasher; later he learned the rudiments of cooking; and, by the time his wife arrived in Boston, he owned his own restaurant. His restaurant did well for a while. Ann recalled in her interview that her father worked all the time and was rarely home. When she was eight or nine, she recalls, things got very bad for the family financially. Her father's restaurant burned down during this period, and he did not open up another one. Instead he began working as a chef for other Greek restauranteurs, but only on a sporadic basis. He invariably got into an argument with his employers and quit or was fired. It was the beginning of the Depression of the 1930s. Antonia reluctantly found that she had to work outside her home as a seamstress for a few hours a week in order to supplement her husband's meager and irregular earnings. She placed her eldest daughter Christine in charge of the other children while she was away.

Arguments between George and Antonia over his inability to earn enough money to maintain his large family became progressively more frequent and more intense. All the Nicholopoulos children in their respective interviews agreed that conflict between their parents permeated the family atmosphere while they were children and through their adolescent years.

George's explanation for not working regularly, which his wife never accepted, was that he was not well. He felt weakened by recurrent asthma attacks and by a diabetic condition. The severity of the latter could not be determined by the information proffered by Ann and her siblings, but we were left with the impression that psychosomatic features seemed clearly evident.

George gradually gave up his role as wage earner entirely. By the time Ann was thirteen years old, her mother had taken full-time employment as a seamstress and became the family's chief wage earner. Christine was given the responsibility of caring for the children while her mother was away working. Her father spent his time playing poker in a Greek coffee shop in town or playing the numbers pool at the local variety store. He spent the better part of each day there. When his children wanted him, they looked for him there. Antonia, then, virtually became head of the household.

In addition to the role of wage earner, she also, with the help of Christine, assumed the full responsibility for the rearing of her children. She was described consistently by her children as a strict disciplinarian who, though she delegated this function at times to Christine, ruled her household in a matriarchal fashion. She suffered little disobedience from her children. The girls were expected to assume responsibilities for the upkeep of the house, which was kept meticulously clean, as soon as they were old enough to do so. When the boys were old enough, they were expected to work after school and in the summers in order to contribute financially to the maintenance of the household.

Ann remembered her mother as tense and overwrought during her childhood period. She related how her mother had frequent headaches and hypertension and attributed this to the fact that Antonia was overworked and fatigued. Ann's siblings, in their interviews, however, tended to be, at times, obliquely critical of their mother. Thalia, the third daughter, described her mother as depressed most of the time. She could not recall much humor in her mother, who maintained an emotional distance from the children.

This somber and joyless picture of the family circumstances surrounding Ann's early childhood was alleviated by the frequent celebrations they had in their home on the occasion of Greek Orthodox religious holidays. All the children helped their mother with the preparations for these celebrations, and in spite of their strained financial situation, Greek food was prepared for at least fifty people. In addition to their relatives, their Greek friends in the neighborhood were invited, as well as friends from surrounding areas, and the parties were very gay.

These celebrations were very important to Antonia. Ann felt that her mother invested so much in these affairs because they enhanced the family's reputation and social position among the Greek community. Ann also reflected with some trace of dissatisfaction that had her mother spent less money on these parties, more might have been left for her and her brothers and sisters to go to college.

Also, these celebrations made it possible for George to participate with the rest of the family in a common activity. He entered into them with a great deal of verve, having invited his cronies from the Greek coffee shop, and assumed for a brief period of time the role of the gracious host. In his interview, he recalled these celebrations with a great deal of joy and lamented that the younger generation, that is, his children and their families, did not see fit to continue this custom.

At Antonia's insistence, the family had moved from the flat they originally occupied to one near the Greek Orthodox Cathedral. Antonia wanted to be near the church so that her children could attend the Greek language school held there every afternoon and church services held on Sunday. Their proximity to the church facilitated the early socialization of the Nicholopoulos children into Greek culture. In addition to Greek school five days a week, they also belonged to youth organizations sponsored by the church. Ann joined the choir, and this required her to attend rehearsals at least one evening a week, as well as singing every Sunday. And, of course, there were many other Greek families who had chosen to rent flats and apartments near the church.

As the children grew older, however, their social activities were not limited to the Greek neighborhood and community. Ann and her sister Thalia joined the YWCA, and Gregory and James the YMCA. The boys were engaged in a great variety of sports, belonged to athletic teams sponsored by their high school, and were very much involved in "American" activities. As they grew older, the boys involved themselves less in the social activities sponsored by the church. Ann described them as "real all-American boys."

There was some variation in the socialization patterns of the two older sisters, Christine and Angela, as compared with the rest of the children. Since Christine was a mother surrogate for the younger children, and Angela immigrated to the United States at an advanced age, they tended to remain closer to Greek customs and to spend a great deal of time in domestic pursuits around the house. Both these sisters, however, internalized the high value on education described below. Their younger sisters, Thalia and Ann, developed close ties with non-Greek friends and, like their brothers, engaged a great deal in sports like baseball and swimming.

Antonia maintained close ties with her sister Garoufalia and brother-in-law, George Kallistou, who was a teacher of Greek in a parish school in one of the Greater Boston communities. This sister, Antonia's only close relative in the United States, bore four children, three girls and one boy. The close contacts between their two families, nurtured by both Antonia and Garoufalia, also helped relieve the somber family picture and enriched the childhood of Ann and her siblings. Ann recalled frequent visits between the two families. Her cousins spent long visits with them in their flat in Roxbury. Ann and her sisters especially enjoyed the companionship of their girl cousins, with whom they still maintained close ties at the time of the interviewing. George Kallistou assumed a paternal role toward the Nicholopoulos children. He was looked up to by both the boys and the girls as a learned man, and he counseled them often. Garoufalia Kallistou was also highly respected by her nieces and nephews. She is reported to have been better educated than their mother, having progressed to a higher level in normal school in Greece before she immigrated to the United States. Antonia often expressed the wish that she could have furthered her education, and she said she envied her sister.

This theme, Antonia's valuing of higher education, is one that appears in the interviews of all her children and was especially dominant in Ann's interview. It was a theme that was further underscored by the presence of Mr. and Mrs. Kallistou in the home. Antonia obviously presented them as role models whom she hoped her children would emulate. She also conveyed to her children, however, the feeling that her hope would be frustrated. She made clear that their financial situation, due to the irresponsibility of her husband, precluded the possibility that there would be money available for them to go to college. If they were to achieve this highly valued goal, they must do it on their own. She was not able to help them.

The adolescent period was a difficult one for the girls in the Nicholopoulos family. The mother, and for that matter Christine, did not prepare the younger girls for menstruation, and no information was given to them about sex. What was made very clear was that they were not allowed to go out on dates alone with boys. Their contacts with boys were to be limited to Greek-American community functions where they could be monitored by Antonia. This issue was a continuing source of conflict in the family. Angela rebelled by getting married at the age of eighteen without her mother's consent. She and her husband, in fact, eloped. Thalia dated secretly, and the frequent discovery of her transgressions resulted in the eruption of bitter battles with her mother. Ann went to her high school senior prom with a Greek boy whose family were acquaintances of the Nicholopouloses. "He was the best looking boy at the prom, but I was bored to death with him." Ann also dated secretly but less frequently than Thalia, and somehow it never became a major source of conflict with her mother. Christine seemed to have escaped this area of conflict. She did not report it to have been a problematic area. Her husband was a frequent visitor to the celebrations held in her home, and she married him with the blessings of her parents when she was twenty-seven years old.

The boys also did not report difficulty with their mother around the issue of dating. No great problems were created regarding whom they dated. Like their sisters, however, Gregory and James received no counsel about sex, except admonishment to be good and not to get into trouble.

They were given preferential treatment in other areas too, as their sisters were quick to mention in the interviews. The girls were expected to "wait on them hand and foot," to make their beds, and mend their clothes. The boys had a good deal more freedom in what they did and were not required to give an account of their comings and goings as was the case with their sisters.

Another theme that appears in the interviews of Ann's brothers and sisters was the preferential treatment that she, the youngest, received from the mother. Thalia especially reported with some mild resentment that Ann was never required to take care of her room and that her mother often did her laundry for her. The financial strain in the family had lessened somewhat by the time Ann reached adolescence, for the older children were all working. Ann apparently was not expected to pitch in and work as hard, and, in fact, it seemed Ann was actively protected by the mother from the rigors endured by the rest of them. As the result of this favored treatment, Ann was the one least expected by the rest to have emotional difficulties later in life.

At the time the purpose of the study was first explained to Ann, the symptoms of thought disorder were no longer evident. Her thinking was lucid and her affect was more bland than depressed. She maintained a clear emotional distance from the researchers but agreed, albeit reluctantly, to cooperate in the future interviews that were planned.

During this initial discussion, Michael was also present; he tended to interrupt his wife frequently and to correct statements that she made. While she became visibly irritated at these interruptions, she made no effort to limit her husband's behavior.

In her first individual interview with the social worker, Ann initially maintained her distant, detached stance, but gradually she relaxed and related in a warmer, more interested fashion. It became progressively more evident to the social worker that Ann was attempting to establish a therapeutic relation with her in which the expectancy of emotional support became evident. This behavior was in marked contrast to what had been described by the male psychiatrist. With him she remained distant; their interviews were punctuated by long silences, and she never really, at this juncture at least, was able to establish a therapeutic relation with him.

Subsequent interviews were held in the Constantine home. Located in a middle-class suburb of Boston, the house was a typical split-level, four-bedroom structure in a new development. The furnishings were modern in design; all the floors were covered with wall-to-wall carpeting. The house was neat and clean and undistinguishable from other houses in the neighborhood. The interviews were held in the living room. Ann chain-smoked during the interviews but manifested no other signs of anxiety or discomfort. While the information she proffered about the atmosphere in her home when she was growing up was in general not inconsistent with that given by her brothers and sisters, there was one important exception. She viewed her father's not working when they were children as due to chronic illnesses he had. In her eyes, he frequented Greek coffee houses the way other Greek men of his age and time did, and there was nothing unusual about this. Her mother she saw as overworked and therefore overwrought. Ann recalled vividly her mother's going to work, and the sad feelings she experienced in not having her mother around enough. Antonia was not seen as cold and indifferent toward the children, however; she merely had no energy left to give to them, Ann believed, because of the burdens she carried for all of them. Her mother, furthermore, suffered from frequent headaches which incapacitated her and which were probably caused by hypertension. Her hypertension in turn was caused by overwork.

This attitude assumed by Ann in discussing her parents did not go so far as to include a denial of strains in her family when she was growing up. Her parents' continued quarreling and the economic deprivation, however, were discussed with a detachment that suggested she was not as affected by them as her siblings, especially her sisters. The report of her siblings that she was spared a good deal of the suffering they experienced is corroborated by Ann, albeit in an oblique and indirect manner. She considered herself to be favored by both her mother and father but not at the expense of the others. She recalled enagaging a great deal in sports as a child, often joining her brothers in playing baseball. She loved swimming and did a lot of this at the YWCA with girlfriends.

Looking back on her family's close ties with the Greek-American community, she wondered whether that had been a good thing. Though she expressed gratitude to her parents for sending her to Greek school (she speaks and writes Greek well), she asserted that she herself was first of all an American and her parents should have invested more time in learning American ways.

She was a good student and did so well in grammar school that one of her teachers urged her to apply to the city's Latin High School when she graduated. This was a public school that admitted only scholastically high-ranking grammar school pupils from the school system and charged a nominal tuition for special textbooks and other expenses. Antonia was pleased with this honor but told Ann that they could not afford the extra money required. This inability was a serious disappointment for Ann.

During adolescence, Ann usually conformed to her mother's strict rules about dating without much resentment. She did date occasionally, but if this was detected by her mother, no issue was made of it.

She described herself as the bookworm type who spent a great deal of her time at home studying. She established close relations with girlfriends and still maintains a relation with two of these who are Greek. Ann strongly emphasized to the interviewer that since her mother was not around much, she got into the habit of making her own decisions. This independence remained, she said, an important facet of her personality, and to that day, she maintained, she could not stand having anyone tell her what to do.

When she graduated from high school, she wanted to go to college, but again there was no money for this. She and her brother Gregory were the only two who had aspirations for continuing their education. Gregory had natural talent as a pianist and wanted to pursue this as a career. Neither of them received any encouragement. Their aspirations were noble, it was clearly intimated to them, but college was out of the question.

Ann decided to go to a business school instead and took the secretarial course. Her first job as a secretary was in an office of a state agency where she worked for five years, after which she worked at an office of a different state agency for two years. She talked little about her experience in these jobs except to say that she enjoyed being out of the home and coming into contact with different kinds of people.

When she was nineteen years old, two years after graduating from high school, she enrolled in the evening program of a local university. She attended regularly for one year, taking courses toward a Bachelor of Arts degree. The reason she gave for not continuing was that she lost interest, realizing it would take her a very long time to get her degree in this manner. Also, she said this particular university was not fully accredited. Her mother, again, was delighted that her daughter had decided to pursue higher education but did not interfere when she decided to abandon this plan.

Her mother also encouraged her, paradoxically, in another direction. Ann announced that she had decided to join the WACS. The Second World War was underway, her brothers were in the service, and some of her girlfriends had already signed up. The interviewer expressed some surprise at Antonia's willingness to support this plan, given the close supervision she exercised over her daughter's behavior. Ann responded by saying that her mother trusted her completely and was confident she would handle herself responsibly in the WACS. She also said that her mother loved America and considered it a worthwhile effort on her daughter's part to make a contribution in this way.

Ann, however, did not carry through with this plan. She

got as far as the recruitment office and filled out some forms, but then abruptly decided not to go through with it. She could not tolerate the regimentation, she said, that would have been required in the service. She decided instead to contribute time to the USO and attended dances for servicemen regularly. It was at this time that she enrolled herself for a secretarial course at a business school as a kind of substitute to joining the WACS.

Michael Constantine was interviewed after his appointments at the state hospital where he was seeing a social worker as part of the prescribed treatment for his wife.

He made an effort from the first to ally himself with the interviewer and to present his case regarding his wife's illness. He approached the interview energetically, and his recollections and statements were reflected visibly on his face and through gesticulating. At times, when discussing upsetting issues, he became so obviously depressed that the interviewer found herself alternating between supporting him and shifting the focus of the interview to another topic. In discussing his personal history and later in discussing his relation to his wife, two overriding themes emerged: The first was that he came from a healthy, loving and stable family. The second was that Ann's illness was the fault of her crazy family. He had suffered for a long time because of his wife and her family, and he looked to her therapy at the state hospital to solve once and for all his wife's problems. He also indicated he hoped that this study would in some way contribute to his wife's cure.

He felt that his own therapy with the psychiatric social worker he was seeing at the state hospital was a superfluous effort and he was attempting to terminate his sessions at this time. This was discouraged by the psychiatrist seeing Ann and by his own social worker. When he was asked for information about his background, he prefaced the information he gave by indicating that he did not want his own family contacted. He said that he did not want to alarm them and added that Ann did not like them and he was sure they did not like her much either.

Michael's father, Sam, was born in a Greek village and immigrated to the United States alone in 1919 when he was twenty years old. His reason was the same as that of other Greek immigrants—to realize a better life for himself in "the Promised Land with the streets flowing with milk and honey and everyone eating well." In making this comment, Michael smiled in a wry manner. The father came to a town in New Hampshire where there was a Greek population and worked in the woolen mills there. He had a brother and a sister who came over later. His education was limited to two or three grades in a primary school in his village in Greece.

The marriage between Michael's parents was arranged by their mutual relatives in Greece. His mother, Amalia, was born in a village in the same part of Greece as his father. His father did not meet his mother until a week before they were married. She arrived in the United States to marry him after the father had been here for five years. Michael made the point very emphatically that, in spite of the fact that this was an arranged marriage, his parents were very compatible with each other. "They have the same compassion, love, lots of love for the children, are dedicated to their family, and they both enjoy giving more than they receive. My mother idolizes my father. Even today, she waits on him, gets his slippers, and takes care of him like a baby."

Michael was the first-born child. The next sibling was Phyllis, born three years later. She married a man of Greek descent, a clothing salesman. They had two children, ages sixteen and fourteen at the time of the interview, and lived in a Boston suburb. Michael felt especially close to this sister. Next was Margaret, who eloped with a man of Polish descent who worked as a salesman. At the time they had five children, ranging in age from fourteen to two. Michael had been helping this sister and her family with money because they were having a very bad time of it financially. His youngest sister, Electra, married a Syrian boy who was a white-collar worker. They had two children at the time of the interview.

Michael spoke with pride of his father's industriousness while the children were growing up. The elder man worked two jobs as a bartender for many years in order to provide an adequate income for his family. There were difficult times, however, in spite of this. During the Depression of the 1930s, his father worked for the WPA for a time, and Michael remembered vividly the economic strain on the family. His mother never worked outside of the home with the exception of a six-month period at the beginning of war when she worked in a laundry.

There were other strains as well, although not severe. His father, he said, was definitely more Americanized than his mother, who adhered closely to Greek ways and customs. His father was also better educated in that he could read and write both in English and Greek while his mother could neither read nor write in any language. Sam had gone to night school when he first came to the United States in order to learn enough to become a naturalized American citizen. He enlisted in the United States Army during World War I and was sent to France. For the most part, however, he was self-taught. He, of course, was exposed to non-Greeks daily in his job as bartender, but his wife's activities were limited to the home. She insisted that the children speak Greek in the home. Michael's father, on the other hand, often spoke to the children in English, and this occasionally provoked loud arguments between his parents.

Michael pointed out, however, that his father did not reject his Greek heritage. He was proud of being a Greek and was not adverse to letting his customers at his job know it. Although he did not belong to any Greek organizations and attended church only infrequently, mostly on holidays, he did, as was the custom among Greek men his age, frequent the local coffee shop when he could. Because he was out of the house a great deal working, he turned over to his wife the running of the house and the rearing of the children. This pattern is not inconsistent with family patterns in Greece. He remained, however, in accordance with Greek cultural patterns, the head of his household. He exerted his authority when he was there, and Michael remembers that at family meals he demanded strict obedience and no nonsense from his children. They never questioned his authority, and their mother would hold out the spectre of punishment from their father whenever she wanted to exert control. She depended on her husband completely, and her authority was clearly one that was delegated by him.

Sam did not interfere much with his wife's insistence that the children be brought up according to Greek customs. She made sure that they all attended Greek-language school in the afternoon and church regularly on Sundays. Amalia was herself a devoutly religious person. Their room was covered with icons, and a votive light shone perpetually over their bed. There were frequent gatherings to which relatives and Greek friends were invited. Michael's activities, however, were not limited to the Greek-American community. He became interested in sports at an early age and played baseball, basketball, and football. He had many friends, few of whom were Greek.

A very important factor in his early socialization was his involvement with a settlement house located near their neighborhood, which provided a broad range of recreational experiences for the children of working-class families. He describes this settlement house as a sanctuary away from home where he had many friends. This settlement house sponsored a camp that he attended for several summers. He remembers the college boys who served as counselors there and recalls wanting to grow up to be like them. Michael used the word *sanctuary* without elaborating. He made it clear, however, on different occasions in his interview, that he felt constricted by his mother.

His mother kept a tight rein on him as well as his sisters and was always concerned that they would get into trouble with the law. Whenever a police car came down the street, she would rush him to the window and point it out, saying that she never wanted the police to come looking for her children. In fact, some of the children in the neighborhood did get into trouble with the law. All the Constantine children had to be in the house before dark, and their mother would become hysterical if she didn't know where they were.

This behavior of the mother became more intense, or was felt as more intense by Michael and his sisters, during their adolescent years. Michael dealt with it by getting even more involved in sports outside the house. He dated non-Greek girls almost exclusively and was never seriously questioned about this. His sisters were not as fortunate. Constant battles were fought over the issue of dating, with the mother getting every excited and shouting that they would one day come home pregnant and bring disgrace on the whole family.

As a consequence of this attitude, his second oldest sister

eloped when she was eighteen and was married to a man of Polish descent in the Catholic Church. What upset the mother most was not that he was Catholic but that he was not Greek. In addition, he was a penniless non-Greek. Her parents did not attend their daughter's wedding, nor were any of the children allowed to go. The disgrace that Margaret had brought on the family was the chief concern in the Constantine family for months. It was only after the birth of Margaret's first child, a year and a half later, the first grandchild for Sam and Amalia, that a reconciliation came about.

Margaret's elopement seemed to weaken the mother's resolve considerably. She became much more tolerant of her daughters' dating and in general relaxed her control of them considerably. When her youngest daughter Electra married a Syrian, three years before this study was begun, she was able to accept it with little, if any, protest. After all, her other two children, Phyllis and Michael, had all married Greek-Americans.

Michael mentioned the strong emphasis in his family on education as a means to individual achievement. His parents both encouraged him to pursue a college education. This encouragement, however, seems to have been limited to him. The girls were expected to get married and have a family, so they did not need an education. Michael also expressed the feeling that Phyllis, who married a Greek-American, was pushed into an early marriage by their mother. He explained that because she was so unyielding in matters of dating, his sisters became involved with the first men they dated in order to get out of the house. In any event, none of his three sisters progressed educationally beyond high school.

Michael entered the service for the duration of World War II after finishing high school, and he enrolled at a local university on his discharge. His tuition was paid by the G. I. Bill, but he worked to supplement the living allotment he received. He graduated in the normal four-year period with a B.A. degree in business administration.

Ann and Michael started dating when they were both in their senior year in high school. She was the first Greek-American girl that he ever dated. They went to parties and dances together, but a serious relation had not developed at the time Michael went into the service. Michael was not sent overseas, but his furloughs were few and far between and he did not see Ann on his infrequent visits home. He did not correspond with her until near the end of his service in the Army when he wrote at the urging of an aunt of his who was a close friend of Ann's family. When he was discharged, he did not resume dating her until he had been home for about five months and only then at the urging of this same aunt.

During the courtship which gradually began, Michael was attending college. They went to college parties, and Michael describes his wife as having been a lot of fun when they were with other people. When they were alone, however, he said that Ann would withdraw and not talk with him much. On some occasions, she would fall asleep when he visited her. He found that he had to take the initiative during their courtship as to where to go, what to do, and so forth; she merely complied and did what he decided. Michael expressed the view that his wife had not really been ready for marriage. She was embarrassed about and unprepared for the sexual aspects of marriage. Probably the fact that all her girlfriends had gotten married while she grew older convinced her that marrying was the thing to do.

Ann became visibly tense and nervous in discussing this courtship period and her subsequent marriage to Michael four years later. Her version of this period differs in one important respect. She said that it was she who had pushed for the marriage and not her husband. He was reluctant to get married but was, according to her, pressured into it by his family. During the first two years of their courtship, and prior to their engagement, they had a quarrel and broke off for a time. Ann recalled the rupture as lasting only a few days, whereas Michael said it lasted a few months. During this time when they were not seeing each other, Michael dated another Greek girl, also named Ann. According to Michael, this second Ann really liked him. She adored him, he said, and followed him around like a puppy dog. Although pleased by this, he felt that she presented no real challenge. Ann finally called him, and soon they were engaged. Both sets of parents approved of the match, and a large engagement party was held in the Nicholopoulos home with elaborate Greek festivities.

They were not married, however, until two years later. Michael said the reason for the long engagement was that he had to finish school first.

The wedding itself apparently caused tension between Michael and Ann. Each discussed the events around the wedding with a good deal of feeling. Ann's recollections, however, were accompanied by the expression of a good deal more resentment than was the case with Michael.

She and Michael, she said, had decided to have a small, modest wedding to which only their families and close friends would be invited. They had agreed to conserve their limited financial resources for furnishing an apartment. When Ann's mother-in-law heard about this, "She hit the roof." She wanted her son to have a big wedding and felt that he would be shortchanged by anything less. Michael's father took a neutral stance during the arguments between the two families that were precipitated by his wife's unyielding position on the matter. In their interviews, Christine and Thalia mentioned this wedding as a bid by Michael and his family, always conscious of social status, to impress people. There was no mention, however, by any of Ann's siblings of Ann's parents offering to contribute money toward meeting the expenses of the wedding, even though, traditionally, the father assumed the major financial responsibility for his daughter's wedding in Greek culture. Ann, it should be noted, the last girl in her family to be married, had been working for several years prior to her marriage. Given the financial strain in the Nicholopoulos family, it is quite possible that she had to bear the whole cost of her own wedding.

Ann reluctantly gave in to her mother-in-law in the end and spent the entire $1300 she had saved. As an afterthought, she reported to the interviewer that her mother-in-law did contribute four hundred dollars toward the wedding expenses. In discussing this event, she referred to her mother-in-law as a very limited person with narrow horizons and very little understanding of life outside her home. The older woman was described as always concerned about "putting on a big show" for the Greek community. Michael's mother insisted on big celebrations after the christenings of each of Ann's children, although she did not do so when her own daughters' children were christened. Ann thought that this was because Michael was the only son and that made a big difference.

Michael's account of the issues around their wedding virtually contradicted what his wife reported. His family, he said, was not interested in a big wedding, he also said that he had contributed four hundred dollars toward the expenses because his wife's family could not contribute. According to him, the wedding cost around five or six hundred dollars in all, and most of the guests were his wife's relatives and friends of their family.

Michael reported that their sexual adjustment was poor from the beginning. Sexual relations were never satisfactory from Michael's point of view. Ann remained unresponsive for the most part, and this was a continual source of strain between them. Ann herself said only that she had some difficulty in getting pregnant, worried over this, and finally went to a doctor about it.

When they were first married, the young Constantines lived in a modest apartment in a lower-middle-class area of Boston. After their first two children were born there, they bought their home in a suburb of Boston. The modest apartment was part of a plan for savings rather than the result of financial strain, for Michael always made a very good salary in his job. Strains became rapidly evident, however, in the major areas of their interactions.

Ann reported feeling pushed and railroaded by her husband in everything she did. She said that he tried to make all the decisions for her about the management of the house, the rearing of the children, relations with their extended families, and their recreational and social activities. She was in a state of continual rage about this but could not stand up to her husband. For example, she complained she should never have been hospitalized at the private hospital in the first place. She had been seeing a psychiatrist in the town in which they lived, and he could have taken care of her recent upset. Also, it was Michael who had recently decided she should get a job when she talked of being bored. He made arrangements with a business firm he had dealings with for her to work from nine to two in the afternoon. He then said the boss there needed her from nine to four. How was that possible if she wanted to be home at three when the children got home from school? She said that he always did things like that, arbitrarily made decisions for her that put her under a great deal of stress.

She described her husband as too energetic and active for her. He was always on the go, wanted to step out constantly and socialize with many people, while she preferred to spend more time at home. She told of being forced to entertain business associates of his for dinner at home, and each time this happened she was thrown into a panic for days preparing for the event. She often thought of her mother having fifty people to a party and she shuddered.

In talking about Michael's family, she focused on his sister Margaret, with whom she never got along well. In arguments they had, Michael invariably sided with Margaret, which infuriated Ann and characteristically led her to withdraw. Ann found her mother-in-law hard to communicate with. Michael's mother was said to be full of old-world superstitions and to push for old-fashioned Greek remedies when Ann's children got ill. Her father-in-law, on the other hand, was rated by Ann as a sweet and loving man.

Ann's daughter, Cynthia, was twelve years old at the time of the interviews; her son, Sam, named after her father-in-law, was seven. Ann's first delivery was a difficult one. It was a dry birth, and she had no labor. Headaches persisted for a month or two after, and Ann could not nurse. Her mother moved in to help after Cynthia was born, and the mother-in-law dropped in once a week. The second pregnancy and delivery were uneventful. Both her pregnancies were planned, and she really wanted to get pregnant each time. She and her husband agreed that two children were enough. Ann said she came from a large family and didn't feel the children got enough of their parents when there were so many siblings to compete with. (She stopped working when her first child was born. In fact, she looked forward to getting pregnant the first time because she was tired of working.)

The two Constantine children were doing well in school. Cynthia was described by her mother as the quiet type. She was said to read a great deal and take over the management of her brother when her mother was away from home. Sam was called a "cute little thing" and a good boy. They were involved in a great many activities such as art lessons, ceramic classes, Girl Scouts, and sports. They had both been going to Sunday school at the Greek Orthodox Church, and Ann intended to start them in the afternoon Greek school in September. She maintained she would keep them in Greek school only if they liked it and if it did not interfere with their other activities. She and her husband, she said, agreed that the children should be involved in as many activities as possible.

Ann mentioned that she kept a close relation with her mother even after establishing her own household. Mother and daughter went shopping together often and were in almost daily contact. Her parents had moved in with Christine in the suburb where she lived about five years earlier when her mother began to have strokes. Ann and her children visited there at least once a week. She was very solicitous of her mother and tried to help in her care as much as she could. The relation with her brothers and sisters was not as close since she had gotten married. They saw each other principally on holidays. Michael never got along well with Ann's family and communication with them over the years became less and less frequent. She regularly saw a Greek girlfriend she had known since childhood, however.

Michael referred to Ann's family as being "all crazy." On visits, he invariably got into arguments with them. Christine and Angela, the older sisters, constantly accused him of thinking he was too good for them and not wanting to associate with them. He denied this accusation to the interviewer and said it was their own problem if they thought this. He got along best with Thalia, the sister he called first when Ann was hospitalized.

From the outset of their marriage, in Michael's opinion, Ann never wanted to associate with his family. She didn't want to visit his family because his parents were old-fashioned ("As if hers weren't") and the mother spoke only Greek. It hurt him a lot that his parents always treated her like a daughter and she never reciprocated. Michael added that, though he was no psychologist, he felt Ann's inability to show affection toward his family originated in the fact that she never received any from her own parents.

Ann also never got along well with his sisters, Michael protested. He always felt it was because she was jealous of them.

They were good housekeepers and good cooks, and Ann to him was a poor housekeeper and a bad cook. He helped her with the cooking on weekends so he could have a decent meal and he suggested she take cooking lessons. She flatly refused to do this.

With a great deal of obvious exasperation, he went on to say that he could not understand Ann's antagonism toward his mother. She never thanked his mother for taking care of the children during her recent absence from the home. She even refused to talk to Michael's mother if that lady happened to answer the phone when Ann called to see how the children were. In the past, well before Ann got sick, whenever his mother visited them, she would insist on helping out in the house. She washed the dishes, waxed the floors, and even raked the leaves in the yard. He saw his mother as a lovable person, and he was certain that everyone who knew her in his town "thinks the world of her." Ann's neighbors praised her to Ann, and she responded by just "clamming up." They had never spent a holiday at his home, meaning his parents' home, with their children.

Michael described how he felt very close to his family, meaning his parents and his sisters. He visited his parents every Monday night for dinner but only stayed for an hour because he knew Ann disapproved of it. He was also close to his sisters. They came to him for advice with problems, and he helped his sister Margaret financially when her husband was not working regularly. His father, officially retired and receiving a Social Security allotment, continued to work two and a half days a week because he couldn't sit without doing anything all day. Michael stated that because of his father's advanced age, he himself had become the head of the family, and he acknowledged responsibility to support his parents and sisters if necessary. They also supported him. He had borrowed a thousand dollars from his father to pay Ann's hospital bill, money he planned to return as soon as possible. He had borrowed six hundred dollars from his father a couple of years before and never got around to returning it. No issue was made of it by his father.

A recurrent theme in Michael's interview was his deep disappointment in Ann's reluctance from the beginning of their marriage to participate with him in the many activities he was engaged in. He had hoped she would be an asset to him in his work by entertaining his business associates. His work required him to be in contact with many people, and socializing with them was an important way in which good will could be developed. Ann understood this but only reluctantly entered into these social engagements. Mostly she wanted to stay home, and when they did, it was hard to keep conversation going. At one point he had suggested they take dancing lessons together, and she had flatly refused. She wanted him home at five sharp, and she could never realize, he claimed, that his income depended on his being able to work evenings and to take trips out of town. He had been going out of town more frequently the last three or four years. Ann reacted angrily at first; later she said nothing when he announced imminent trips, but he felt her hostility.

She also had been unwilling to participate with him in the many civic activities he was engaged in. Nor did she pay attention to the athletic activities he was engaged in; she would not even participate in sports he encouraged their children to engage in. He had started teaching his children to ski, for example, and wanted Ann to join in to make it a family activity. He finally got her to learn to play tennis at the club he belonged to. In talking to the interviewer, he added at this point that it was not a "ritzy country club" but only a tennis club with very modest dues. She learned to play and actually began to enjoy it. It was the fact that she had to relate to the people at the club that distressed her, not the tennis itself.

Michael spoke very fondly of his children. "They are the greatest." He expressed concern about the fact that Cynthia was not working in school at a level commensurate with her potential. She was not asked to take a foreign language that year, which is a privilege offered to students who are excelling in their other work.

In a somewhat philosophical tone, Michael expressed the hope that his children would have a better life than he had. He explained that he had no guidance from his parents scholastically and he was trying to give this to his children. He wondered, however, where the younger generation was going. He said that his own children received "everything" and were protected from the struggles and hardships he had had to endure to get an education and get ahead. "Perhaps having it so easy is not a good thing for the young people these days," he mused. He thought they would not be properly equipped to handle life when they were adults.

In discussing his job, Michael related having some difficulties with his current boss and the owner of the firm. This individual supposedly was not the man the former boss was, with whom Michael had a close relation. He found he did most of the thinking for the new boss but did not get the credit he deserved. Lately he had gotten very disillusioned with people, feeling them to be exploitative and uncaring about each other. He felt that during his absence from the office during Ann's illness, so many bad decisions had been made by his employees that it would take him six months to straighten things out.

As a result of his sessions with the psychiatric social worker, Michael came to realize that his wife had been sick a long time. Back when his son was born, for example, and his mother could not stay because she had the flu, Michael took Cynthia to be cared for at his sister Margaret's house. Ann had become very agitated about this and expressed the fear that Margaret would poison her. He was now optimistic about Ann's psychiatric treatment, however, and hoped that her problems would be solved once and for all. Lately, since seeing her psychiatrist, she was becoming more affectionate.

The Family Grown Up

At the time of the investigation, Ann's brother James lived in a duplex apartment next to his brother, Gregory, in a lower-middle-class suburb of Boston. He was a tall, thin man, then forty-one, who appeared somewhat tense and apprehensive about the interview. Ann had arranged it, and he had reluctantly agreed to a visit at his house.

The interviewer was struck by the marked contrast between his apartment and Ann's modern furnishings. There was more furniture than seemed necessary in the living room, and it was arranged haphazardly. A desk placed against the wall at one end of the room was covered with school books and papers, and a spinet piano sat imposingly at the other end. The piano was obviously new compared with the rest of the furniture.

The informality of the living room was matched by the informality of the interview itself. James's two-year-old daughter snuggled up to her father on the couch, and his other two children—Nicky, age thirteen, and Tula, eleven—came in and out of the room. They were introduced to the interviewer, and James indicated he was ready to begin the interview only after his wife had collected the children for bed. James's wife, Alexandra, was an attractive Greek-American girl who conversed in a buoyant, friendly way. She put the children to bed and returned about half an hour later and sat next to her husband to participate in the interviewing.

James worked at various jobs during high school and joined the Army after graduation. He went to a local state university on the G.I. Bill after his discharge. He graduated with a degree in economics and had been working for the same insurance firm since graduation. Despite occasional problems at work, he reported enjoying what he was doing.

James made the point clearly that he received no financial help and little encouragement from his parents when he went to college. His father, especially, was uninvolved with the entire thing. This statement was the closest James came to being negative about his parents. Though he mentioned quarrels between his parents, he attributed them to the financial strain caused by the Depression. His avowals of feeling toward his father especially were quite warm, and he reported contributing financially toward the older man's medical care. Any tension or nervousness in the mother, James explained, had been caused simply by financial strain.

James had looked to his older brother for the little guidance he got when he was growing up. He also talked about his aunt's husband, George Kallistou, in a warm way. James remembered Gregory and Ann as being the most talented of the children and with the most ambition to get ahead in life. Christine also would have been quite capable of furthering her education, he felt, had there been money for this. When they were kids, James felt closest to his sister Thalia, and while he was in the service, he sent his checks to her to save his money for him. Here James mentioned a fact that does not appear elsewhere in the interviews with Ann or his other siblings. For the past few years, he had felt especially close to Ann and had managed to visit her at least once a week (since the firm he works for is close to her town). He professed, however, to know nothing of her present difficulties or about any problems she may have been having with her husband.

In a subsequent interview, James's wife, Alexandra, participated fully with her husband in talking about their own family and the kind of life style they had. She had met her husband at a Greek dance where he had reluctantly taken his sisters. She had been working at the time in her father's restaurant. Although her parents were enthusiastic about the match, she made it clear to the interviewer that their parents had nothing to do with their decision to get married. Nevertheless, they had a large Greek wedding with over two hundred guests. Their children were all baptized in the Greek Orthodox Church.

The children were doing well in school, and both James and his wife emphasized that they guided them in school matters and expected them all to go to college. When discussing this, the wife winked and said "the girls too." James smiled and responded with "especially the girls." Alexandra was accustomed to going to PTA meetings and had served as a Cub Scout den mother. James had been an adviser in the Junior Achievement Program for two years.

James's children were encouraged to participate in as many sports as possible, and he said that he hoped Billy would take a special interest in baseball, although he doubted it because Billy tended to be a bookworm.

The children had been attending Sunday school as well as Greek school at the local Greek Orthodox Church. James expressed the feeling that his children did not do enough on their own. When he was a kid, as he remembered it, he was on the streets all day long. His children were being driven everywhere, were not as active as he'd like them to be in sports, and spent too much time watching TV at home.

James and his wife were reluctant to discuss strains in their own family, but two themes emerged in the course of the interviewing. The first had to do with the wife's dissatisfaction with James's unwillingness to help with domestic tasks. According to her, he would not even see to it that the children picked up after meals and helped to keep the house clean. In response, her husband could see no reason why he or the children should have to do any of these things. She talked about feeling overwhelmed with the care of her three children, their outside activities, the shopping, and so forth. She talked about all this in a good-natured way, almost as if she were confused about her role and wanted some kind of feedback from the interviewer.

James's major recreational activity was playing golf on Sunday, often with his brother. He said he often felt guilty about this, and at least one Sunday a month he gave it up and spent the day with his wife and the children.

The second source of strain was James's mild resentment that his wife spent so much time concerning herself with her parents. They lived in the same town and were quite old. His wife called her mother every day and went frequently to help her with her father, who was ill a good deal of the time. When his wife said she talked to her mother in Greek on the phone, James interrupted to disagree, saying that he had heard her talking in English to her mother for at least a half hour.

James had little to say about his relationship to his own parents and to his brother and sisters since his marriage. When his mother was living, they had family get-togethers around holidays, but no sense of closeness was conveyed. His closeness to Ann was mentioned as an afterthought. Also his contribution to his father's medical expenses was talked about as a duty performed rather than as one aspect of an ongoing warm relationship.

Gregory, the older of the Nicholopoulos sons, lived next to James in a duplex apartment. He was a muscular, stockily built man who related in a frank and easy manner. From the beginning, he evidenced a willingness to cooperate in giving whatever information he could. His apartment, like that of his brother's, was furnished in a functional manner with little attention given to style. A well-worn oriental rug covered the living room floor, and no particular effort was made to pick up in preparing for the interviewer's visit.

His wife, who was also of Greek descent, made only a brief appearance in order to be introduced to the interviewer. Gregory had three children at that time, ranging from eighteen to twelve. His daughter Tessie, age fourteen, sat on the living room couch watching TV with her brother Phillip, who was twelve. Their eldest son, Harry, eighteen, was attending classes at a vocational institute, learning to become a mechanic like his father.

Gregory's description of life in his home when he was growing up was consistent with that given by his brother and sisters. He justified his father's withdrawal from the family by saying his mother was a strong person who left little for his father to do in the house. He emphasized that he was surprised to learn that Ann was having emotional problems. As a child and before she got married, she manifested no signs of being in any difficulty. In fact, his mother was not as strict with Ann as she had been with the rest of the children.

He talked about his own hardships as a child. He very much wanted to become a pianist and was allowed to spend some of the money he made after school on lessons, but it was not enough. When he finished high school, the Depression was at its worst, and he could not find a job. Finally he had to give up his piano lessons entirely, and he was deeply saddened by this. When he finally did get a job, it was as an apprentice machinist in a factory, and the manual labor bruised his hands so that his dream of continuing his piano practice was completely given up. His mother had originally encouraged him to take up the piano on the grounds that she wanted him to stay off the streets and keep out of mischief. Later, both parents began to express the hope that he might make a career out of music, but they were unable to assist him financially in realizing this hope.

Gregory met his wife at a church dance and married her two years before he went into the service. He picked up his trade as a mechanic when he got out of the service and had been employed by a large industrial firm ever since.

James turned to Gregory, as the older son, for guidance since their father was never around. His mother also relied on Gregory to help "keep his brother in line." He was often sent out to find where family members were and to assure her they were not getting into any trouble. Gregory also talked about his aunt's husband, George Kallistou, as a great help to his mother in guiding the children. He described George as a kind person whom he looked up to and respected a great deal. Gregory also felt that his brother was now the one the rest of them turned to when a family issue came up. He did not elaborate this point.

Gregory was not maintaining close relations with his family except for James. He visited his father strictly in the spirit of a dutiful son discharging an obligation. In fact, he usually spent a great deal more time with his wife's family. They visited her parents and her brothers and a sister quite regularly; they all lived in towns around the Boston area.

Gregory and his wife encouraged the children to participate in sports, and they engaged in many outdoor activities together as a family. They closely supervised their children, and Gregory manifested some of the same concern as his parents that his children stay out of trouble. His children attended Greek school and went to church faithfully on Sundays.

Gregory expressed the hope his children would go to college, but he gave no evidence that he was actively planning for it. His son was in a vocational training school, and his daughter was taking the vocational rather than the college sequence in high school.

He would like, he said, for his children to marry Greeks but was quick to add that he did not insist that his children limit their association to children of their own ethnic group. His daughter had an Italian girlfriend with whom she was close.

Angela Kontos, the second oldest of the Nicholopoulos children, lived on the second floor of a two-story house on the outskirts of Boston. At the time of the interview, she was in her early fifties but looked younger. She was a dark, vibrant, and engaging woman. She spoke with a slight Greek accent, rapidly and with constant movement of her hands. In fact, all of her was in constant motion. She addressed the interviewer with a mixture of warmth and uneasiness undergirded with mild skepticism about the worth of the whole interviewing effort. Michael was the person who should be talked to, she scolded. He was the crazy one, not her sister Ann. Why bother her with these questions anyway? She said she was uneducated and ought not to be expected to inform the interviewer. She added that since the interviewer was from Harvard, the interviewer should be teaching her, not asking questions. And what nationality was the interviewer anyway?

Angela's daughter-in-law Persephone, the wife of her youngest son, was present at the initial interview. She was an attractive young woman who obviously was there to provide support for her mother-in-law. The two of them carried on a humorous interchange with much joking and laughter.

Once Mrs. Kontos got started, it was impossible to interrupt her, and the interviewer was exhausted after about an hour. Angela postponed the second interview three times but again gave information freely once she had begun.

She related having been left in Greece when her mother immigrated to the United States with her sister Christine. She was raised by her maternal grandparents in the village. Her grandfather, the village priest, valued education highly but more for boys than girls. She attended grammar school through the eighth grade and was always an honor student. She had to walk each day for three-quarters of an hour in bare feet to get to school. An aunt, the wife of her uncle Gregory, was a school teacher whom Angela loved very much. This woman, whose children she minded after school, had a profound influence on Mrs. Kontos. She also worked on her grandfather's farm and thus had led a busy life. She voiced regrets over not having been encouraged to continue school. The theme of education permeated Mrs. Kontos' two interviews. When she arrived in the United States, she was only thirteen and so by law was obliged to go to school. Her parents, however, somehow managed to convince the city officials that she was attending night school and thus freed her to go to work as a stitcher with Christine in a shop that manufactured men's clothing.

She came into conflict with her mother soon after her arrival in the United States. Her mother was unbelievably strict and narrowminded, which Mrs. Kontos attributed to the older woman's lack of education.

Mrs. Kontos was referring specifically to her mother's attitude toward the opposite sex when she used the word *strict*. Not

only were the Nicholopoulos girls not allowed to date, but even at
dances sponsored by the Greek community they were not allowed to
dance with the men there. At one of these functions she met her
husband, James. He was quite forward and took her onto the dance
floor. Her mother, who was present, was furious and she heard
about nothing else for a week. Angela dated her future husband
secretly, and they fell in love. Her mother, when she learned about
the dating, became even more furious since she considered the Kontos family beneath them socially and categorically objected to the
marriage.

James's family accepted Angela from the start and treated
her like a daughter. Angela and James decided to elope. They were
married by a justice of the peace and left without Antonia's or the
rest of the Nicholopoulos family's knowledge for a brief honeymoon
in New York City. They slept in separate beds, however, and did
not consummate their marriage until later, when their union was
blessed in a wedding ceremony at the Greek Orthodox Church. Her
daughter-in-law laughed when Angela related this part of the story
and said, "Good for you, ma!"

This event had struck the Nicholopoulos family like a thun-
derbolt. Antonia was unconsolable for days. She alternated between
complete withdrawal and periods when she screamed invectives at
her daughter for her sinfulness and ungratefulness in bringing disgrace on the family. What compounded the girl's sin was the fact
that she had gotten married before her older sister. In Greek families, if a younger daughter were to marry first, the chances of marriage of the older sisters would supposedly decrease. No one from the
Nicholopoulos family dared attend the wedding. Angela moved in
with her in-laws, and there was no communication with her family.

Shortly thereafter, Angela decided to write to her grandfather in Greece about the circumstances of her marriage. He
wrote back and was supportive. He told Angela to remind her
mother about what she did, referring to Antonia's elopement with
George. Perhaps, the grandfather speculated, this was God's way of
repaying Antonia for what she had done many years before.

The local Greek Orthodox priest in the meantime was trying
to bring about a reconciliation between the two families, but Antonia remained recalcitrant. Finally the priest threatened to prohibit

her from taking Holy Communion if she persisted in her position. Antonia gave in at last, further softened by the prospect of a first grandchild, for Angela was six months pregnant. A formal reconciliation was arranged at Antonia's house with members of both families present on a Sunday afternoon with everyone dressed in their best attire. There was much crying and hugging by everyone, especially Angela and her mother.

Angela, however, continued to be close to her in-laws and to spend most of the holidays with them. She and her husband took the first-floor apartment in the house owned by her father-in-law, who spared them rent because her husband earned little money at his factory job.

The Kontoses had two sons, one of whom, Spyros, became a successful physician in a neighboring suburb. The other one, Bill, became an engineer with an executive position in a large firm also in a nearby town. Angela spoke with great pride about her two sons, both of whom married Greek-American girls.

She raised them both to respect the church and to have pride in their Greek heritage. They attended Greek school faithfully throughout their grammar school years and both served as altar boys at the local church. They were also active in sports, which their father especially encouraged. When the younger son, Bill, became interested in football and played on the high school team, Mr. and Mrs. Kontos attended all the games. Angela remembered sitting in the stands and cringing with fear that her son might be injured. Mr. Kontos, however, supported his son's playing and pointed out to his wife that sports would keep their sons out of trouble. If they had too much time on their hands, they would start playing with girls instead. This argument was a convincing one for Angela. She, like her brothers, was continually concerned that the children not get into trouble by associating with bad company.

Mrs. Kontos continued to work while the children were growing up and yet always managed to get home before they arrived from school. Although the family had little extra money, there was never a question about Spyros and Bill's going to college. They were good students and managed to get scholarships for college, but their parents also assisted financially at some sacrifice to themselves.

In rearing the boys, Angela tried not to be too strict like her mother. She expressed some confusion about whether she may have been a little too controlling. She and her husband often had arguments about discipline, with Angela feeling he was too lenient. She expressed the view that American parents were too permissive and that was why their children got into trouble so often. In her eyes, the children were never taught to respect their elders, and they did whatever they pleased.

Her sons chose their wives and she raised no objections except that because Spyros was in college when he met his future wife, his mother at first tried to persuade him to wait until he finished school. He became quite upset about her objections, however, and Angela relented, remembering her own experience with her mother.

Angela was never close to her family even after the reconciliation. She was accepted warmly by all her husband's relatives. She maintained contact with her brothers and sisters, but their lives were not intertwined in any significant way. She visited her mother regularly in Antonia's declining years and was keeping in contact with Christine now that her father lived with her sister.

Angela had definite views about Ann's illness. Michael, in Angela's opinion, gave his wife a hard time. He was too close to his own family and put them ahead of Ann in all things. Moreover, Michael, she thought, felt he was better than Ann's family and did not want to associate with them. Ann had never showed any signs of emotional disturbance when she was growing up. She had it much easier than the rest of them. Furthermore, Angela could see nothing wrong with her sister now. She felt that Ann was better off than any of her brothers and sisters and was living in a better house than any of them. When Ann was discharged from the private hospital and before she was admitted to the state hospital, she stayed at another small private hospital which was not an expensive facility located near the town where the Kontoses lived. At that time, Ann left the hospital without the knowledge of the staff and visited Angela, who saw nothing wrong with her. Ann did tell her that she thought Michael was trying to poison her, and Angela recognized that this was not normal; but otherwise her sister's thinking was perfectly rational. Michael, she felt sure, was the one the interviewer should be talking to.

Christine Demetriou initially resisted the prospect of being interviewed. When the interviewer arrived, she was dressed in a housecoat and announced that she had felt bad all day. She referred to dizzy spells which were probably, she thought, related to her high blood pressure. She had tried to phone the interviewer to postpone the appointment but could not locate her. Since the woman was now here, Christine would struggle, she hinted, to do the best she could to answer questions. She then settled back in a large armchair, placed a pillow behind her head, lifted her legs up onto a footstool, and looking much the invalid indicated she was ready.

The Demetriou home, a single-family house, was located in an attractive neighborhood in a middle-class suburb of Boston. It was furnished well and was obviously well kept and maintained. Christine was a somewhat overweight woman in her middle fifties who, when she finally relaxed, had a warm, effusive manner. She gave information in a direct, candid manner in marked contrast to her initial resistance.

During the initial exchange of amenities with the interviewer, she mentioned her son, Milton. She informed the interviewer that he was currently finishing his Ph.D. work in chemistry at a midwestern university where he had been an outstanding student. His major professor, in fact, had asked him to join the faculty when he completed his doctoral research study the coming June. As Christine talked about her son, her headache seemed to be relieved; she sat up in her chair and was obviously pleased that she had a receptive listener. She rewarded the interviewer by responding from that point on with a readiness to answer all questions.

She described in a more candid way than did her brothers and sisters the strains in their family when they were growing up. Her father, she recalled, was casual about working and thought nothing of telling his bosses off and leaving a job on the spot if he got angry. Her mother assumed the breadwinning role with a great deal of resentment. Antonia worked all the time, at the job and at home, and had little time left over to be involved with the children. The mother paid attention to them only to censure them when they did something wrong.

Christine reported that her mother had often expressed disappointment in not having been allowed by her father to further her education in Greece. Antonia's father, who was a priest, felt that it was more important for the boys to get an education. Somehow Antonia's sister, Christine's aunt, had managed to be allowed to go further in school than Antonia. This fact intensified the mother's disappointment. She conveyed her high regard for education to her own children but also made it clear that, given their financial circumstances, they would have to find their own means of continuing school.

Christine was an excellent student throughout grammar school. In high school she got all A's but had to drop out after her first year to go to work. If her father had not been the kind of man he was, she believed, she would have gone to college.

All the family worked hard, in Christine's judgment, and they were geared to trying to better their position. They were imbued with the determination to find solutions to problems through hard work. Of course, Chrisine noted, Ann had it easier. Christine herself had made sure that her little sister always had decent clothes when she went to school, and the girl was spared a great deal of the financial strain the rest of them experienced. In any case, Ann never showed any signs of emotional difficulties when she was growing up. She was always a bit shy, the quiet, listening type, but that was the way she was, as Christine saw it.

Christine had met her husband at one of the parties her parents held at their house. She had never been allowed to date, even when she was twenty-seven and was assuming a major portion of responsibility in the house. Her marriage was not arranged, however. Her parents approved from the outset; they knew her future husband's relatives, who came from the same village in Greece as they did.

Shortly after Christine married, her in-laws bought a two-family house in Boston, occupied one floor, and invited the newlyweds to move into the other. Christine's husband owned a florist shop, and she worked with him to build up the business. She was still working with him in the florist shop. Her parents had moved in with them in their current house about five years previously, when her mother began having strokes. Her father, who was eighty at the time of the interview, also worked in the florist shop weekdays when it wasn't busy. It took him out of the house and relieved Christine of having him around all the time.

She talked glowingly of her daughter, then in high school and getting all A's and B's. She, too, was headed for college. She was a good girl, her mother stated, who listened to her parents and gave them no trouble. Christine was counseling her about sex matters and discouraging her from dating. Americans were too lax with their children, she felt, and she did not agree that being popular with boys was a good idea. The temptations were many, and it was too easy to get pregnant. Her son knew a girl he dated at college, she reported, but she was only a good friend. Christine had told her son that when he finished his degree and settled in his job and found a girl, then they would sit down and talk about marriage.

In discussing Ann's illness, Christine pointed to the marriage with Michael as the source of the trouble. She was not, however, as overtly hostile toward him as was her sister Angela. She expressed her views in a questioning way as if she were considering various alternatives in trying to understand why Ann got ill.

At times Michael seemed to her courteous, gentlemanly, and generous. At other times, especially in relation to Ann and Ann's family, he became critical and difficult. For example, he blamed Ann's current difficulties on her own family. In order to substantiate this charge, Christine described an incident that occurred when she was driving home with Michael after a visit to Ann at the hospital. Michael had become agitated as he expressed his feeling to his sister-in-law. Ann, he said, was upset because of her family. She was ashamed of the fact that Thalia had been divorced and about the fact that she, Christine, had a child twelve years after her first child. Ann, he continued, was also ashamed and upset about the fact that Christine worked in her husband's shop. At this point in the interview, Christine with great exasperation asked what was wrong with conceiving later in life. "Was this a sin?" Certainly her working was nothing to be ashamed of.

Christine wondered aloud whether these were Michael's own concerns and not Ann's. Ann often told her Michael aspired to be what he wasn't, "a big shot." His joining the tennis club was an example, according to Ann, and as his wife she felt that he "looked like a jerk there with all those professional people and high-class people." Ann had also told Christine that Michael got angry at her and shouted at her at home with the windows open so that the neighbors could hear.

Christine was sure that the strain of living with Michael had made Ann sick, not her own background. Michael had recently told his sister-in-law that he thought Ann would never get better. Christine related this statement in an inquiring fashion, obviously wanting feedback from the interviewer about the accuracy of this prediction. The interviewer assured her that people recovered from Ann's illness and that, as far as could be told, the therapy was progressing well.

Christine also expressed the view that her mother's death could not have caused Ann to get ill, inasmuch as it was expected. Ann was prepared for the death because her mother had had several heart attacks before she died.

Christine talked at length about her sister Thalia's first marriage and divorce, which were clearly perceived by her as a major crisis in the family alongside that of Angela's elopement. Thalia, the third daughter, had been in continual conflict with their mother about dating. She was the only one of the daughters who took a stand on this issue and openly challenged her mother's strict rules. She dated frequently in high school, and, shortly after, she met Bill at a church picnic and she began to date him steadily. Her mother objected because she was not sure what Bill's intentions were. More arguments followed when Bill went into the service and thus confirmed Antonia's suspicions that he had no intention of marrying her daughter. On one of his leaves from the Navy, Bill announced suddenly to Thalia that they were getting married. With no time for a big Greek wedding, they were married in a small ceremony in the Greek Orthodox Church with only their parents and immediate family present. Antonia had mixed feelings about this wedding, but her experience with Angela's elopement seemingly made her less willing to oppose it.

Bill's return to duty two weeks after the marriage kept him and Thalia separated for about a year. After his discharge he got a good job with a large insurance company in Boston. He was a college graduate with a degree in business administration.

Thalia became pregnant shortly after he returned home. Bill had confided to her that he had been with other women during their separation, but she dismissed his infidelity as caused by his loneliness and was glad he could confide in her. Gradually realizing, however, that he was continuing to have affairs, she got a divorce after three years of marriage.

Antonia reacted to her daughter's divorce with a mixture of shame and bitterness. She shouted that she knew the divorce would happen and that Thalia's disobedience had brought disgrace on the whole family. She tried to warn her, the mother went on, but she would not listen. Thalia moved back into her parents' home and went back to work. Five years later she married Carl Martin. She had been married to him for about ten years at the time she was seen by our interviewer.

Thalia made an impression as a very attractive woman who looked considerably younger than her forty-five years. She moved around the kitchen as she talked, preparing her husband's supper in an efficient manner. She seemed all the while to be sizing up the interviewer, and apparently she concluded that the woman could be confided in. When she finally sat down, she related in a disarmingly frank and open manner.

Thalia was the sister Michael first contacted after the episode when Ann ran to the neighbor's house in the middle of the night in her pajamas. Thalia had taken Ann out for lunch the next day, and Ann, who was driving, was so distraught she almost wrecked the car on the way home. Thalia then urged Michael to get Ann to a hospital.

Thalia was aware of the problems that Ann and Michael were having. Michael had called her several times during the past two years to confide in her that Ann wasn't talking much and wouldn't cooperate with him in anything. Thalia tried to help by having lunch with Michael and inquiring what the problems were. Ann knew about the lunches and felt uncomfortable when she was with Thalia. Ann's hospitalization upset Thalia so much that she stayed awake several nights trying to figure out how she could help the couple resolve their differences. Finally she decided that the doctors at the hospital would take care of things, and this reassurance enabled her to fall asleep.

Thalia was less critical of Michael than her brothers and sisters were. She did say Michael thought he was superior to them and that he blamed her family for Ann's illness, but she also recognized that Ann could be difficult to live with. She recalled that Ann was spoiled by her mother when she was growing up. She was never expected to do house work like the rest of the girls, and Antonia used to do Ann's laundry. Thalia had fought a great deal with Ann about this issue when they were girls. Ann's early experience might explain Michael's complaints about his wife as housekeeper and cook.

In discussing her mother, Thalia was direct in saying that she was in constant conflict with her about many things. Antonia had disapproved not only of dating but of anything the girls did outside the house. Her mother didn't want her to play ball, which she loved, because it wasn't ladylike or to take part in the after-school activities planned by her teachers, such as going on picnics or visiting the museums in Boston. Her mother wanted her to stay home and do housework.

What saved her, Thalia felt, was her relationship with her aunt and the aunt's husband, George Kallistou. This aunt took her on vacations with her own daughters, Thalia's cousins, and they frequently visited back and forth between the two houses. She was able to confide in this aunt in a way that she was unable to with her mother. She loved her cousins, who were a lot of fun. In fact, it was her cousins who first told her the facts of life. She was not prepared for menstruation and to this day cannot understand why Christine and Angela, at least, had not informed her. Thalia mused aloud at this point, as a kind of afterthought, that it was too bad Ann had not been so close to her aunt and cousins as she was because her sister missed out on so much as a result.

Thalia described with obvious pleasure the good times they had on Greek outings and Greek dances. Christine and Angela in those days could do Greek dances beautifully, and she was proud of them. She and Ann, who couldn't dance Greek style as well, used to proudly watch their sisters doing the intricate steps of these dances.

Thalia unhesitatingly stated that her father was not a competent wage earner. "It's the women in our house who wore the pants." The only time her father brought home money was when he hit the jackpot in the numbers pool, and these times did not occur often.

Thalia was a good student in school and always got excellent grades. When she graduated from high school, however, she knew there was no money for college. As an alternative, she at first wanted to become an airline stewardess because it was glamorous work and she could travel. However, she decided to take a job instead in the sales office of an auto parts company, and there she was still employed. She took time off to have her child by her first husband and didn't work for about a year after. After her divorce, she went back and worked herself up to her present position of sales manager, a key position in that company. Hers was a "man's job" with a great deal of responsibility. She bossed several salesmen and loved the work.

At the beginning of the second interview, Thalia deftly shifted from the questions posed to her to the unburdening of the many problems she was facing in her current life. It was as if she had prepared for this opportunity, having tested out the interviewer in the first session and found her to be someone she could confide in.

Thalia's second marriage had not turned out any better than the first. Carl, she said, was a near alcoholic. She had met him in the auto parts company, where he had been working at the time as a salesman. There had been no children by this second marriage. She wondered aloud why it was she married the wrong man twice. She then answered her own question by saying that it was because her own parents quarreled all the time and so she never had an opportunity to learn how happily married people live.

She described Carl as an immature man who was angry all the time and who did not get along well with her son, Manny, who was seventeen at the time of the interview. The constant friction between them left her distraught and drained all the time.

Her son was also a constant source of worry to her. He had barely graduated from high school, having been a marginal student all through the four years. She hoped eventually he would go to college, but he was planning to go into the service first. She felt guilty, she said, because she knew some of Manny's difficulties in school were based on the fact that his own father never saw him.

Also, after her divorce, Antonia, with whom she lived, could not cope with Manny, and he had to be boarded out while Thalia worked. When she needed her mother, Thalia said, her mother let her down.

Manny had been seen at the local mental health clinic once when he was about fifteen because he could not concentrate on his work in school and one of the guidance counselors suggested he be evaluated. She worried that perhaps her nagging about studying may have contributed to this problem.

Thalia married her second husband in the Greek Orthodox Church although he remained a nominal Episcopalian. She and her son were members of the Greek Orthodox Church but did not attend regularly. One of the reasons she gave was that her mother had taught her it was a sin to go to church when she was "unclean," that is, menstruating. She did not seem concerned whether her son married a Greek-American girl or a girl from a different background.

Thalia said that she felt close to her own family and maintained close contact with them. She was closer to Angela than she was to Christine, however.

Ann, she felt, was doing much better lately. She had talked to her just that day and Ann told her she was working part time for a company that supplied secretarial help. Thalia expected to see her the coming Sunday when all the family met for the memorial mass for George Kallistou. A get-together after the mass would take place at the home of one of his daughters. Michael would not be there, however, because he was playing tennis that day.

Conflicting Values

The diagnostic evaluation of Ann's mental status, made when she was brought to the hospital, focused entirely on intrapsychic factors. A causal relation was posited between her observed ego disorganization and the perceived psychological deficits that characterized her developmental history. Specifically, the psychological withdrawal of her mother during a critical period in her developmental history was seen as a central factor that resulted in poor ego development and weakened Ann's capacity to deal with stresses in her adult life. The death of her mother and the concomitant onset of menopause were seen as interacting precipitants of the psychotic episode itself.

When they are examined in relation to the cultural and social characteristics of the family in which she was born and in which she developed, the psychological stresses Ann was experiencing take on new meaning. Her extended family as well as that of her husband continued to constitute a field of cultural and social forces within which the new nuclear family they created was functioning. Ann and Michael were also subject to cultural and social forces outside both their nuclear and extended families. This was the American middle-class value system in which husband and wife were socialized in a wider sense and which continued to exert a patterning effect on their behavior. The conflicting roles expected of them and which they expected of themselves reflected discord between the Greek and American value orientation system upon which they were attempting to draw.

The origins of the stresses experienced by Ann in her marriage are found in the presence of conflict in her grandparents' generation. The family of her maternal grandfather, who was the village priest, enjoyed higher social status than her paternal grandfather, who was a sheepherder and a farmer.[1] Furthermore, Ann's maternal grandfather, while not educated to an advanced degree himself, clearly held education in high regard. This value on education was mediated to his two daughters, Antonia and Garoufalia. The elopement of Ann's parents is explained as having been, at least in part, precipitated by this social status discrepancy. In any event, George, by eloping with Antonia, clearly abrogated the authority of his bride's father, whose lineal position traditionally entitled him to decide whom and when the women of his household would marry. It should be underscored that elopement is severely censured in

---

[1] Village priests in Greece have always themselves relied on farming as a means of supporting their families. There is no doubt, however, that they have always enjoyed a high social status in their village communities. While they are not themselves highly educated, they traditionally have more education than their parishioners, for they are required to be able to read and to write. (See Sanders, 1962.)

Greek villages because it reflects a direct challenge to the Lineal > Individual > Collateral value orientation profile that orders interpersonal relations. Elopement is an affront to every Greek father, who is expected to maintain a position of authority in his role of chief provider and protector of his family members. Elopement in this setting also implies irresponsibility in sexual matters, with the assumption that one or both partners must be driven by lust. The shame that this generates is, of course, borne by the entire family.

George's stealing away with a priest's daughter, then, represented a doubly audacious disregard for Greek values and customs and clearly marked him as a deviant in the village community in which he lived. One can speculate that his decision to immigrate to the United States to seek his fortune may have been, in part, motivated by this fact. That Antonia was willing has no bearing on the issue as it would be seen traditionally, for a woman was not expected to be fully responsible for her behavior.

George separated himself from an extended family network in which his father-in-law clearly held the dominant position and in which he was obviously viewed as of low status. He may have hoped, by making money in the United States, to elevate his social position vis-à-vis his family unit in a new world.

George Nicholopoulos in the end, however, did not reject the traditional Greek value orientation pattern as would at first seem to be the case. He did not rebel against authority on principle. Rather, he rejected the low position to which he was delegated in the Lineal hierarchy represented by his wife's extended family and the values of the village. He was determined, it seems, through strong Individualistic drives to create a replica in the United States with himself at the head of the family.

His decision to emigrate by himself and to move quickly from the position of a hired worker for others to the proprietor of his own restaurant reflects his strong individualistic orientation. He is described as working day and night in his restaurant in his effort to make it a success. His corollary Doing and Mastery-over-nature orientation are manifest in this effort. He was not contented, as many of his compatriots were, to hold down a steady job in a factory with an assured income. Nor did he save the money he made in order to return to Greece and resume his life there with his family. He was determined to become a success in the new country through hard work.

Unfortunately he failed. It was the Depression period, when many businesses failed, but George could not see this; when his restaurant burned down his hopes went with it. He could not stand working for other men; emotionally he could not bear to be relegated again to a lowered position in someone else's business. Furthermore, his wife's constant complaining that he was not earning enough to support his family doubled the agony. For her, her husband's failure as a breadwinner must have been a confirmation of her parents' strong objections to her marrying him. She was, indeed, now paying for her sins, as they had warned. He was, beyond doubt, below her socially; her parents were right. In his despair, George Nicholopoulos gave up the battle and withdrew.

He gave up his Individualistic, Doing, Mastery-over-nature, and Future oriented strivings. These orientations that had motivated his entrepreneurial behavior no longer seemed relevant. After that, he behaved very much like a Greek farmer whose crops failed. He withdrew to the coffee shop and allowed the women to work for the bare essentials needed for the family to subsist on. His Doing behavior gave way to Being and his Mastery-over-nature orientation to Subjugated-to-nature, the traditional first-order positions in the Greek village. Consistent with chance and the Subjugated-to-nature position, he relied on the unpredictable winnings that his occasional good fortune would bestow on him in the numbers pool he played at the local variety store. His Being orientation was reflected in the fact that his pleasures came from the companionship of his cronies at the coffee shop and from the celebrations his wife planned at their home rather than from work toward achievement. And since for him there was no longer a hope for the Future, he lived from day to day, in the Present.

In Greece it is possible for a man to retain his Lineal position in the family structure along with a Being, Present-time, and Subjugated-to-nature orientation. In fact, these first-order orientations provide a good fit with a first-order Lineality in the relational orientation modality. This is not the case in the United States. Here one's authority derives from one's demonstrated capacity to achieve an Individualistic orientation. George Nicholopoulos sensed this, and when his efforts at achievement failed, he relinquished his rights as the head of the household.

It seems at first glance that these rights were then assumed by his wife, who is described by Thalia as "wearing the pants in the family." Closer scrutiny of the family structure and functioning after George withdrew shows, however, that this was not the case. The relational value pattern itself was abandoned in the face of the stress that was precipitated by his withdrawal. Antonia assumed a very special breadwinner role which called for Christine, Angela, Gregory, and James to share the responsibility. In other words, a first-order Collaterality become the orienting value in the Nicholopoulos family. The children were expected to collaborate with their mother in the maintenance of the family unit. This collaboration encompassed a broad range of other activities as well. The role of disciplinarian, which was relinquished by the father, was shared among the other family members and was not assumed exclusively by Antonia. Christine is described as exercising this function in relation to the younger children, who also looked to her for guidance and help with the different problems they faced. Gregory described himself as being looked up to by his brother and he was expected by his mother at times to exercise a corresponding disciplinary role. The Collaterality that characterized the family was best described by Christine when she talked about their common determination to better their lot in life. There was a shared preoccupation with finding solutions to the problems that confronted them. All except Ann felt a strong responsibility to contribute economically and emotionally to the maintenance of the family system.

It is also true, however, that Antonia reserved for herself the prerogative of the final authority in critical issues. She decided unilaterally what her daughters' behavior had to be in matters regarding the opposite sex, and she determined how the sparse financial resources would be spent. Lineality, then, is still evident in the patterning of relations among the Nicholopoulos family members but clearly is of secondary importance to Collaterality. The mother's authority was successfully challenged by both Angela and Thalia in their choice of husbands. This is significant, for Antonia had a strong investment in maintaining control over her daughters in these matters because of her own "bad marriage" as she perceived it. She felt she was suffering doubly paying the price of defying her parents' authority but unable to exert sufficient authority of her own to stop her daughters from going their own way.

Individualism was also evident in the patterning of relations in the Nicholopoulos family but in a tertiary, weak fashion. Although the children were encouraged to get more education and through this means to make their own way in the world, this was not supported in any tangible way by Antonia. She mediated to her children the high value set on education by her father. Yet, concurrently, she conveyed the feeling that advanced schooling was out for them because of the lack of financial resources. Ann at one point complained that the money her mother used for the big Greek celebrations they had at their home might have been better used to send the children to college. Even when the financial strain on the family was lessened as the children became adult wage earners, no effort was made by Antonia to encourage any of the younger generation to further their education. Their father, of course, was no help in this matter. He had abandoned his own Individualistic strivings and could not be expected to transmit them to his children. The new value pattern that emerged in the Nicholopoulos family, then, was Collateral > Lineal > Individual. This is the typical pattern that emerged in the group analysis of the value orientation responses of the first-generation members of the with-patient families.

George's economic failure takes on a new significance in the light of his wife's own commitment to achievement values in the form of Doing, Individualism, Mastery-over-nature, and Future orientations. It meant that cherished values she learned from her father would never be realized, and she could not forgive him for this. It was his fault, she believed, that her children were denied the chance to go to college and make something of themselves. Was she not already overburdened with the responsibilities of making money and rearing her children? How could she be expected to do more? Furthermore, only a father, according to the traditional value pattern in Greek culture, could exert enough authority as head of the household to see to it that individualism, in the sense of achievement, was encouraged in his children.

Antonia, therefore, turned to her brother-in-law, the teacher

George Kallistou, as the natural father surrogate. In George's family, the traditional value pattern was maintained. He was clearly the head of the household and as such saw to it that Individualistic strivings in his children were implemented. All of George's children went to college, even though three of them were girls. And it was through George that the hope of achievement was kept alive. In fact, this hope was actualized by Gregory and James after the war when financial resources became available through the G.I. Bill. Christine and Angela actualized this hope through their children. Thalia, in her own way, actualized it in her own successful achievement strivings in business. It was Ann who had the most difficulty in this effort. In a way she was caught in the middle between two conflicting value systems that made the issue of achievement and the issue of choosing in general a very difficult one.

Ann's assigned role in the Nicholopoulos family was clearly different from that of her sisters. Christine, Angela, and Thalia related to the mother more like sister surrogates than daughters. They worked alongside their mother in the factory as seamstresses; and they shared equally the household tasks and child-rearing functions in relation to their younger siblings. In other words, they maintained for the most part a Collateral relation to their mother. Christine and Angela were also identified with Greek culture more than their younger sisters and brothers. They attended Greek functions and were experts in Greek dancing. Ann was the baby of the family, separated from her older sisters by almost a generation. In this role she was not as involved in the Collateral strivings and was even freed from the routine household tasks that her older sisters were expected to do. She was, in fact, actively protected by her mother from these tasks. She was clearly her mother's child.

Why Ann was singled out in this fashion is not entirely clear. Certainly her being the youngest daughter and the youngest child was a factor. It is also consistent with a pattern evident among large families in rural Greece for the parents to assign to one of the children, usually the youngest, the role of provider and supporter of the parents in their old age. This is the child who is expected to remain close to the aging parents and to provide for them when they are too old and infirm to provide for themselves. Certainly Ann, in some ways, served this function for her mother.

Being protected from the obligations of Collaterality exposed Ann to Individualism and the other achievement-oriented values of Doing, Mastery-over-nature and Future time, which her sisters could not be expected to implement. Her mother's own frustrated hopes in this direction must have been mediated to her favored daughter. Furthermore, Ann, in contrast to Christine and Angela, was allowed to finish high school. She therefore experienced the socializing effect of the American school system to a greater extent than they.

Tragically, Ann partly adopted Doing values without acquiring the ability to live with them. She made some feeble attempts to implement these orientations but failed. Her mother encouraged her to join the WACS; considering the strong control Antonia exerted over her other daughters, this was, indeed, a surprising position for her to take in regard to Ann, but nothing came of it. She also encouraged Ann's decision to go to college in a night school program. Ann was not able to see this effort through to successful completion either. The favored daughter had internalized the Individual > Collateral > Lineal pattern and the corollary values in the other areas characterizing American society but lacked the requisite skills. Since the Collateral > Lineal > Individual pattern and the corollary values were the orientations that patterned the behavior of her family, Ann was exposed to a contrasting pull that must have created a great deal of strain.

One result of this strain was the inhibition that characterized Ann's approach to a great many issues. As a young woman she was not willing to be the "good Greek girl" like Christine, content and able to work hard and skillfully in the home. Yet neither was she able to handle higher education and the upward social mobility that this could make possible. She chose instead to work in a bureaucratic system as a secretary until the time she met her husband.

The courtship of Ann and Michael was marked by long separations and obviously a good deal of ambivalence on her part. Michael was probably right when he said that his wife was not prepared for marriage. Ann chose a man who was obviously ambitious, driving, and geared very definitely in the direction of achievement and upward social mobility. He clearly engaged the part of her that placed a high value on these traits. She presented herself to him as a cool, attractive, and sophisticated woman who would surely be an asset to him in realizing his ambitions in the business world.

Ann, however, lacked the interpersonal skills that would have been necessary for her to realize her husband's expectations in this regard. Moving out into "American" society had been problematic for her before marriage. She had skirted activities that would have made demands on her to behave in the Individualistic, Doing manner that her husband now expected. Now, not only was she unprepared, but the inhibiting effect of anxiety blocked her from learning. Preparing dinner parties for Michael's business associates, meeting community leaders, and participating in recreational activities such as those at Michael's club were beyond her capacities. They created stress because she had not been socialized sufficiently into the myriad interpersonal skills that these activities required. She had not gone to college where she could have learned these skills. In fact, she lived at home up to the time she was married.

Michael was not consistent, however, in his desire to have his wife be the ideal middle-class American housewife. He assumed a Lineal, authoritarian position in relation to her and expected her to behave like the dutiful, dependent Greek housewife of the village. He assumed a patriarchal position, in place of his aging father, in his own family and expected his wife to take her place, alongside his mother and sisters, in this extended family unit. Ann was not prepared for this role, either. She saw herself as an independent and resented deeply her husband's assumptions of supremacy. She likewise resisted her mother-in-law's intrusions in her home and said she could not communicate with her because the woman spoke only Greek. Ann was saying, in effect, that she was too Individualistic and too "American" to be placed in this role by her husband. Furthermore, she had not learned the household skills that would have made it possible for her to implement the role of the good Greek housewife even if she wanted to.

Ann's marriage, then, exacerbated conflict between her American and Greek values. She was unable to function competently in either system, whereas her husband expected her to function effectively in both at the same time. The marked inhibition she showed before she became ill is understandable in the light of the conflicting pull of expectations based on discrepant value orientations. These stresses gradually must have become too much to bear, and Ann had few resources with which to deal with them.

There was one way in which she could find some relief. She could become her mother's child and find some purpose and some feeling of efficacy in ministering to her aging parent. Ann then, fulfilled the role she had been in one way prepared for and alleviated in this way the stresses that her marriage had exacerbated for her. But this was, at best, a precarious resolution of a continuing conflict. She tried awkwardly to please her husband in his relentless demands that she participate in the many social activities he was constantly planning. Her relation to her mother provided a refuge from the stresses that this effort engendered. When her mother died, this source of support was taken away, and she could no longer contain the anxiety that finally engulfed her.

The critical importance of Ann's relation to her mother becomes clearer when we look at her relation to her family after she married. She was described by her sisters and brothers as being better off than the rest of them. She lived in the nicest house, in a suburb, and was economically better off than they were. The life style sought by Michael and Ann, in contrast to the way Ann's siblings lived, had all the earmarks of the American middle class. Collateral ties to Ann's extended family were at best weak. Ann's extended family, after her marriage, was not available to her as a support system on which she could rely in times of crisis. Michael would not have it, for one thing. He clearly disdained Ann's family. His own life style was different from theirs. He considered himself more "American" than they were, and their perception of him as feeling superior to them was based on this orientation. It is not clear, either, whether Ann herself saw her siblings as potential sources of support. She saw herself as the independent middle-class matron leading a modern life in the suburbs. Michael's relation to his own family was more Lineally oriented than Collateral. He was a source of support to his parents and his sisters.

His mother, in fact, tried to make herself available when Ann had her children. The older woman came into their home to help out. Ann, however, would have none of it. She reacted violently to this "intrusion." The support she got from her own mother did not really reflect the operation of Collateral values either. Her mother had never been a source of emotional understanding and support. Theirs was rather a relation in which her mother had fostered a dependence and allowed a very passive form of feeling protected and cared for to develop. It was only when Ann became acutely ill that Michael relented and allowed Ann's siblings to become involved and to provide the support they now both needed to get through a difficult situation.

Even when the crisis struck, however, Michael's middle-class values reinstated themselves. He wanted his wife to have the best treatment in a hospital that served primarily a wealthy clientele and that, incidently, he could not afford. Ann's discomfort in these middle-class surroundings was an extension of the stress that brought her there in the first place.

Michael's inconsistent behavior in his relation with Ann reflects the alternate effect of the middle-class American and traditional Greek value orientations that operated in his life. In the work situation he behaved very much like the Individualistically oriented, Doing, middle-class businessman. He behaved this way also in his relation with the community in which they lived, where he was constantly planning athletic activities. This emphasis shifted, however, when he assumed the role of husband in his own home and father surrogate with his siblings and parents. In these situations his strong Lineality asserted itself, and he became very much the Greek patriarch. This inconsistency reflects the competing force of the two value systems that he was responding to and the transitional point in the acculturation process he found himself in.

For the most part, Michael was able to handle this conflict reasonably well by compartmentalizing the two behavior spheres in which he operated. He was not always successful, however, in this effort. In the business situation, for example, he had difficulty with his boss and with those who worked for him. His very weak Collaterality made collaboration with both difficult. He resented being exploited by a boss whom he felt had little competence. Michael's strong Individualism was preceded in importance by a strong Lineality. His strong and successful Individualistic efforts meant to him that he had to be in the position of leadership. He could not easily tolerate being in a secondary position of power in his company. By the same token, he felt that in his absence those working for him would take advantage of him. They had to resent him for being boss and could not be expected to act responsibly in his absence. Michael, then, in many ways was much more "Greek" in the sense of Lineal > Individual > Collateral than was Ann. Though she was not able to implement an Individual > Collateral > Lineal pattern in her own life, she felt correctly that her husband was behaving toward her in an authoritarian manner that was not consistent with the correct way an American husband ought to behave. She could not accept, therefore, the role he tried to cast her in.

Family Style

Let us now examine how Ann's sisters and brothers coped with the acculturation stress that they also were subjected to. In the case of Christine and Angela the issues are the most clear. By retaining the Collateral > Lineal > Individual pattern, they were able, for the most part, to bypass the acculturation stresses. They had no other choice. They worked hard, but Doing and Individualism in the sense of achievement were postponed until the next generation. Through their sons and daughters these cherished values came to fruition.

Christine married a Greek-American who was approved of by her parents and who was himself born in Greece; they bought a two-family dwelling and moved her parents and younger siblings in with her. The first-order Collateral pattern was reinforced. She became the major power in her new family, simulating her own mother's role, and she provided concurrently for her extended family, which is a clear sign of her strong Collaterality. Her own children, however, achieved—and with a vengeance. The old hopes and dreams of her mother and her father and herself were at last fulfilled.

This was no less the case with Angela. Her husband was also born in Greece; she adopted her husband's family and perpetuated the strong Collateral orientation of her own family. She lived with her in-laws in the same house; they took care of her children, and she worked hard to be sure the children went to college and achieved. Again the dream was fulfilled. Her own husband seemed also to be somehow in the background. It was Angela who, like Christine, provided the driving force for achievement in her sons.

Both Christine and Angela saw to it that their children attended the Greek Orthodox Church and Greek school regularly. Their mother had learned to value education from her father, who was a priest, and the children's uncle, George Kallistou, had reinforced this orientation. The Greek church and the Greek school, therefore, were, for them, vehicles for the maintenance and development of orientations to higher education and achievement. As we pointed out in Chapter Six, for Greeks living in the United States, the monumental accomplishments of the ancient Greeks are a continuing source of pride and motivation for achievement in the "land of opportunity." Christine and Angela's children were exposed to this Greek heritage in Greek schools, and this exposure must have buttressed the value orientations that their mothers inculcated at home.

In contrast to Christine and Angela, Thalia took a decidedly American direction in resolving the conflict between Greek and American value orientations. She early challenged her mother's authority to dictate in these matters. She did not escape from the conflict by eloping, as did Angela, but insisted on dating openly and finally choosing a husband who seemingly showed promise of achieving in middle-class American terms. Since she herself could not go to college, she chose to achieve in a job that required a high degree of independent capability. When her first marriage did not work out, she did not hesitate to get a divorce in spite of the strong disapproval of her mother. Her second husband was not Greek, and her ties to the Greek community in this marriage were weak.

Her difficulties with her second husband she identified as psychological problems for which she sought help from the research interviewer. This is a neutral view of human nature that is the preferred orientation in middle-class America. She questioned what the cause of these problems might be and described her own role in a way that reflected her ability to achieve psychological distance from those problems. She was able to see that her parents' difficulties were related to her own. In other words, in seeking expert advice from the interviewer and in identifying the difficulties she was having as psychological problems she took a Mastery-over-nature and Doing attitude.

She had supported her son when he sought professional help for his problems, and she concluded that his difficulties were caused by the absence of a stable father figure. She was in these matters evaluating and behaving in a typical American fashion— calling upon experts to solve problems through technical knowledge and skills.

Also, in relation to Ann and Michael's difficulties she could at last relax her efforts to help them when she decided that the psychiatrists at the hospital would, as experts, assume the responsibility for solving their problems. This approach of Thalia's is contrasted with the reaction of Christine and Angela, who blamed Ann's difficulties on Michael's "bad" character. Theirs was the more traditional Greek approach, where the source of interpersonal difficulties is believed to lie in the bad character of one or several of the individuals involved. This evil-good view of human nature characterizes traditional Greek culture. Mental illness, too, in Greek culture is viewed as reflecting the "bad," imperfect nature of an individual and carries the corollary stigma. For Angela and Christine, then, it was not Ann who was "crazy" (that is, "bad"), it was Michael.

Michael's own position in relation to Ann's illness also reflected a conflict between the traditional Greek way and the American middle-class value orientation. On the one hand, he saw a need for Ann to get expert medical care to solve her psychiatric problem; on the other hand, he attributed her illness to her family's character. They were all "crazy," so Ann was crazy. No doubt he too was imbued with the good-evil view of human nature typical of traditional Greek culture.

Thalia, like her sisters Christine and Angela and unlike Ann, assumed a dominant—that is, Lineal—position in relation to her second husband. She clearly wore the pants in her family and in this respect she identified with her mother. In the relational area, the pattern that emerges is Individual > Lineal > Collateral.

Although a second order Lineality worked well in Christine's and Angela's marriages, in Thalia's relationship with her husband, it was a source of continuing strain. For Christine and Angela the first-order Collaterality made for a collaborative effort between husband and wife in the work area that mitigated the effect of the second-order Lineality. Christine worked with her husband in the shop, and Angela worked as a stitcher from the beginning of her marriage. Their dominance in family matters was not felt acutely by their Greek husbands, who must have believed that they were relegating the affairs of their households to their wives. Also it seems Christine and Angela must have given them their due in Greek cultural terms—that is, treated them with the respect they needed to have as Greek males in their homes.

For Thalia however, the situation was quite different. Her strong Individualism and her high level of accomplishment in her job resulted in a competitive relationship with her American husband. The presence of the son from her first marriage in the home accentuated this competitive struggle. Mr. Martin's position vis-à-vis his wife was never secured. He constantly had to prove his worth to a wife who was obviously more competent in the occupational area than he was. She maintained her dominant position further by playing her son off against him. His heavy drinking was probably related to the stress that this struggle engendered in him. Whatever intrapsychic conflicts he brought with him to the marriage must have been accentuated by this conflict.

Thalia, like her sisters, wanted her son to go to college. The strong drive for success in American terms was also mediated by her to him. She was deeply distressed by his emotional difficulties, in part because she saw them as an impediment to his furthering his studies and achieving.

Let us look now at the modes of adjustment that characterized the men in the Nicholopoulos family. The two brothers, Gregory and James, pursued advanced education through the G.I. Bill when they returned from the service. They also, then, moved in the direction of implementing achievement values in American terms. However, only James obtained a college degree. Gregory, who was described as the most gifted son academically, attended a four-year vocational school; he acquired skills in a manual trade and worked in what were essentially blue-collar jobs. And even though James's degree in economics meant professional status in the occupational area, his life style was the same as that of his brother. They lived in working-class neighborhoods, and they married Greek-American wives and maintained close ties to the Greek Orthodox church and the Greek community.

Thus, Gregory and James did not adopt middle-class American value orientations fully. They moved further in this direction than did Christine and Angela, but the value orientations they had internalized in their home when they were growing up continued to have strong valence for them.

The clear family centeredness in their respective households suggests that Collaterality remained a strong first-order orientation. This Collaterality was also evident in the relation between their households. They lived in the same two-family dwelling and so communicated with each other daily. The brothers saw each other frequently and did things together in an extended family manner.

Gregory and James were both clearly the heads of their households. A second-order Lineality is seen in their roles as husbands and fathers. James's wife complained that he was unwilling to help her with household tasks, and she resented being left on Sundays when he played golf with his brother. He was not, in other words, behaving in the egalitarian manner expected of an American husband. He, in fact, was exercising the prerogatives of a Greek—that is, Lineal—father.

Both Gregory and James and their wives disapproved of American permissive child-rearing practices. They could not accept the American notion of fostering independence if that conflicted with parental (Lineal) authority. As far as they were concerned, parents still knew what was best for children.

There was evident, then, an ambivalence and a resultant confusion as to which behavior, Greek or American, was to be the approved one in their households. Gregory and James both expressed the hope that their children would marry Greeks. In this respect they did not differ from Christine and Angela, and they obviously did differ from Ann and her husband, whose ties in the Greek culture were weak.

Since Gregory and James wanted their children to pursue a college education, achievement values were also present. For Gregory, however, this desire appeared to be more of a wish than a goal that was being realistically planned for. His son in fact was going to a technical school as he had done. James, who was himself college educated, had internalized these values in a more complete fashion. In contrast to his older brother, then, he seems to have moved a bit further in the adoption of American achievement orientations. His children probably have gone further in that direction than he did, while Gregory's offspring have not. Perhaps the fact that Gregory was older, and therefore in one sense more exposed to parental influence, may account for this difference.

8

The Ethnic Family and
Culture Change

I n this chapter we shall consider the unique problems of adaptation faced by ethnic families in the changing American scene. Our major focus is on the 1960s as a decade of significant social and cultural changes in the United States. We analyze also, from the point of view of cultural value orientation theory, the special character of the problems faced by nonwhite ethnics, principally Blacks, Mexican-Americans, and American Indians, and contrast them to those faced by so-called white ethnics such as Italians, Greeks, Jews, and Poles. We discuss the interrelation of these two major segments of ethnic America, as each attempted, through different yet connected pathways, to meet the new demands of a social order that they themselves were changing and that in turn was changing them.

The modes of acculturation employed by ethnic groups and illustrated in the three case histories were presented in relation to American core value patterns. (See Table 9 for an interpretive key to value orientation preferences.) Ethnic subcultures resolve the discordance between the traditional values they bring with

Table 9.

VALUE ORIENTATION MODALITIES AND PREFERENCES: AN INTERPRETATIVE KEY

Modalities	Value Orientation Preferences		
Activity	*Doing:* Emphasis is on activity measurable by standards conceived as external to the acting individual, i.e., achievement. (American core culture)	*Being:* Emphasis is on activity expressing what is conceived as given in the human personality, i.e., the spontaneous expression of impulses and desires. (Mexican rural society)	*Being-in-Becoming:* Emphasis is on the kind of activity which has as its goal the development of all aspects of the self as an integrated whole. (Classical Greek Society, Yoga, Gestalt psychology)
Relational	*Individualism:* Individual goals are preferred to group goals; relations are based on individual autonomy; reciprocal roles are based on recognition of the independence of interrelating members. (American core culture)	*Collaterality:* Individual goals are subordinated to group goals; relations are based on goals of the laterally-extended group; reciprocal roles are based on a horizontal, egalitarian dimension. (Italian extended family)	*Lineality:* Group goals are preferred to individual goals; relations on a vertical dimension are hierarchically ordered; reciprocal roles are based on a dominance-submission mode of interrelation. (British upper-classes)
Time	*Future:* The temporal focus is based on the future; emphasis is on planning for change at points in time extending away from present to future. (American core culture)	*Present:* The temporal focus is based on the present; the past gets little attention; the future is seen as unpredictable. (Italian and Latin American societies)	*Past:* The temporal focus is based on the past; tradition is of central importance. (Traditional Chinese society)
Man-nature	*Master-over-nature:* Man is expected to overcome the natural forces and harness them to his purpose. (American emphasis on technology to solve all problems)	*Subjugation-to-nature:* Man can do little to counteract the forces of nature to which he is subjugated. (Spanish rural society)	*Harmony-with-nature:* Man's sense of wholeness is based on his continual communion with nature and with the supernatural. (Japanese and Navaho Indian societies)
Human nature	*Evil:* Man is born with a propensity to do evil. Little can be done to change this state, so the only hope is for control of evil propensities. (Puerto Rican culture)	*Mixed:* Man has natural propensities for both good and evil behavior. *Neutral:* Man is neither good nor bad innately. He is shaped by the environment he is exposed to. (American core culture)	*Good:* Man is innately disposed to good behavior. Society, the environment, etc., corrupt him. (Neo-Freudians)

them and those that confront them in the United States through intragroup social structural changes that make it possible to retain some of the old ways while effecting a degree of adaptation to the new ones. The peer group in Italian-American culture and the enclave community in Greek-American culture are two primary examples of such social structural arrangements. Both these forms have their origins in the traditional societies of the respective groups but have been modified to meet the value orientation demands of American society. In the case of the Italian-American peer group, Individualism and independence are expressed through the Collaterally structured group. The peer group makes it possible to express one's independence and separateness from the family without the necessity of divorcing oneself from it through achievement-oriented strivings in American middle-class terms. The psychological stress that this latter course would entail is therefore muted. Greek-Americans utilize the enclave community to reaffirm those aspects of traditional culture that are congruent with American core values, that is, the emphasis on individualistic, achievement-oriented behavior. At the same time, the Greek community provides a buffer against the shock of culture change, an arena where Greek Being-oriented behavior can be expressed through the reaffirmation of ethnic identity and the sense of intragroup solidarity that this involves.

These intragroup structural changes are only partially successful, however, in reducing the stress of acculturation. Stress is especially pronounced in the relations between generations because of the varying degrees to which traditional value orientations are abandoned and American ones are adopted. It is also evident in role conflict within the same generation. A spouse, for example, may adopt American values at a more rapid rate than his or her marital partner. Tony Tondi, for example, adopted American value orientations in certain areas, whereas his wife, Celia, remained close to the Italian rural patterns. In addition, intraindividual stress results when a person adopts particular American value orientations while retaining others of his traditional culture. For example, adopting Doing and Individualism while retaining a Present-time orientation can make for a considerable amount of inner conflict and frustration as one attempts to engage in achievement-oriented behavior. The case of Ann Constantine provides a good example of the nature of internal stress which such a resolution generates.

The stress of adapting to a new culture can be great. But what if that new culture itself is undergoing change, compounding the stress of adaptation? We discuss this consideration here in the light of a changing American culture.

Changing Sociocultural Conditions in the United States

The traditional American pattern, with first-order emphasis on Doing, on Individualism, on the Future, and on Mastery-over-nature, is being challenged by important segments of American society. The challenge is two-pronged. First, the Protestant ethic itself is being questioned for demanding individual achievement at the cost of other human needs, principally in the aesthetic and affective areas—that is, the Being, Collateral, Present-time, and Harmony-with-nature value orientations. The Subjugated-to-nature alternative seems not to have ever been a viable one in the United States since the whole thrust of the cultural change process was toward less dependence on authoritarian structures. The second aspect of this challenge is the unmasking of the covert authoritarian relational values that pattern institutional arrangements in much of American society. Behind the overt Individual > Collateral > Lineal pattern that guides the formal socialization process in American institutions, it has become apparent that a covert Individual > Lineal > Collateral pattern exists. Though Individualism continues to be the first-order preference in this covert pattern, it is backed by a second-order Lineality, while Collaterality is relegated to a third-order position. Supposedly abhorring authoritarianism in any form, Americans in fact function in hierarchically structured settings. The school system, for instance, teaches children to be individualistic and independent while the system itself is administered through a hierarchy that includes a superintendent, principals, department heads, and so on. Administrative decisions, to be sure, are arrived at through numerous committees that provide the trappings and feeling of a second-order Collaterality. However, in the last analysis, one's position in the hierarchy determines how much power he or she can employ in decision-making for the system as a whole.

A close look at the social structure of industry, of bureaucratic agencies, and of the executive and legislative branches of the federal government confirms the point. Although the Constitution is based on the principles of open elections, majority rule, and a balance of power between the executive, legislative, and judicial branches of government, the observance of these principles in practice does not conform in all respects to the intentions of its founders. The country's democratic institutions, it seems, are not as democratic as had been believed.

Awareness of the high cost of demanding achievement above everything and awareness of the gap between democratic theory and authoritarian practice has been stimulated by various social movements over the past two decades. These movements have been mobilized for the purpose of confronting one or the other of these two aspects of American culture. The so-called youth movement of the sixties was guided clearly by both of the above considerations.

The issues that motivated youth to take group action against the "system" varied. Young people protested against the war in Vietnam, discrimination against minority groups, pollution of the environment by large industries, and "authoritarian" administrative structures in a broad range of institutions. These protests ranged from direct confrontation—sometimes violent—against the power structure in high schools and universities to peaceful demonstrations such as those against the war in Vietnam staged in the nation's capital. Alternative life-style arrangements and various communal patterns in part also constituted a protest and a clear rejection of middle-class norms. The drug subculture represented another way of "dropping out" from the system. Timothy Leary urged his audiences to "tune in, turn on, and drop out," and the thousands that followed his direction created a major social problem in our times. The appeal of the encounter group movement with its emphasis on the expression of feelings and learning to be oneself reflected the perception that the established modes of interaction in our society do not provide adequate opportunity to meet these needs.

The themes that undergirded the various manifestations of rebellion against the "system" are not difficult to discern. The dominant one is a growing awareness among young people of the discrepancy between the professed values of their society, which they internalized in their formative years, and the actual functioning of the various institutions that confront them as they reach maturity. Though conflict between the old and the young has cropped up at all times and in all places, its manifestations in the United States in the sixties had far-reaching effects on the evolution of the culture itself. What was at issue here was not principally the abhorrence of authoritarian values themselves. That was taken for granted. What produced outraged response was the discovery that the national behavior was at variance with what they had been socialized into believing was the reality. The cognitive dissonance (see Festinger, 1962) that this realization created and the pain that it engendered found its expression in various manifestations of protest against the "establishment." The unbearable dissonance needed to be resolved. Things had to be made "right" again.

The momentum provided by the youth movement spread to other issues as well. The women's liberation movement (see Greer, 1971; and Friedan, 1963) and the community mental health movement (see Ryan, 1969) are two of the more visible examples. The drive for equal rights for women, originating late in the nineteenth century, became an effective social movement in the sixties. Male chauvinism was the immediate target of attack; the social system which relegated women to an inferior status was the main focus of the movement. Women organized effectively to change hiring practices and salary scales. They vociferously challenged the role of mother and housewife assigned to them and fought successfully for the right to be viewed in terms of individual merit and not of sex. The success of their continuing effort is evidenced in the increased frequency with which women now appear on boards of directors of large corporations, in prestigious government positions, and in other spheres of activity previously limited almost entirely to men.

The community mental health movement is based on equal opportunity for adequate mental health services for all citizens.

The "middle-class" nature of traditional psychiatry was described in a study by Ryan (1969). It became progressively more apparent through this and other studies that the mental health establishment was geared to providing psychotherapy to those who, by virtue of their education and ability to pay high fees, were in a position to avail themselves of it. Mental health clinics provided only limited service to the select few who could adapt to the psychotherapeutic situation, that is, those who could learn to interact on a one-to-one basis with a therapist and were able to "work through" their problems over an extended period of weekly sessions. Since the poor and uneducated were not oriented to this mode of getting help for their problems, they were labeled "noncooperative" or "antitherapeutic" and summarily dropped. Principally, the clinics served to train in individual psychotherapy mental health professionals who then practiced it on a private basis. (See also Bellak, 1964.)

The climate of the sixties brought the intrinsic undemocratic (that is, Individual > Lineal > Collateral) nature of this system into sharp relief. The realization that the needs of all citizens could not be served in this way led to a reexamination of the entire structure of the nation's mental health delivery system. The changes embodied in the community mental health movement were reflective of the underlying value shift that the country as a whole experienced. The emphasis now was on "primary prevention," on community-based programs and on community control of the system itself. The primary-prevention approach saw the sources of psychological stress in the environment, that is, the "system," and geared its efforts to devising epidemiological methods for reducing the incidence of mental illness in large populations. Community-based programs were designed to provide services for citizens in their own neighborhoods, not in clinics in middle-class areas where they usually never ventured or in hospitals to which they were transported only when they became too ill to function. And community control allowed the average citizen to judge the system based on his, and not a professional's, needs.

The youth movement of the sixties was not limited to a challenge of the authoritarian, that is, the second-order Lineal, value orientations that patterned the relational area in American culture. It was directed also to the reexamination of the value orientations that patterned life in the other areas, that is, the activity, time, and man-nature modalities. The Protestant work ethic with its emphasis on achievement (Doing > Being > Being-in-becoming), on planning for the future (Future > Present > Past), and on overcoming problems by technological means (Mastery-over > Subjugated-to > Harmony-with), also was brought into question. These middle-class orientations, it was felt, did not produce the happiness and sense of individual fulfillment that they promised. Young people had only to look at the older generation to find confirmation for their emerging doubts. The youth movement provided a stage for experiencing value orientations that were not available to them through conventional life styles. These were the Being, Collateral, Present-time and Harmony-with-nature orientations. The emergence of these value orientations as the preferred patterns for living is described by Kenniston (1968). In the summer of 1967, an organization called Vietnam Summer was organized by young men and women for the purpose of opposing the war in Southeast Asia. Kenniston was asked to study the group from a sociopsychological perspective, and, in the course of doing so, he interviewed several members. Revealing insights emerged.

These young radicals were not motivated in their anti-establishment efforts by a clearly formulated political ideology. The New Left was not interested in attacking the capitalistic system as such and was not interested in an alternative, socialistic political philosophy, as some of its critics have suggested. Its adherents talked instead of the alternate ways of experiencing life that their movement provided. It allowed them to recognize and express a broad range of emotions that were previously neglected or shunned in conventional settings. Individualistic needs were subordinated to group purposes, freeing the individuals involved to "be themselves." No longer burdened by any strivings for success in career terms, they could dedicate themselves instead to effecting changes in what they saw to be an unjust system. This made it possible for them to enhance their individuality and discover the unique emotional and intellectual resources they already had instead of shaping their behavior to meet the demands of the marketplace.

These views are expressed in the comments of one person

interviewed by Kenniston (1968, p. 25), who was asked by him whether she had ever thought about abandoning the work of the movement:

> No, I've been really very happy. This is one of the things I feel very positive about . . . One of the things I've learned in the last two years is that you don't need very much to live on. . . . It gives me a completely different perspective on what it is that I decide to go into. I wouldn't mind having a car, but I would have to learn to drive first. I can think of ways to enjoy a nice way of life, but I don't feel obsessed by it. . . .
>
> I sort of feel myself to be open and I feel very happy. It is like I have built a whole new world. It has been a very good transition. I feel I have a solid foundation. . . . I just saw a friend of mine from ten years ago the other day, and it was very difficult to talk to her. . . . You realize that the people you want to be your friends are the people where you don't have to go through the whole process of justifying why you're doing what you're doing. . . . You end up eliminating a lot of your old friends. . . . The kind of people who get involved in the movement are really people who have a strong need for friendship. . . . I don't feel as politically conscious as maybe I should. Maybe I'm approaching things much more pragmatically. How do you build something? How do you get things done?

The value orientations underpinning these expressions of a new philosophy of life are readily seen. They reflect a commitment to a Collateral orientation as the preferred mode of interpersonal relations and the abandonment of the first-order Individualism that characterizes American core culture. This Collaterality is buttressed by acceptance of the Being-in-becoming over the Doing orientation. The spontaneous experience of individuality in the group is preferred over Doing in the sense of working for the achievement of individual goals independently. And the major time focus of the movement is the Present; changes must take place now and not in some distant Future. The Mastery-over-nature orientation, with its emphasis on technological competence to overcome problems, is dropped in favor of a Harmony-with-nature emphasis.

Kenniston also points out another important feature of the

attitudes expressed by members of the New Left. They believed that the new radicalism they were advocating was in fact consistent with the basic philosophy of America—a philosophy from which the country had deviated. They saw their movement as a return to the real values of the past.

Ethnic Groups in the Sixties

For members of ethnic groups in the United States in the sixties, the situation was indeed a confusing one. The American dream they were striving to achieve was being rejected by those Americans who were already in possession of it. Second- and third-generation members of ethnic groups who were striving to make it into the system were confronted with the spectacle of thousands of their contemporaries rushing to leave it in one form or the other. In the process of trying to "make it" in American middle-class terms, many ethnics had separated themselves from their own subcultural groups. Now they became aware that their native American contemporaries were advocating a return to those very Being, Collateral, and Present-time orientations that undergirded the ethnic subcultures they were leaving. The sense of alienation experienced by America's radical youth and their efforts to find meaning through the formation of various movements, that is, subcultures of their own, provided the impetus for "hyphenated" Americans to reexamine their own particular heritages in a different light. What was previously viewed as an impediment to their striving for upward social mobility was now seen as a resource they could turn back to in order to reaffirm their own distinctiveness and "personhood."

Black Americans took the lead in this direction. In the early days of the civil rights movement in the fifties, the major goal of Martin Luther King and his followers was the integration of the Black population with the rest of American society. His crusade was a continuation of the work of the National Association for the Advancement of Colored People (NAACP), which had labored for many years to combat anti-Negro prejudice in the United States and further the opportunities for Blacks to gain a firm position in American society.

This vision, however, led to disillusionment in the sixties. Integration, it was argued by many Blacks, was not proceeding fast enough in spite of the Supreme Court decision of 1954. Despite new opportunities for upward social mobility, the dissatisfaction of Blacks showed signs of increasing rather than decreasing. The riots of the middle sixties gave testimony to the rage felt by Blacks at the discrimination they had experienced over the past century. The eruption of violence in Watts and Newark gave full vent to this rage. As the violent protest in the Black ghettos mounted, the push for full integration into the American social system lost its momentum. Militant Black leaders argued for a movement toward separatism, the rejection of the white society that had for so long rejected them. Some of the more extreme advocated a return to Africa, while the majority looked to strengthening the Black community itself and developing its economic and social resources. Social scientists took positions on opposite sides of the integration-segregation controversy that emerged.

The course that Blacks intended to follow, however, soon became clear. The measure of freedom from discrimination they had achieved would be employed to reaffirm their ethnic identity. They revitalized an interest in their African heritage and the slogan "Black Is Beautiful" became a symbol of their determination to be viewed as a group with unique and valuable characteristics. The push now was for upgrading the standard of living in the Black community itself. Black businesses, aided by federal funding, increased in number and in the range of services they could provide for the Black community. Through Model Cities and other federally funded programs, new housing in Black areas was built and old housing rehabilitated where possible. Moving to the suburbs, for Blacks who could afford it, became less attractive than remaining in the core city and improving living conditions there. The decision to remain in a Black community now became a viable alternative to being subjected to white prejudice in a non-Black suburb. More importantly, the Black community provided that sense of group identification and group solidarity that could not be found elsewhere. It was here that people could be themselves and enjoy the experience of living with those of a common heritage, with interrelated needs and aspirations and hopes. The feelings of alienation experienced by radical youth had been more poignantly felt by Blacks. Black youth could not commit themselves to the cause of furthering the welfare of their ethnic group except from the context of the Black ethnic subculture itself. They now derived the strength to fight the system from their participation in the "Black experience" and their evolving sense of Black consciousness. They no longer had to view their color as a necessary handicap in the effort to forge a place for themselves in the white core society.

In universities throughout the country Black studies programs were created where Black history was taught and the African heritage of American Blacks rediscovered. Black students organized themselves to combat discrimination in their respective institutions and demanded and received the right to participate in the formation of administrative policies that affected them. Certain television programs were produced specifically for Black audiences. Black culture was promoted, and the achievements of Black leaders in various spheres of activity were given primary exposure. The message was clear. Blacks could no longer be viewed as second-class citizens.

The Black community, then, intensified the two-pronged challenge to American core values discussed above. They opposed both the overt Individual > Collateral > Lineal and the covert Individual > Lineal > Collateral. The Black example helped to counteract the sense of alienation experienced by many Americans. The isolation and loneliness, the muting of spontaneity and joy which the Doing and Individualistically oriented middle-class society required, was counterbalanced by the Being, Collateral, and Present-time orientation of the Black subculture. This does not mean that strivings for individual achievement were abandoned. It means, rather, that the consolidation of the Black subculture provided an "ingroup" where spontaneous feeling could be expressed, where one's sense of individual value could be affirmed, and where one could be psychologically strengthened to cope with the demands of the Protestant work ethic more effectively. Individual achievement now was experienced within the context of a first-order Collateral orientation. One's individual achievements became a reflection of group membership, of Black identification which enhanced the status of all Blacks. The challenge to the covert Individual > Lineal > Collateral pattern is, of course, reflected in the collective movement against the continuing paternalistic policies and practices in American society which deprive Blacks of equal opportunities.

White ethnic groups reacted initially with hostility to the Black movement. Lower-income groups continued to resist the expansion of the Black community into previously all-white neighborhoods. The inroads made into previously all-white labor unions also created anxieties and predisposed many negatively to the Black movement. However, a development corollary to the consolidation of the Black community gradually became evident. This development was the emergence of white ethnic groups reaffirming themselves as distinctive minorities.

While white ethnic groups have always maintained subcultures of their own in America, they have rarely taken open stands to emphasize those characteristics that distinguish them from "native" Americans. The trend, rather, had been to deemphasize differences in accordance with the "melting pot" demands of American core culture in the occupational and social spheres. The reinforcement of one's ethnic identity was reserved by hyphenated Americans, if at all, for associations within their respective subcultures. Many ethnics were associated with institutions of their subculture from birth until death, and took their primary social relations from among members of their own ethnic group.

Cultural pluralism, then, as Gordon (1964) and others (see Glazer and Moynihan, 1963) described it was certainly always a reality on the American scene. The reality of it, however, was rarely advocated overtly as the preferred mode of living. Ethnics viewed themselves as Americans of this or that background, and reference by others to their ethnicity was felt, at best, to be an act of bad taste. The dearth of research by social scientists on this reluctance to be studied as an ethnic subculture. Undoubtedly, American ethnic groups in the past fifty years bears testimony to this sensitivity derives from the aversive consequences of being viewed as "foreign"—that is, different and alien.

This picture began to shift in the sixties. The vociferous determination by Blacks to be valued because of, rather than in spite of, the color of their skin earned the respect of white ethnics in whom a responsive chord had been struck. A trend now became evident. Ethnic groups began to assert themselves in terms of the distinctiveness of their cultural background.

The Blacks were followed in this trend first by the Mexican-Americans and by the American Indians. The talk was of Brown Power and Red Power. The Chicano movement in the Southwest was organized around the issue of the exploitation of migrant Mexican-American farm workers by their white employers. Under the dynamic leadership of Cesar Chavez, broader issues relating to the economic territorial rights of Mexican-Americans in the Southwest were later raised. A direct challenge was mounted against the past and present exploitative practices of the United States government, which was accused of illegally appropriating lands that rightfully belonged to Mexican-American farmers and either leasing them to white farmers or designating them national forests. The Chicano movement took on a more comprehensive character in the form of the open assertion of pride by Mexican-Americans in their heritage. They served notice that the stereotype of the lazy Mexican basking in the sun under his sombrero would no longer be tolerated. Mexican-American studies programs appeared in universities in the Southwest where young second- and third-generation Mexican-Americans rediscovered their heritage and identified in a new way with the culture of their forefathers.

The American Indian also asserted himself. Loss of territorial rights, humiliation by the Bureau of Indian Affairs, and any number of long-endured injustices became fighting issues. The squalor of the reservation could no longer be tolerated. Indian leaders attacked the stereotype of the Indian savage scalping women and children until he is brought down by the guns of the hearty Western frontiersman. With the American Indian Movement (AIM), the cause of Indian rights was reaffirmed on the foundation of Indian history and culture. Indian studies programs now were revitalized in schools on reservations. American Indian intellectuals came forth to lend their support to a group effort to improve the educational standards of schools supported by the Bureau of Indian Affairs and to institute courses on American Indian history and culture in colleges and universities.

The directions taken by white ethnics in asserting their cultural identity varied from those taken by the Black, Mexican, and Indian Americans. Discrimination against Italians, Irish, Greeks, Poles, and Jews was, after all, not institutionalized in the manner that it was for the more culturally distinct groups, at least not in the sixties. Though the larger groups, such as the Italians, the Irish, and the Jews had long controlled pockets of political power in the different cities and states in which they lived, this became manifest only during election periods. The rest of the year the existence of clearly defined enclaves of ethnics in their various neighborhoods throughout the cities and states was an invisible reality. After elections a kind of mass denial was reinstituted by both the ethnics and "native" American society that any differences could be discerned in the cultural composition of the "American people."

Denial had a functional purpose. It facilitated the steady progress being made by white ethnics toward securing for themselves a permanent place in the economic and social structure of America. Trade unions were their domain in some parts of the country. Life was good in the sixties: a blue-collar worker could earn good wages and provide well for his family; he could buy many of the material goods he was exposed to in the marketplace; and he could even think of putting money aside to send his children to college. Furthermore, the road to upward social mobility was more accessible to white ethnics. The first post-World War II generation reached college age in the sixties, and the numbers of second- and third-generation "hyphenated Americans" who went to college, the first of their families to do so, increased markedly.

What could be the issues, therefore, around which white ethnics would mobilize to assert their particular cultural distinctiveness? The immediate rallying point seems to have been the threat presented by Black and Puerto Rican blue-collar workers in large cities who were making significant inroads into previously white ethnic neighborhoods and occupations. In these areas, ethnicity had the functional relevance of combating a perceived social and economic threat. Ethnicity represented the bond that held together a group in its effort to maintain the social and economic interests that had been gained, they felt, through hard work and much sacrifice. Of course, ethnicity also resulted in a special kind of bigotry and prejudice. One category of minority group, white ethnics, opposed a second category of minority group, Blacks, within a social system that was, to a greater or lesser degree, discriminatory toward both. (See Levine and Herman, 1972a, 1972b.) It is indeed a paradox that out of this confrontation of Blacks and working-class whites, the latter found the opportunity to assert their particular ethnic identities and to awaken their sense of group cohesiveness.

And while this happened as a response to the immediate threat of Black and Puerto Rican encroachments into economic spheres of ethnic white activity, it also represented the surfacing of long-festering resentments against a broader middle-class American social system that tended to devalue the white ethnics' traditional cultural background. (See Novak, 1971.) The sense of alienation that they felt was now, for different reasons, being articulated dramatically by middle-class college men and women through the youth movement. It was all coming together, it seemed, through the very process of all coming apart in a society marked by group divisions, by violence, and by the erosion of official values.

The acculturation of white ethnics within American core society thus turned out to have been more apparent than real. The surprising fact that emerged in the sixties was that it was the third-generation ethnics, the grandchildren of the original ethnics, who were the most energetic in turning to their traditional cultural roots and reaffirming their ethnic identities. They were not motivated by any special wish to oppose the Black and Puerto Rican movements. The primary impetus came instead from the subjective feelings of alienation they had long felt and that they shared with their young counterparts in all the rest of American society who were neither ethnic nor of working-class origins. The Protestant ethic had caught up with them, too.

Both the working-class ethnic on the assembly line and the professional ethnic in the middle or upper class experienced the same dissatisfaction. Their ethnic backgrounds served, in the first instance, as a base against which their current feelings of isolation and anomie were experienced in sharp relief; they had known a different life when they were growing up in their ethnic homes and neighborhoods, and now they remembered it. Feelings of solidarity and spontaneity were sought, a sense of joy in interpersonal relations that were not cultivated for purposes of "connection." In value orientation terms, they were searching for a life style based on a Being orientation within a Collateral relation framework, geared to the Present rather than the Future. This was the third-generation ethnics' alternative to the encounter groups, group family living arrangements, and drugs used by the youth movement in its reaction to traditional core values.

Open manifestation of ethnic feeling took a variety of forms, and varied in intensity, in different white subcultural groups. In New York City, the Italian-American Fraternal Society organized itself to combat the prejudicial stereotyping of Italian gangsters in movie and television films. Its program was also positively geared to affirming the contributions made by Italian-Americans to American society. Polish-American cultural and fraternal organizations also took aggressive stands against the mass media for stereotyping their ethnic group. Pulaski Day in the sixties drew an unprecedented number of second- and third-generation Polish-Americans who in previous years had left the celebration of the memory of the Polish hero in the American Revolutionary War to their fathers and grandfathers.

Greek-Americans organized themselves into a nationwide organization called the Greek Orthodox Youth of America (G.O.-Y.A.). It is important to note that the primary impetus for this effort of Greek-Americans did not come from the fraternal and cultural organizations founded earlier by their immigrant fathers and grandfathers. Nor did it come from the Greek Orthodox Church. It came from the second- and third-generation youth themselves who felt the need to unite for the purpose of deepening their sense of Greek consciousness.

Perhaps the most dramatic manifestation of this reaffirmation of ethnic origins was the response of young American Jews to the Israeli-Arab conflict, first in 1967 and then in 1973. The war in 1967 stirred a deep interest in thousands of young American Jews and the Israeli victory after only six days of fighting was experienced by them as a personal triumph. Many followed up their emotional involvement in this conflict by going to Israel and working, with the clear purpose of making a contribution to Israel. They believed that in the process they were also renewing themselves. It felt right to commit themselves to a cause outside the realm of their individual social and economic advancement. It satisfied the need for the "mutuality" that Erikson had taught them was an essential ingredient of a healthy personality. When the Israeli-Arab conflict was activated again in 1973, the response of American Jews was overwhelming. Young men and women left their schools and jobs and professions and traveled to Israel to participate in whatever way they could.

The movement of members of American subcultural groups toward renewed pride in their ethnic origins then represents part of the broader reaction of the youth of America to the endemic strains present in contemporary society. We have conceptualized these strains in terms of value orientation theory. The strain incumbent in the discrepancy between the overt Individual > Collateral > Lineal and the covert Individual > Lineal > Collateral value orientation patterns in the relational area, we have argued, is one of the main sources of strain in the American social system. The other is the intrinsic strain in the traditional emphasis on achievement values— that is, Individualism, Doing, Future-time and Mastery-over-nature orientations, which do not foster group solidarity or Collaterality, individual commitment to group goals, or the spontaneous expression of feelings through trusting interpersonal relations and the joy of just Being. However, what are the implications of this theoretical analysis for the future course of adaptation by American ethnic families in the United States?

Sociologists such as Glazer and Moynihan (1963) and Gordon (1964) have pointed out that the United States has always been a culturally diverse and pluralistic society. The melting-pot notion of ethnic and national groups' eventually amalgamating into a homogeneous culture is not supported by the facts.

Before the Black movement, Italians, Irish, Poles, Greeks, Jews, and in particular the Chinese maintained separate cultural identities in the United States. In the past, however, the maintenance of ethnic subcultures was based partly on the defensive sociopsychological needs of the subculture members. Ethnics affirmed their value and worth as a group in covert or purely symbolic ways in reaction to the discrimination they faced from the white Anglo-Saxon Protestants who preceded them. In the sixties the situation was quite different. The issue became one of positively affirming ethnic patterns of life to meet a different configuration of sociopsychological needs: those not being met by that white Anglo-Saxon society, which the ethnics had now joined. In addition, many of the second- and third-generation ethnics had achieved middle-class status. Thus, in the sixties, affirmation of ethnicity was associated with the protection of political, economic, and social interests. Cultural pluralism in the sixties was more than symbols.

In a conference in San Francisco in 1971 sponsored by the American Jewish Committee and entitled "Consultation on Ethnicity," issues relating to the need for a "new pluralism" in the United States were discussed by various scholars and community leaders. (See American Jewish Committee, 1971.) Irving M. Levine, the director of the National Project on Ethnic America of the American Jewish Committee, stated the issue as follows: "We need to work out a new system of relationships between groups, a new 'pluralism' that accepts uniqueness and balances identification with a small group against commitment to society as a whole, while protecting the individual who does not wish to identify as well. America has too often failed to deal honestly with the ethnic group factor, and this has weakened our nation's legitimate claim on its citizens to join in the common good. Fragmentation results not from recognizing difference, but from ignoring it" (American Jewish Committee, 1971, p. 16).

The appeal here is for open recognition that ethnic variation is and always has been an integral part of the American social scene. More important, however, the speaker calls for "acceptance" of the uniqueness and value of American subcultural groups on an equal basis with that of the core middle-class culture.

The appeal to a "new cultural pluralism" is a response to the implicit devaluation of differences from the American cultural norms supported by the covert Individual > Lineal > Collateral value orientation profile with its implied "superior-inferior" patterning of group relations within the various subgroups of the society. Ethnic groups were once clearly on a lower rung of a lineal hierarchy in the United States, their position being determined by how closely, through skin color, country of origin, and religion, they approximated the Anglo-Saxon Protestant white norm. The insistence on shifting to the overt, official Individual > Collateral > Lineal pattern evident in the culture protest movements of the 1960s signals the "new pluralism" advocated by Levine. The egalitarian nature of the Collateral orientation dictates that all groups within the system are entitled to equal status and therefore are entitled to assert their individual and collective uniqueness within the broader social system.

This shifting orientation is clearly a first step toward eliciting the commitment of members of divergent subcultural groups, ethnic and otherwise, to a sense of national purpose. The current fragmentation of American society into competing interest groups of divergent cultural and ideological character is certainly not a viable arrangement for either the subgroups themselves or for the country as a whole. The refusal of thousands of American youth to participate in the "immoral" Vietnam War shocked Americans into the realization of how divided they had become on the issue of national purpose and direction.

It is the second aspect of the culture change process in the United States, however, that poses difficult problems for members of ethnic groups in their efforts to adapt to American core society. How can one internalize the value orientations characterizing the agrarian societies that his forebears came from while at the same time trying to find a place in the social and occupational structure of a technologically advanced urban society? (See Gutman, 1973.) Furthermore, what direction will technological society take now that the Protestant ethic has been challenged? Culture change in the United States has clearly not proceeded to the point where Individualism, Doing, Future, and Mastery-over-nature orientations have disappeared from the important institutions. How are the alternative value orientations characterizing ethnic subcultures— that is, Being, Collaterality, Present, and Harmony-with-nature—to become viable in America? In other words, what can the new pluralism live on, and what are the psychological implications?

In addressing this fundamental question let us reexamine an aspect of Kluckhohn's value orientation theory that bears on this issue. (See Kluckhohn and Strodtbeck, 1961.) Though every society has a dominant configuration of values that differentiates it from other societies, it is also true that within a particular society there can be a wide divergence among the different subgroups. Kluckhohn theorizes that variation in cultural value orientations is a necessary condition for the effective functioning of the society itself. Variation would be expected, for example, among different occupational groups within a society. In the United States, entertainers are more Being-oriented than businessmen while artists are more oriented to the Being-in-Becoming pattern. Both artists and entertainers, however, tend to be more Doing-oriented than artists living in a more Being-oriented culture such as Greece. There are, furthermore, obvious regional differences within a country of origin so that northern Italians, emigrants from an industralized area, are likely to be more Individualistic, Doing, Future, and Mastery-over-nature oriented than southern Italians, born in farming areas where Collaterality, Being, Present-time and Subjugated-to-nature orientations are primary.

The concept of variation in value orientations is not limited to occupational and regional differences within a society. It applies as well to the different stages of development that an individual traverses in the course of his life. It is almost too obvious to state that children everywhere are more Being than Doing oriented and more focused on the Present than the Future, even though these distinctions become blurred very early in middle-class American society through the inculcation of achievement values in school and in the playground. Also, in the United States, middle age blunts the goals of Future and Doing orientations for individuals whose future has decreased in scope and who have attained as much success as they can realistically hope for. The time parameter, then, is important in considering the stresses imposed by value orientations on an individual in the course of his lifetime.

Finally, value orientations vary within individuals during the course of a single day, a week, or a year. Conditions that emphasize one or another are related to the activities in which individuals engage. During working hours, those orientations that fuel competitive, striving, and achieving behavior are in the ascendancy. In recreational situations, usually in the evening and in the company of family members, Being, Collaterality, Harmony-with-nature, and Present-time orientations are more salient. These leisure time values in the United States, however, are clearly reflective of dominant core values—competitive sports and achievement pursuits are emphasized more than in other societies. Nevertheless, the most dedicated American businessman has periods when he relaxes his Doing orientation and is reinforced by Being.

Such variations in value orientations are manifest in the social role patterns through which individuals function. In functioning as a father, for example, an American middle-class male will show more feeling and give more emotionally than he will in functioning as a wage earner in competition with his peers. In his role as husband, he can be expected to be more Collateral, that is, egalitarian, with his wife than he will be in his relation with subordinates at work. In his relation with parents, he may adopt a more respectful role as son, reflecting the operation of a Lineal orientation. There is fluctuation, in other words, in the salience of one or the other value orientation for the social role in which an individual functions at a particular time.

The implications of these theoretical considerations point to how the new pluralism might affect the culture of the United States. Members of ethnic groups already do behave differently in relations within their respective ingroups. Depending, of course, on the particular ethnic group in question, they can be more spontaneous, freer in emotional expressions, can commit themselves to the attainment of group goals—in short, relate to each other in ways that are sharply at variance with those that characterize their relations with the "outside" American core community. In the past, however, shifting back and forth between ingroup and outgroup, between ethnic subculture and American core society took a heavy psychological toll from ethnic Americans. In the three case studies presented in this volume, we tried to illustrate some of the psychological effects that have accompanied the strain of coping with divergent or conflicting value systems and role expectations within a single society. Individuals found themselves having to make the choice of identifying with their ethnic subcultures and isolating themselves from the mainstream of American society or becoming completely "Americanized" and so rejecting an important part of themselves. While they rarely made a choice of either extreme, rarely were they able to integrate the two options either. Neurotic and even psychotic compromise responses emerged from the continuing conflict they had to endure.

Now culture change in the United States has made it possible for ethnic Americans to move in and out of their subcultures without the aversive consequences of previous years—and this, it seems to us, can constitute the essence of the new pluralism in the United States. It is now realistic for ethnic Americans to openly accept the variation in value orientations that characterizes their subcultures and to view these variations as positive, as important, indeed, as psychologically healthy. It can even be argued that shifting back and forth between ingroup and outgroup in this new context constitutes an integrative, ego-strengthening process. It does so because the ingroup can now provide a structure in which those psychological needs not met by the achievement-oriented American culture can be satisfied. The strains incumbent in functioning within a psychologically demanding social system can be relaxed within subsystems whose values allow for more Being, Collateral, Harmony-with-nature, and Present-time oriented thoughts, feelings, and behavior.

The new pluralism conceptualized in this fashion constitutes, then, a new kind of buffer against the stress of acculturation faced principally by second- and third-generation ethnic Americans. Acceptance of their subcultures in a conflict-free manner can liberate energies for identification with broader national purposes and directions. It can also serve another important function, and that is the facilitation of culture change in the United States—that is, the relaxation of those values that undergird the Protestant ethic to the exclusion of humanistic considerations.

The new pluralism can serve a two-way process of cultural modification between ethnic subcultures, on the one hand, and the American core society on the other. When American ethnics operate within their respective subcultural communities, they do not experience them in pure form. Italian or Greek culture in Boston is clearly not identical to that of contemporary Italy or Greece. In Boston these ethnic communities have been modified to a degree in their essential character by virtue of their existence within an "American" environment. An Italian from Italy moving into the North End of Boston (an Italian neighborhood) would still need to go through a period of adaptation before he would feel comfortable among his Italian-American neighbors. First-generation Greek-

Americans who return to Greece in their old age to retire find that they, too, need a period of acculturation to their original homeland. The ethnic experience in the United States, then, is an ethnic-American experience in which the original subcultural values have undergone some degree of shift toward the American core patterns. The Italian-American in the North End of Boston is more Being and Collaterally oriented than his counterparts in the WASP suburbs but less so than his relatives in rural Italy. Members of Italian-American peer groups in the West End of Boston, described by Gans, may spend long evenings socializing with each other in the manner of their counterparts in Italy, but they still have to get up early the next morning to go to work. National, political, and economic conditions also affect and condition the status of their ability to earn money and maintain themselves in this society. These factors permeate their existence and interfere with the essential Being and Collateral orientations that they internalized in their Italian-American homes.

By the same token, the challenge to core American values by the youth movement has sensitized "native" Americans to the "ethnic experience" as a potential source of personal fulfillment. Ethnic themes have emerged in the theatre, in motion pictures, and in television productions where subcultural variations in behavior are treated in a positive light. The partial transformation of Individual > Lineal > Collateral to Individual > Collateral > Lineal, which has made ethnicity more acceptable in the United States, may also contribute finally to the relaxation of that intolerance in American middle-class core value orientations that has been a source of individual and intergroup strain.

9

Implications
for Practice

In this final chapter we shall re-focus our attention on the therapeutic process itself and consider some of the implications of transactional systems theory for the practitioner engaged in the work of helping people with problems. In the three case histories of ethnic families, we attempted to illustrate the complex interrelation between cultural values, social role patternings, and the personality functioning of individuals facing the difficult task of adapting to American core society. These case histories made it possible for us to bring into sharp focus the relations between the cultural, social, and psychological dimensions as foci in a field of transacting processes. These interacting dimensions are not limited, however, to ethnic families facing acculturation, but characterize human relations in a broad range of situations or "systems." The therapist-patient interaction is the system that will concern us in the remainder of this chapter.

The patient-therapist interaction sets in motion a transaction between two fields of life processes, those that characterize the therapist and those that characterize the patient. The therapist's conceptualization of the origins of the presenting problem, the disordered behavior, and the therapeutic strategy he designs for change is not wholly contingent on the theory of personality that he has internalized in the course of his training. It is related also to what is sometimes termed his assumptions about the "nature of man" and what in this book has been termed his "cultural value orientations." The cultural value orientations of the therapist, the definition he gives to his social role as therapist, and his own personality organization transact with corollary processes in the patient beginning with the initial interview and continuing to the termination of treatment. Psychotherapists, especially those who are psychoanalytically oriented, are especially sensitive to the psychological dimension that characterizes their transactions with a patient. They are aware of transference and counter-transference problems, and so they are careful to maintain a certain degree of emotional distance between themselves and their patients. They are rarely sensitized, however, to the variations in cultural and social role dimensions that are also important features in the field of transacting processes that characterize the patient-therapist interaction (Spiegel, 1971).

When the value orientations of the therapist are American core values, they pattern his perceptions of the therapeutic process in certain predictable ways. He expects the patient to be prepared to "work through" his problems (Doing), for the purpose of attaining a better level of independent functioning (Individualism) sometime in the distant future (Future) and to be motivated in this endeavor by his belief that all problems lend themselves to solutions (Mastery-over-nature). He also relates to the patient in an overtly egalitarian manner as he helps him to strengthen his independence from others (Individualism > Collaterality > Lineality) while, in fact, covert lineality characterizes the patient-therapist relation (Individualism > Lineality > Collaterality). Regardless of psychotherapeutic persuasion, the role of psychotherapist, as patterned by covert Lineality, is prescribed in a manner that assures his control of the therapeutic situation. He is the expert, the doctor who defines what is right and wrong and good and bad, however indirectly and imperceptibly, since the overt democratic nature of the relation must be maintained. When the patient has internalized these same core

American values in the course of his socialization, the transactions
between patient and therapist can proceed with the focus on the
psychological problems of the patient. Therapist and patient understand each other well and, in fact, the transference and counter-
transference issues can appropriately occupy their full attention.
There can be full congruence between them also as regards issues
such as the definition of what constitutes the problem to be solved
and what the goal of therapy is to be. Invariably the goal of therapy is conceptualized in terms of more effective functioning in areas
of work and love which, of course, is itself a definition based on the
Doing, Individualistic and Mastery-over-nature value orientations
that therapist and patient share. They are also both oriented to the
Future attainment of therapeutic goals, that is, after several years
of treatment.

When the patient has not internalized these value orientations in his socialization, however, communication with the therapist becomes, at best, tenuous. Unawareness of an incongruence in
the cultural values of the therapist and patient can be a primary
source of ineffective relations between them. In the therapeutic interaction, the therapist's expectations of the patient are not met, and
the patient is confused and frustrated by expectations that he does
not know how to meet. When the patient, for example, has internalized first order Being, Collateral, Present time and Subjugated-
to-nature orientations, which are common to many rural communities of Europe and South America, his perceptions of the
therapeutic situation are markedly variant from those of the Ameri-
can-trained therapist. In the first place, he would be unlikely to perceive psychological disturbance, such as anxiety or depression or
difficulties in interpersonal relations, as a problem that could be
solved with the help of an expert. The concept of psychological
causation is predicated on a problem-solving perceptual set that is
based on Doing, Mastery-over-nature, and Future value orientations. Therefore, the concept is not available to him. He perceives
affective disorders as having an organic basis—they "just happen"
and he himself cannot be expected to exert any control over them
(Being). He is the victim (Subjugated-to-nature) of an illness as
he might be the victim of appendicitis. It is his fate that this should
happen to him. He expects the doctor to give him medicine to make

the pain go away now (Present). Interpersonal conflict is perceived as caused by the "badness" of the other person or persons. Human nature is viewed as Good or Bad and little can be done to change this fixed state. The adolescent who rebels is bad; and it is incomprehensible how a good girl could have a schizophrenic reaction—her bizarre behavior is evidence that she was not so good after all.

The mutual frustration of therapist and patient that can result from this incongruence in value orientations is not difficult to discern. The therapist must separate himself from his own value orientations in order to be able to understand his patient. His ability to design an effective therapeutic intervention strategy for his patient is predicated on his ability to do so.

While this strategy would, of course, correspond to the nature of the presenting problem, some general directions seem clearly indicated. Empathy with the patient is contingent on the awareness of the therapist of his own value orientations and of the therapeutic situation in particular. It is equally important for the therapist to understand the cultural milieu to which the patient is trying to adjust. Is the patient an Italian-American whose significant interpersonal relations occur in his ethnic community and whose parents and siblings are centrally important to his life? Or is he an Italian-American whose major preoccupation is with "making it" economically and socially in the nonethnic, that is, American core society? In this latter case the significant interpersonal relations may be with non-Italian-Americans and so the conflicts—and adjustment to them—are radically different from those in the former case. The therapist may focus his efforts on making this more rapidly acculturating patient aware of the discrepancy between the value orientations to which he was socialized in the Italian family, and those of the core American society to which he is trying to adapt. This clarification of the variations in values can facilitate the task of helping the patient resolve his "culture conflict." The focus of treatment would, by definition, be on strengthening behaviors patterned by core American value orientations—Doing, Individualism, Future, and Mastery-over-nature. The culturally sensitive therapist can help the patient, attempting to adjust to American society, avail himself of those ego strengthening resources available in the ethnic community. The therapist can help his patient to accept in himself those aspects of his ethnic heritage that consolidate his sense of identity and strengthen him psychologically so that he can cope with a demanding, technologically advanced social system.

In the case of the individual whose goal it is to adapt to his ethnic community more effectively, the goals of therapy would be, by definition, quite different. Efforts at conscious clarification of the value orientation issue would be inappropriate and probably ineffective if it were tried. The therapist's focus in this case would be to move the patient as quickly as possible back into his ethnic community and explore with him the ego strengthening resources that would be naturally available to him. In this case, the family and peer group would be the appropriate social supports that would have to be mobilized to help the patient readjust to his environment. Impaired relations in these two social areas would require the primary attention of a therapist sensitive to the special characteristics of Italian culture.

While we have chosen examples from ethnic subcultures to illustrate the importance of the cultural dimension in transactions between patient and therapist, its importance is not limited to therapy with members of ethnic groups. Value orientation discrepancies are evident in the relations between generations and between social classes as well. In the previous chapter we discussed the youth movement at length and argued that it was the awareness of the discrepancy between overt and covert values in American society that generated the social disequilibrium of the sixties. It is interesting to note that during this period, many therapists and other mental health professonals felt that the youth movement was a manifestation of "rebellion against authority" (Bettelheim, 1970). In other words this basic upheaval in a society was conceptualized as a "psychological" problem; the cultural dimension was totally ignored. Psychological motivations have been attributed also to the women's liberation movement and other social change movements that are continuing to grow and develop during the seventies. (See Chapter Eight.)

The therapist who cannot discriminate between cultural and psychological determinants of conflict in his patients because of his own cultural and generational rigidities may find that he is unsuccessful in reaching his patient. He will define his difficulty as resistance in the patient or as a transference problem and he will interpret his own anger toward the patient as a counter-transference problem. In fact, the therapist and the patient are operating from two divergent sets of assumptions about what is valuable and therefore what is the proper goal of treatment. The patient may assume, for example, that American core values are undesirable orientations for living and he is attempting a life-style change based on Being, Collateral, Present time, and Harmony-with-nature orientations. He is living with a woman to whom he is not married, refuses to commit himself to a career, and is heavily committed to social change. He is, in short, a radical of the kind described by Kenniston (1968). He is in treatment because all of this is making him very anxious and he is not aware of the origins of his distress. He is experiencing "culture shock" similar to that of the European immigrant acculturating to American society. He has not completely given up one set of value orientations for the ones in the culture to which he is attempting to adjust. The therapist sees all of this as a psychological problem. The young man hasn't "worked through" his Oedipal conflict, and the therapist determines, albeit implicitly, that that is the area that must be worked on with the patient. The therapy fails. The patient remains more confused than ever and the therapist conceptualizes the Failure as unresolved resistance on the part of the patient. The appropriate identification of the cultural aspects of the problem by the therapist would have made it possible for him to deal with his patient's anxiety in a more effective manner. The therapist who can take distance from his own value orientations, then, can be free to employ whatever psychotherapeutic techniques necessary to reduce the anxiety of the patient and support him in efforts to effect the life-style change that was his goal for seeking help in the first place.

Many of the new therapies that emerged in the sixties such as the encounter group movement and the other "gestalt" approaches are predicated on basic cultural value orientation shifts from dominant American patterns. These shifts were discussed in detail in the previous chapter. Traditional modes of treatment, based on core American value orientations, are viewed by the groups advocating these newer therapies as counterproductive because they do not provide a medium for the expression of spontaneous feeling (Being) and are too individualistically oriented (therapy is done on a one-to-one basis). Gestalt therapy, however, is done in groups (Collaterality) where people learn to relate to other people in meaningful ways. The goal of gestalt therapy is to help people be free from the constraints imposed by a technologically geared society so they can experience life (Being) in a more full and meaningful manner. Its goal is not to free people to "achieve" in American middle-class terms.

The variations in value orientations that separate social classes in America is another important source of strain that is reflected in the therapeutic situation. Traditional modes of psycho-dynamically oriented treatment approaches have been consistently ineffective in treating the working-class and the poor who have been labelled "hard to reach" (Pavenstedt, 1967). This problem is blamed on the patient and his family rather than on the discordance in value orientations that distorts the communication between him and the therapist. The value orientations of working-class individuals in America are closer to those of agrarian societies than they are to those of the middle class. A significant proportion of the working class are, of course, ethnic Americans. Since there is a greater emphasis, therefore, on Collaterality and Lineality, on Being, Present, and Subjugated-to-nature orientations, there is a predictable difficulty in benefitting from traditional psychotherapy.

When treating the working-class and the poor, the therapist needs to reexamine the functions of his traditionally patterned social role of therapist. For example, taking a more direct, that is, Lineal approach in the therapeutic interaction could be effective since this would correspond with the expectations of the patient. Short term approaches such as "crisis intervention" strategies and behavior therapy would be expected to engage the Lineal and Present time orientations of the patient and so ensure his commitment to following a therapeutic regime.

It is in the family therapy situation itself that the dynamic transactions between the value orientations of family members, their social roles, and individual psychological processes are played out. The therapist must be able to separate these three distinct parameters conceptually and design an appropriate intervention strategy that will bring about a homeostatic balance of forces in the family field. He must know when the source of strain is located primarily in the imbalance of power in the family, that is, in the social role dimension. When he learns this, he can help individuals redefine their roles in terms of privileges and responsibilities and effect a more satisfactory interpersonal arrangement within the family structure.

It may not be possible to redefine social roles, however, until family members become aware of the discordance in the value orientations that pattern mutually contradictory expectations of how those roles ought to be lived. The Lineally oriented father, for example, may need to understand that his expectations of submissive behavior from his son (formalized respect) are inconsistent with the Individualistic values his son has internalized outside the family. Alternatives to confrontation that would help the father-son inter-action coalesce into a more mutually reinforcing arrangement would be sought. (The methods with which the therapist brings this about should, of course, be geared to the value orientations of the patient.) The family therapist may decide, on the other hand, that cultural values and social role considerations in the family dynamics cannot be dealt with until some progress is made in helping the "disturbed" member resolve some of the psychological problems that initiated the treatment in the first place. The treatment is then centered on the psychological dimension. In this case, the alleviation of stress in the "disturbed" member can be expected to reverberate positively throughout the family system and reduce the stress located in value and social role conflicts between family members.

To illustrate, let us consider the hypothetical case of an Italian-American husband and a wife of old American stock who seek help from a family therapist because of the sexual impotence of the husband. (In order to simplify the complexity of the family transactions in this hypothetical example, we will not consider the roles of children or the extended family members, which would normally need to be included.) The family therapist determines from his study of the family process that the husband's impotence is related to rage toward his wife, which in turn is related to conflict at the cultural and social dimensions. The husband feels coerced and intimidated by his wife, who expects him to be more achievement oriented (Doing) and to earn more money so that she

can be provided with all the accoutrements of middle-class life. He
wants to earn an adequate amount to provide a "decent" living for
his wife and children and to work only enough to make this possible. He wants and expects to have plenty of free time to enjoy
himself (Being), and much of his enjoyment comes from being with
his family. He expects also to maintain close ties with his extended
family and he expects his wife to enjoy herself by spending long
Sunday afternoons with his parents and his sisters and brothers. She
will have none of this. Furthermore, she is threatening divorce because he cannot function adequately as a man in bed.

When the therapist comes to understand all of this in the
initial, exploratory phase of treatment, he may decide to work first
on the presenting problem, the symptom since both marital partners
are firmly fixated on this as the major source of conflict. The therapist knows he can turn to the other loci of strain—the cultural
value orientation of the family members and the structure and
function of their social roles—at a later point. The major focus now
is on relieving strain in the sexual area. The behavior therapist does
this through "desensitization" and other behavioral techniques
while other therapists might use other methods. For example, it
might be suggested, where appropriate, that sexual relations not be
attempted for a prescribed period of time. The reduction of stress
in this psychological sphere could be expected to have reverberating
effects on the social role and cultural value orientation areas and
the therapist can now turn his attention to them. Where appropriate, the clarification of value discrepancies and the corollary discordance in role expectations can be pointed out to the couple.
Where this insight approach is inappropriate, the therapist can be
more "directive," and "contract" with the couple to alter the behaviors that characterize their interpersonal relations. The latter
"behavior exchange" technique is a standard method employed by
behavior therapists. In this manner, social roles are restructured
since the behaviors subsumed under them are changed and a more
harmonious dovetailing of role expectations in different situations
is brought about. Communication is increased and all of this positive change reverberates throughout the family field and further
reduces what residual strain remains in the sexual, that is, psychological, dimension.

In discussing therapeutic intervention strategies from a transactional systems perspective, we have simplified the description of the therapeutic change process. It is closer to reality to say that the transactions between therapist and family members involve inputs in the three dimensions simultaneously. It is the clinical judgment of the therapist that must guide him as to where and when to apply his major effort. He must also sense when to abandon work in one of the dimensions for work in another. The environment of the patient and his family is in constant flux. Conditions change, people lose jobs, finish school, move away, become ill, recover from illness, etc. Since these changes affect the family field of the individual or individuals being treated, the focus of therapeutic intervention must not be rigid and fixed.

Bibliography

ACKERMAN, N. W. *Treating the Troubled Family.* New York: Basic Books, 1966.

AMERICAN JEWISH COMMITTEE. "Pluralism Beyond the Frontier." Report of the San Francisco Consultation on Ethnicity. San Francisco, 1971.

BANFIELD, E. C. *The Moral Basis of a Backward Society.* New York: Free Press, 1958.

BARZINI, L. *The Italians.* New York: Atheneum, 1965.

BATESON, G. "Minimal Requirements for a Theory of Schizophrenia." *Archives of General Psychiatry,* 1960, *2,* 477–491.

BATESON, G., JACKSON, D., HALEY, J., AND WEAKLAND, J. "Toward a Theory of Schizophrenia." *Behavioral Science,* 1956, *1,* 251–264.

BELLAK, L. *Handbook of Community Psychiatry and Community Mental Health.* New York: Grune and Stratton, 1964.

BENEDEK, T. "The Psychosomatic Implications of the Primary Unit: Mother-Child." *American Journal of Orthopsychiatry,* 1949, *19,* 642–654.

BETTELHEIM, B. *Obsolete Youth: Toward a Psychograph of Adolescent Rebellion.* San Francisco: San Francisco Press, 1970.

BOSZORMENYI-NAGY, I., AND FRAMO, J. *Intensive Family Therapy.* New York: Harper and Row, 1965.

CHRISTENSEN, H. T. (Ed.) *Handbook of Marriage and the Family.* Chicago: Rand McNally, 1964.

COVELLO, L. *The Social Background of the Italo-American School Child.* Unpublished doctoral dissertation. New York University, 1944.

DE VOS, G. A. "A Quantitative Rorschach Assessment of Maladjustment and Rigidity in an Acculturating Japanese-American." *Genetics Psychology Monographs,* 1955, *52,* 51–87.

ERIKSON, E. H. *Childhood and Society.* New York: Norton, 1950.

FESTINGER, L. *A Theory of Cognitive Dissonance.* Stanford, Calif.: Stanford University Press, 1962.

FORESTER, R. F. *The Italian Emigration of Our Times.* Cambridge: Harvard University Press, 1919.

FRANK, L. K. *Personality and Culture: The Psychological Approach.* New York: Hinds, Hayden, and Eldredge, 1948.

FRIEDAN, B. *The Feminine Mystique.* New York: Norton, 1963.

FRIEDL, E. *Vasilika: A Village in Modern Greece.* New York: Holt, Rinehart, and Winston, 1962.

FROMM, E. *Escape from Freedom.* New York: Holt, Rinehart, and Winston, 1941.

GANS, H. J. *The Urban Villagers.* New York: Free Press, 1962.

GLAZER, N., AND MOYNIHAN, D. P. *Beyond the Melting Pot.* Cambridge: Massachusetts Institute of Technology Press, 1963.

GORDON, M. M. *Assimilation in American Life.* New York: Oxford University Press, 1964.

GRAY, W., DUHL, F. J., AND RIZZO, N. D. (Eds.) *General Systems Theory and Psychiatry.* Boston: Little, Brown, 1969.

GREER, G. *The Female Eunuch.* New York: McGraw-Hill, 1971.

GRINKER, R. R., AND HUGHES, H. M. (Eds.) *Toward a Unified Theory of Human Behavior.* New York: Basic Books, 1956.

GROUP FOR THE ADVANCEMENT OF PSYCHIATRY. *Integration and Conflict in Family Behavior.* Report 27. Topeka, Kan., 1954.

GROUP FOR THE ADVANCEMENT OF PSYCHIATRY. *The Case History Method in the Study of Family Process.* Vol. 6. Report 76. New York, 1970.

GUTMAN, H. G. "Work, Culture and Society in Industrializing America, 1815–1919." *American Historical Review,* June 1973, *78.*

HALEY, J. "The Family of the Schizophrenic: A Model System." *Journal of Nervous and Mental Disease,* 1959a, *129.*

HALEY, J. "An Interactional Description of Schizophrenia." *Psychiatry,* 1959b, *22,* 321–332.

HALLOWELL, A. I. "Acculturation Processes and Personality Changes as

Indicated in Rorschach Technique." *Rorschach Research Exchange*, 1940, *6*, 42–50.

HATT, P. K. *Backgrounds of Human Fertility in Puerto Rico.* Princeton: Princeton University Press, 1952.

HOLLINGSHEAD, A. B., AND REDLICH, F. C. *Social Class and Mental Illness.* New York: Wiley, 1958.

HOWELLS, J. G. (Ed.) *Theory and Practice of Family Therapy.* New York: Brunner/Mazel, 1971.

JACKSON, D. D. "The Study of the Family." *Family Process*, 1965, *4*(1).

JACKSON, D. D., AND WEAKLAND, J. "Schizophrenic Symptoms and Family Interaction." *Archives of General Psychiatry*, 1959, *1*, 618–621.

JACKSON, D. D., AND WEAKLAND, J. "Conjoint Family Therapy: Some Considerations on Theory, Technique and Results." *Psychiatry*, Suppl., 1961, *24*, 30–45.

KARDINER, A., WITH LINTON, R., DU BOIS, C., AND WEST, J. *The Psychological Frontiers of Society.* New York: Columbia University Press, 1945.

KENDALL, M. C. *Rank Correlation Methods.* (2nd ed.) New York: Macmillan, 1955.

KENNISTON, K. *The Young Radicals.* New York: Harcourt Brace Jovanovich, 1968.

KLUCKHOHN, C. "Values and Value Orientations." In T. Parsons (Ed.), *Toward a General Theory of Action.* Cambridge: Harvard University Press, 1951.

KLUCKHOHN, C., AND MURRAY, H. A. (Eds.) *Personality in Nature, Society, and Culture.* (Rev. ed.) New York: Knopf, 1953.

KLUCKHOHN, F. R. "The Participant-Observer Technique in Small Communities." *American Journal of Sociology*, 1940, *46*, 331–343.

KLUCKHOHN, F. R. "The American Family Past and Present." In O. H. Mowrer (Ed.), *Patterns for Modern Living: Psychological Patterns.* Chicago: Delphian Society, 1952.

KLUCKHOHN, F. R. "Dominant and Variant Value Orientations." In C. Kluckhohn and H. A. Murray (Eds.), *Personality in Nature, Society, and Culture.* New York: Knopf, 1953.

KLUCKHOHN, F. R., AND STRODTBECK, F. L. *Variations in Value Orientations.* New York: Harper and Row, 1961.

LEE, D. G. "Greece." In M. Mead (Ed.), *Cultural Patterns and Technical Change.* New York: UNESCO, 1953.

LEVINE, I. M., AND HERMAN, J. "The Life of White Ethnics." *Dissent,* Winter 1972a.

LEVINE, I. M., AND HERMAN, J. "Search for Identity in Blue-Collar America." *Civil Rights Digest,* Winter, 1972b.

LIDZ, T. *The Family of the Schizophrenic Patient.* New York: International Universities Press, 1965.

LINDEMANN, E. *Life Stress and Bodily Disease.* Baltimore: Williams and Wilkins, 1950.

LINTON, R. *The Study of Man.* New York: Appleton-Century-Crofts, 1936.

LINTON, R. *The Cultural Background of Personality.* New York: Appleton-Century-Crofts, 1945.

LINTON, R., AND KARDINER, A. *The Individual and His Society.* New York: Columbia University Press, 1939.

LOPEZ, A. *The Puerto Rican Papers: Notes on the Re-Emergence of a Nation.* Indianapolis: Bobbs-Merrill, 1973.

MC CLELLAND, D. C., BRONFENBRENNER, U., HARDING, J., GALLWEY, M., KALTENBACK, J. E., STRODTBECK, F. L., AND BALDWIN, A. L. *Talent and Society.* New York: Van Nostrand, 1958.

MALINOWSKI, B. "Parenthood, the Basis of Social Structure." In V. F. Calverton (Ed.), *The New Generation.* New York: Macaulay, 1930.

MEAD, M. *Male and Female.* New York: Morrow, 1949.

MEAD, M. (Ed.) *Cultural Patterns and Technical Change.* New York: UNESCO, 1953.

MINUCHIN, S., MONTALVO, B., GUERNEY, B., JR., ROSMAN, B., AND SCHUMER, F. *Families of the Slums.* New York: Basic Books, 1967.

MOWRER, O. H. (Ed.) *Patterns for Modern Living: Psychological Patterns.* Chicago: Delphian Society, 1952.

MURDOCK, G. P. *Social Structure.* New York: Macmillan, 1949.

NEIMAN, L. J., AND HUGHES, J. W. "The Problems of the Concept of Role: A Re-Survey of the Literature." *Social Forces,* 1951, *30,* 141–149.

NOVAK, M. *The Rise of the Unmeltable Ethnics.* New York: Macmillan, 1971.

PAPADOPOULOS, T. H. *The History of the Greek Church and People under Turkish Domination.* Brussels: Demeester, 1952.

PAPAJOHN, J. "The Relation of Intergenerational Value Orientation Change and Mental Health in an American Ethnic Group." Unpublished paper, 1974.

PAPAJOHN, J., AND SPIEGEL, J. P. "The Relationship of Cultural Value Orientation Change and Rorschach Indices of Psychological Development." *Journal of Cross-Cultural Psychology,* 1971, 2(3), 257–272.

PARSONS, T. *Essays in Sociological Theory Pure and Applied.* New York: Free Press, 1949.

PARSONS, T. (Ed.) *Toward a General Theory of Action.* Cambridge: Harvard University Press, 1951.

PATTERSON, G. *Families: Applications of Social Learning to Family Life.* Champaign, Ill.: Research Press, 1971.

PAVENSTEDT, E. (Ed.) *The Drifters, Children of Disorganized Lower-Class Families.* Boston: Little, Brown, 1967.

PETRAKIS, H. M. *The Odyssey of Kostas Volakis.* New York: McKay, 1963.

PISANI, F. *The Italian in America.* Jericho, N.Y.: Exposition Press and Federal Writers Project, 1938.

PISANI, F. *The Italians of New York.* New York: Random House, 1957.

RAINWATER, L. *Behind Ghetto Walls.* Chicago: Aldine, 1970.

REICH, C. *The Greening of America.* New York: Random House, 1970.

RIESMAN, D. "The Themes of Work and Play in the Structure of Freud's Thought." *Psychiatry,* 1950, *13,* 1–16.

ROSEN, B. C. "Race, Ethnicity, and the Achievement Syndrome." *American Sociological Review,* 1959, *24.*

RYAN, W. (Ed.) *Distress in the City: Essays on the Design and Administration of Urban Mental Health Services.* Cleveland: Case Western Reserve Press, 1969.

SAGER, C., AND KAPLAN, H. S. (Eds.) *Progress in Group and Family Therapy.* New York: Brunner/Mazel, 1972.

SALOUTOS, T. *The Greeks in the United States.* Cambridge: Harvard University Press, 1964.

SANDERS, I. T. *Rainbow in the Rock: The People of Rural Greece.* Cambridge: Harvard University Press, 1962.

SCHERMERHORN, R. A. *These Our People: Minorities in American Culture.* Lexington, Mass.: Heath, 1949.

SLATER, P. *The Pursuit of Loneliness: American Culture at the Breaking Point.* Boston: Beacon, 1970.

SPIEGEL, J. P. "A Model for Relationships among Systems." In R. R. Grinker and H. M. Hughes (Eds.), *Toward a Unified Theory of Human Behavior.* New York: Basic Books, 1956.

SPIEGEL, J. P. "A Model for Relationships among Systems." In W. Gray,

F. J. Duhl, and N. D. Rizzo (Eds.), *General Systems Theory and Psychiatry*. Boston: Little, Brown, 1969.

SPIEGEL, J. P. *Transactions: Interplay Between Individual, Family, and Society*. J. Papajohn, Ed. New York: Aronson, 1971.

SPIEGEL, J. P., AND BELL, N. "The Family of the Psychiatric Patient." *American Handbook of Psychiatry*, Vol. 1. New York: Basic Books, 1959.

SPIEGEL, J. P., AND KLUCKHOHN, F. R. *Integration and Conflict in Family Behavior*. Report 27. Topeka, Kan.: Group for the Advancement of Psychiatry, 1954.

SPINDLER, G. D. "Sociocultural and Psychological Processes in Menomin Acculturation." *University of California Publications in Cultural Sociology*, 1955, *5*.

STRODTBECK, F. L. "Family Interaction, Values, and Achievement." In D. C. McClelland, U. Bronfenbrenner, J. Harding, M. Gallwey, J. E. Kaltenback, F. L. Strodtbeck, A. L. Baldwin (Eds.), *Talent and Society*. New York: Van Nostrand, 1958.

STUART, R. B. "Operant-Interpersonal Treatment for Marital Discord." In C. J. Sager and H. S. Kaplan (Eds.), *Progress in Group and Family Therapy*. New York: Brunner/Mazel, 1972.

UNITED STATES DEPARTMENT OF COMMERCE. *Statistical Abstract 1972*. Washington, D.C.: Government Printing Office, 1972.

VOGT, E. Z. "Navaho Veterans: A Study in Changing Values." *Peabody Museum of Harvard University Papers*, 1951, *41*.

WALLACE, A. F. C. "The Modal Personality Structure of the Tuscarora Indians as Revealed by the Rorschach Test." *Bulletin of the Bureau of American Ethnology*, 1952 (150).

WALLER, W., AND HILL, R. *The Family: A Dynamic Interpretation*. New York: Dryden, 1951.

WARNER, L., AND SROLE, L. *The Social Systems of American Ethnic Groups*. New Haven: Yale University Press, 1945.

WATZLAWICK, P. "A Review of the Double Bind Theory." *Family Process*, 1963, *2*.

WELLS, H. *The Modernization of Puerto Rico*. Cambridge: Harvard University Press, 1969.

WHYTE, W. F. *Street Corner Society*. Chicago: University of Chicago Press, 1943.

WYNNE, L. "Thought Disorder and Family Relations of Schizophrenics: A Classification of Forms of Thinking." *Archives of General Psychiatry*, 1963, *9*.

WYNNE, L., AND SINGER, M. T. "Thought Disorder and Family Relations of Schizophrenics." *Psychiatry*, 1963, *21*.

Index

Personal names in italics are fictitious names of people in case studies.

A

Acculturation: psychopathology related to, 194-204; stress of, 270-271, 285, 290

ACKERMAN, N. W., ix, x

Activity orientation: of Americans, 30, 36, 98, 269; concept of, 22-24, 269; culture change and, 275; of Greeks, 179, 180, 198; of Greek-Americans, 196, 198, 199, 201, 203; of Italians, 98; of Italian-Americans, 142, 143, 166; of Mexican-Americans, 30; of Puerto Ricans, 47-48, 85. *See also* Being; Being-in-becoming; Doing

Adolescents: in American family, 39-40; and peer groups, 57-58, 105-108, 270

American family, integrations in, 35-45. *See also* American society

American Jewish Committee, 286

American society: activity orientation in, 24, 30, 36, 41, 43, 48, 98, 269, 271, 279, 288-289; culture change in, 271-277; human nature orientation of, 28-29, 52, 98, 269; man-nature orientation of, 27, 30, 32, 36, 51, 98, 269, 271, 288-289; relational orientation of, 25, 35, 36, 37-38, 49, 107, 269, 271-274, 279-280, 288-289; time orientation of, 26, 36, 43, 50, 269, 271, 288-289; values of, contrasted with those of Greek society, 179-205; values of, contrasted with those of Italian society, 97-110; values of, contrasted with those of Puerto Rican society, 46-58

Amoral familism in Italian-American society, 109-110

Index

315

See also Collaterality; Individualism; Lineality

Rescuer. *See* Protector-Rescuer

RIESMAN, D., 36

Role playing and socialization, 13-14

Roles, social: in American family, 36-45; categories of, 14-16; concept of, 11-16; conflicts in, xii, 140-158, 299-300; in Italian family, 100-101; needs related to, 17-19; structuring of, in Mexican-American family, 30-35; theory and structure of, 14; value variations in, 289. *See also* Fictive roles; Formal roles; Informal roles

ROSEN, B. C., 194

RYAN, W., 273, 274

S

SAGER, C., ix

SALAUTOS, T., 183, 184, 186, 188, 191

SANDERS, I. T., 181, 182, 183, 184, 252*n*

SARYAN, A., xv

SCHERMERHORN, R. A., 97

Self-action, 4

Social system: of American family, 36-45; concept of, 3, 6; family related to, 7-19; of Mexican-American family, 30-35

Socialization: of Greeks, 184, 185; of Greek-Americans, 189, 216, 225, 258, 259; needs fulfilled through, 17; role playing related to, 13-14

Spanish society, subjugation-to-nature in, 269

SPIEGEL, J. P., ix, xi, xiii, xiv, xv, 4, 5, 11, 14, 194, 293

SROLE, L., 194

Strains, family: in American family, 38-45; in Greek-American family, 192-193; in Italian-American family, 151; in Puerto Rican family, 49, 52-55

STRODTBECK, F. L., 21, 51*n*, 107, 192, 196-197, 287

Structure and role theory, 14

STUART, R. B., ix

Subjugation-to-nature: to Greeks, 179; to Greek-Americans, 254; to Italians, 97, 103, 288; to Italian-Americans, 106; as man-nature orientation, 26-27, 269, 271; to Mexican-Americans, 30, 32; to Puerto Ricans, 51; in Spanish society, 269; in therapy, 294, 298

Succi, Angela, 128-131, 134, 136-137, 138, 149, 154, 159, 169, 174-175

Succi, Frances, 128, 130, 131, 133, 134, 139

Succi, Henry, 128, 129, 130, 131, 134

Symptomatic episode in Italian-American family, 159-161

T

Therapist: social role of, 298; value orientations of, 293-294

Therapy: family, 298-300; implications of transactional systems theory for, 292-301; intervention strategy in, 295-296

Time orientation: of Americans, 36, 43, 269; concept of, 22, 26, 269; culture change and, 275; of Greeks, 179, 180, 198; of Greek-Americans, 196-198, 199-200, 202, 203; of Italian-Americans, 98, 141-143; of Mexican-Americans, 30, 33-34; of Puerto Ricans, 49-50, 85. *See also* Future; Past; Present

Tondi, Antonio (Tony): background of, 111-116, 118, 120-129; courtship and marriage of, 133-149; roles of, 151-155, 157-159; and Sonny's illness, 161, 163-167, 170-178; value orientations of, 270

Tondi, Antonio, Jr. (Sonny): illness of, 111-113, 115-118; and pathological equilibrium, 156-163, 167; and role conflicts, 148-154